Praise for Charlene Spretnak's *Missing Mary*

"Like Charlene Spretnak, I would like to think of myself as a pro-Mary progressive. I would like to believe that it is the genius of Catholicism to say 'both . . . and.' I would like to be able to persuade myself that one can say 'both ecumenism and Mary,' 'both liturgy and the rosary,' 'both Mary and dialogue with Islam,' and 'both the Council and the *Salve Regina*.' "

—Fr. Andrew Greeley, *National Catholic Reporter*
(front-page review)

"*Missing Mary* 'makes the case' that the meaning and significance of Mary has been downplayed by the Catholic Church over the past forty years—but that Mary's full spiritual presence is alive and well in ethnic parishes."

—*Atlanta Journal-Constitution*

"Spretnak has made the point that Marian devotion has been an unwarranted casualty of the Vatican Council."

—*The Tablet* (UK)

"*Missing Mary* is a brilliant book, one of the best I have read on the subject for many a day."

—Rev. David Rhys, St. Theresa of the Child Jesus, Kent (UK)

"For anyone who has ever loved Our Lady, or desires to, Charlene Spretnak offers a clear vision of the Blessed Mother's true and enormous shape—one that some, over time, have tried to reduce to dust. But the Mother of the Immaculate Heart is a wild one. She refuses to be made small. As in the oldest 'call and response' songs, Spretnak has called on the Blessed Mother's magnitude. And the Holy One has responded with her immaculate love; this is evident on every page. This book and its author are to be treasured as truly enacting the deepest spirit of ¡Viva la Virgen!"

—Clarissa Pinkola Estés, Ph.D.,
author of *Women Who Run with the Wolves* and *The Faithful Gardener*

"If you have prayed for a closer walk with Mary, then this book is an answer to your prayer. Charlene Spretnak serves not just Mary, but all of us, in returning her to her proper place in the cosmos and in our hearts."

—Marianne Williamson, author of *Everyday Grace*

"Passionate and courageous, *Missing Mary* is a rousing call to recover and reclaim the mystical dimensions of the cosmic 'Queen of Heaven.' Spretnak rescues Mary from social conservatives and actually makes it 'safe' for progressives to reclaim the mysteries of Marian spirituality. In a narrative filled with suspense and surprises, Spretnak traces the fate of Mary in the Catholic Church in recent decades and charts a path for revitalizing her spiritual presence in the world today. For all those who have hungered for the power of the Blessed Mother in their lives, Spretnak's book is a banquet."

—Professor Sarah McFarland Taylor,
Department of Religion, Northwestern University

"*Missing Mary* is a joy to read—luscious language, brilliant ideas, and a many-layered wisdom that continually astonishes. Charlene Spretnak has given birth to a work that, if fully apprehended, will change the course of history. Certainly the debate between science and spirituality is now permanently changed. Spretnak offers direct access to a deep spirituality that has the power to tear open modernity's materialist ideology, allow a fountain of grace to flow into the human heart, and save us from plummeting finally into chaos. The impact on a reader of this daring and beautiful book is profound."

—Brian Swimme, Ph.D., author of *The Hidden Heart of the Cosmos*

"Charlene Spretnak skillfully sheds light on the remarkable reawakening of devotion to the feminine in a modern context. Her careful historical analysis and her clear insights into the cosmological implications of Mary make this book fascinating and indispensable reading. With this pathbreaking work the bridges can now be made to the enormous energy of devotion to the feminine in many parts of the world that reflect our new historical moment."

—Professor Mary Evelyn Tucker, Department of Religion, Bucknell University

"In *Missing Mary*, Charlene Spretnak has returned Mary to our midst where she belongs. Spretnak explores the numerous facets of Marian devotion and doctrine with gusto, including Mary's mystical presence. Spretnak's incisive arguments, her careful research into the shifting perception of Mary since Vatican II, and her clear-headed thinking about the variety of responses to this enigmatic figure are indeed welcome. A profound grassroots devotion to Mary has persisted throughout the centuries. This book brings the wisdom of that ancient belief in the 'Mother Who Contains the Uncontainable' into our world today."

—China Galland, M.A., Professor-in-Residence, C.A.R.E.,
Graduate Theological Union, Berkeley, CA

"No matter how you remember Mary, you'll want to read *Missing Mary* . . . Few people have Spretnak's grasp and understanding of the complicated political machinations of the church. Fewer could distill that knowledge into a brief and insightful history lesson that illustrates how quickly Mary could be excised . . . The most exciting part of *Missing Mary* is Spretnak's discussion of the cosmological meaning of Mary . . . By incorporating explorations of art, science, history, and politics, and with a keen understanding of spiritual psychology and personal devotion, Spretnak has written an enlightening, inspiring, and intriguing remembrance of Stella Maris, Blessed Mother, Queen of Heaven, Blessed Virgin, Mary."

—*The Beltane Papers*

Missing Mary

The Queen of Heaven
and Her Re-Emergence in the
Modern Church

Charlene Spretnak

palgrave
macmillan

for my mother, Donna Rose,
named in honor of Her

MISSING MARY
© Charlene Spretnak, 2004.

First published in hardcover in 2004 by PALGRAVE MACMILLAN™
First PALGRAVE MACMILLAN™ paperback edition: October 2005
175 Fifth Avenue, New York, N.Y. 10010 and
Houndmills, Basingstoke, Hampshire, England RG21 6XS
Companies and representatives throughout the world.

PALGRAVE MACMILLAN is the global academic imprint of the Palgrave Macmillan division of St. Martin's Press, LLC and of Palgrave Macmillan Ltd. Macmillan® is a registered trademark in the United States, United Kingdom and other countries. Palgrave is a registered trademark in the European Union and other countries.

ISBN 1–4039–7040–8

Library of Congress Cataloging-in-Publication Data

Spretnak, Charlene
    Missing Mary : the Queen of Heaven and her re-emergence in
the modern church / Charlene Spretnak
        p. cm.
    Includes bibliographical references and index.
    ISBN 1–4039–7040–8 paperback
    ISBN 1–4039–6398–3 cloth
    1. Mary, Blessed Virgin, Saint. I. Title

BT603.S67 2004
232.91—dc21   2003053615

A catalogue record for this book is available from the British Library.

Design by Autobookcomp

First PALGRAVE MACMILLAN paperback edition: October 2005

10 9 8 7 6 5 4 3 2 1

Printed in the United States of America.

Other Books by Charlene Spretnak

Lost Goddesses of Early Greece: A Collection of Pre-Hellenic Myths

The Politics of Women's Spirituality: Essays on the Rise of Spiritual Power within the Feminist Movement
(Editor)

Green Politics: The Global Promise
(with Fritjof Capra)

The Spiritual Dimension of Green Politics

States of Grace: The Recovery of Meaning in the Postmodern Age

The Resurgence of the Real: Body, Nature, and Place in a Hypermodern World

Madonna Platytera / Madonna Misericordia, *Bartolomeo Buon, Venice, 1448–50, Istrian stone, 8′3″× 6′10″. Originally Mary was depicted in this sculpture as Queen of Heaven with a tall crown, but it was apparently chiseled off at some point in the eighteenth century.*

Contents

Introduction

Being Marian

I f I told you I have always been a Marian Catholic, you might well ask, *Is there any other kind?* Not in past times, perhaps, but today the Roman Catholic world is split over the meaning and status of the Blessed Virgin. Her spiritual presence has been drastically reduced, both visually and theologically, since the Church decided forty years ago that it must modernize itself by minimizing Mary.

During the subsequent decades, an intense polarization has developed over Mary: The Catholic right claims the Virgin, especially in her traditional forms, as its own, while most of the Catholic left (who generally call themselves "progressives") defend the radical shrinkage of Mary to strictly biblical delineations as a rational, modern step that was long overdue. Most "progressive" intellectuals in the Church, in fact, tend to consider any glorification of the Nazarene village woman as "Queen of Heaven" to be theologically regressive and even dangerously reactionary — or, at very least, in poor taste.

I encountered that attitude several times while writing this book. Catholic "progressives" expressed severe puzzlement or even shocked disbelief when I told them I feel that too much of the Catholic faith's beautiful Marian spirituality was lopped off by the Church in the mid-1960s. A typical encounter of this sort occurred in April 2001, for instance, when I met a Maryknoll nun while she was on sabbatical from her work in the Philippines. She graciously told me that she admired my books on spirituality, social justice, and ecological thought; I told her that I greatly admire the work of the Maryknoll nuns and priests, who dedicate their lives to the social gospel of Christ by improving the lot of the poor in "developing" countries. When I mentioned that I was writing a book on Mary, she responded with the enthusiastic assumption that I was writing *against* Marian spirituality — that is, writing disdainfully about "that old Mother Mary stuff," "that white-statue stuff so cut off from nature," as she put it. When I explained, on the contrary, my reasons for feeling that the Church made a serious error in suppressing so much of Mary's cosmological dimension and the attendant spiritual practice, this perplexed sister was visibly gripped by cognitive dissonance. She simply found it impossible to conceive of such a position being held by a socially committed, feminist author. She was still struggling with disoriented expectations when we ended our friendly but brief conversation.

I have found, alas, that the polarization concerning Mary among the left and the right orientations within the Church is complemented by an equally dispiriting vacuum in the generation under age forty-five, including many nuns and priests, who neither know nor care much about the full spiritual presence of Mary. They came of age during the heavy silence about the Queen of Heaven. Her great prayer, the "Salve Regina," was deleted from the mass worldwide in the mid-1960s, and her hymns are rarely heard any more except in some ethnic parishes. In surveys today, most young Catholics identify Mary only as a nice woman in the Bible.[1]

A few years ago, when a professor in a Catholic school of theology noticed that the Virgin Mary was absent from the curriculum, she offered a course titled "Perspectives on Mary in Christian Tradition." Several male students enrolled, the younger among them explaining that they "knew nothing about Mary," but not a single female student took the course. Later the professor heard from several of the women that the mention of Mary brought to mind "a sense of betrayal and disillusionment" or "undefined unease" or the conviction that there is "too much baggage" around Mary for her to be of interest.[2]

As for the rosary, that brilliant pathway into the contemplative life, its treasures lie largely forgotten, situated beyond the pale of the far more "rational" — and hence more modern — focus on the text, that is, Scripture. I have been told by nuns both young and old that they keep their beads in a drawer for use only on the evening before funerals, when — they invariably note with a sigh — the families still expect a rosary to be recited in its entirety. In the daily life of many parishes, such as my mother's in Columbus, Ohio, there is no mention at all of Mary or any group recitations of the rosary in the weekly church bulletin — in spite of the fact that half of that congregation is Italian! Even when young people do exhibit an interest in recovering Marian spiritual practices today, they are often discouraged by their "modernized" parish priests. Several diocesan seminaries today, I have been told, discourage or forbid their future priests from gathering in small groups to pray the rosary together. Too Marian, too regressive, too reactionary! Moreover, influential forces within the Church hierarchy seem bent on maintaining the Virgin Mary's minimized version. Some priests are outspoken about a need to go even further than the current diminution and put to rest forever "the Mary problem."

I count myself among the growing number of liberals who have developed a properly "bad attitude" about the Church's drastic reduction of Marian spirituality in our lifetime. The Roman Catholic Church is a container and guardian of mysteries far greater than itself. It had always recognized not only the biblical delineations of Mary, as do the Protestant and Orthodox branches of Christianity, but also what could be called the biblical*plus* perception of her, as do the Orthodox. That is, the Church traditionally held that the Virgin Mary, by virtue of her inherent role in the Incarnation, was an expansive bridge between humans and the Divine. Hence she was associated symbolically with the moon. Having grown the Incarnation from her very flesh, Mary was recognized as a spiritual figure who was more than human but less than divine, a conduit of Christ's grace, a compassionate maternal power, and a loving presence on Earth as well as in heaven. Theologically, she was accorded veneration of an order higher than that for saints but was denied adoration, which is reserved for God. Because Mary's full spiritual presence has cosmological dimensions, she was long honored as the Queen of Heaven, among her other honorific titles. (In this book I use the traditional title "Queen of Heaven" as a shorthand label for the broad and deep traditional perception of Mary's full spiritual presence. Several of her other traditional titles appear at the end of each chapter.)

The spiritual meaning of the Mother of God-the-Son in her mystical and cosmological fullness, whose theology had evolved with the life of the Church itself, was repeatedly expanded, always in response to grassroots spiritual perceptions and demands.

When, forty years ago, the Roman Catholic Church deemphasized and banished an essential cluster of (Marian) spiritual mysteries, as well as the evocative expression of ritual and symbol that had grown around them, a profound loss ensued. Today the theology and liturgy of the Catholic Church is less "cluttered," less mystical, and less comprehensive in its spiritual scope. Its tight, clear focus is far more "rational" but far less whole. We who once partook of a vast spiritual banquet with boundaries beyond our ken are now allotted spare rations, culled by the blades of a "rationalized" agenda more acceptable to the modern mindset.

The biblical*plus,* traditional sense of Mary's full spiritual presence is inclusive, for it includes the biblical delineations of Mary's role in the sacred narrative of the Incarnation, the ministry of Jesus, his Sacrifice and Resurrection, and his spiritual return on Pentecost. In contrast, the strictly biblical sense of Mary, which has dominated Catholic theology since the mid-1960s, is exclusive: It excludes, or disallows, the more than 1600-year-long organic growth of Marian spiritual engagement that cherished the Blessed Mother as a compassionate figure of maternal gravitas and quiet dignity, who, as the God-Bearer (surely a mystical role), was a mediating presence between humans and the Divine. In this book I seek to articulate the rationale for that perception, which was apparent to millions of Catholics for centuries but is often dismissed today as an ungrounded, irrelevant projection. Far from being ungrounded, the traditional perception of Mary as a figure of more-than-human spiritual capabilities derives from the heart of the sacred narrative of the Incarnation, being a logical extrapolation: In growing God-the-Son from her very flesh, Mary *was changed ontologically.* She occupies a unique type of being that did not exist before. Rather than excluding the biblical narrative, this orientation is built on Mary's unique *and elemental* role in the Incarnation and the ministry of Christ. While the cosmological sense of the Mother of God-the-Son is inherent in the Mystery, it is not delineated in the first-century telling of the sacred story, for reasons I discuss. Consequently, the expansive spiritual presence of the Blessed Mother of all the faithful is disallowed by "modernized" Catholicism as being outside the text, or nonbiblical. In using the term "strictly biblical," or "biblical*only*," for the dominant perception of Mary in Catholic theology during the past forty years, I seek to distinguish this position from the traditional biblical*plus* perception of Mary. The two views are significantly different. However, Protestants would be quick to note that the post-Vatican II perception of Mary in modernized Catholicism, while a vast improvement in their eyes, still maintains three elements that are nonbiblical: the teaching that Mary was born without Original Sin, having been conceived as the Immaculate Conception; that after Mary's life on Earth Christ took her body and soul to be with him in heaven (the Assumption); and that Mary, like other members of the communion of saints in the Catholic faith, has intercessory powers (although she is no longer considered to have mediating powers). While it is true that these three aspects, which survived the "rationalizing" of Mary's presence in Catholicism, are not biblical, the primary message of modernized Catholic Mariology is that she is to be regarded solely as a Nazarene village woman. (Within that delineation, many contemporary Catholic biblical scholars find ample reason to honor Mary, while others assert that she is largely unimportant.)

This book argues for an inclusive position that is both biblical and biblical*plus*. I do not expect that the countless numbers of Catholic theologians and other "progressives" who have spent the past forty years in the exclusively biblical orientation will feel inclined to expand their view of Mary to the biblical*plus* orientation. That is, I do not expect them to conclude that the woman who grew God-the-Son from within her own body was consequently in an ontological space that is more than human, possessing more-than-human spiritual capabilities. There is no need for them to undergo such a conversion. Rather, what is needed — for the many reasons I explore in this book — is the recognition that the current grassroots resurgence of traditional Marian spirituality is neither regressive nor in error. The recovery of engagement with Mary's full spiritual presence is a profound correction of the excessive streamlining of Marian theology (or Mariology) and spiritual practice. In *Missing Mary* I both present my perspective on the current resurgence of spiritual engagement with "*big* Mary" and seek to advance that recovery through various observations.

In taking this inclusive position, I do not criticize my feminist-"progressive" sisters and other theologians in the Church for planting themselves, both personally and professionally, so firmly in the strictly biblical orientation of the past four decades and eschewing the traditional perception of Mary. What I do criticize is their frequently expressed assertion that the Church is far better off having deleted the Queen of Heaven (and all related forms of her cosmological presence) and that the strictly biblical view is the sole acceptable position for all Catholics. In their defense, it is easy to see why they would do so: The exclusionary, strictly biblical view of Mary has been the official theological position of the Church for longer than Catholics younger than forty have been alive. Moreover, the argument that removing Mary from her cosmological "pedestal" would be good for Catholic women seems to have won the hearts and minds of feminist "progressives."

Within the biblical reductionism that dethroned the Queen of Heaven, however, feminist-"progressive" theologians discovered that, even after Mary had been vastly reduced to strictly biblical delineations, she was still considered by some of their male colleagues in the Catholic "biblical movement" (or "biblical renewal") to be getting too much attention. The "progressive" feminists found that they must struggle mightily to get Mary any recognition beyond the most minimal level from those male scholars who argue that Mary is mentioned so infrequently in Scripture that she should rationally be set aside as a bit player. Consequently, feminist-"progressive" theologians have produced a stream of well-argued books that explicate Mary's roles, character, and influence in the biblical narrative as textually well-grounded reasons to honor her.

An exemplar of the strictly biblical view of Mary as expressed by feminist-"progressive" theologians is *What Ever Happened to Mary?* (2001) by Mary E. Hines, a short book designed for use in college courses that is a model of clarity. As a past officer of the Catholic Theological Society of America, Hines celebrates the fact that the strictly biblical view of Mary has replaced "the queenly Mary on a pedestal" with someone "women are beginning to rediscover and reclaim as a sister."[3] Now that "Mary is free again to become our truly human sister," she takes her place in the Catholic communion of saints, having no greater intercessory powers than her saintly peers.[4]

Hines's book is particularly noteworthy for its mention of the new direction being cautiously charted by several "progressive" Catholic theologians today: The revulsion expressed in past decades by many at traditional Marian devotions is making way for a bit of guarded acceptance. After noting that statues of Mary and other figures "disappeared overnight" from Catholic churches during the modernizing forty years ago "to allow a central focus on the altar," Hines observes, "Some will have noticed that, of late, the statues have been creeping back in. This is in part a rethinking of the value of popular devotions, such as the devotions to Mary."[5] Surely there is a problem here, though, with theologians in the strictly biblical orientation giving a nod to Marian "popular devotions": Most of those devotions are all about "*big* Mary," not solely the Nazarene woman, who is the only Mary acknowledged by "progressives." If the difference between the inclusive (biblical*plus*) and the exclusive (strictly biblical) versions of Mary is fudged or ignored, the kind words about respecting Marian "popular devotions" become merely an empty expression of political correctness. I suppose one can safely assume that the "creeping" Marian statues approved for readmission by "progressive" theologians are solely those depicting Mary as the Nazarene village woman, never the Queen of Apostles, Queen of Heaven, or Our Lady of anything. Still, the fact that some "progressive" theologians now feel that Marian statues and "popular devotions" are not so bad is a welcome change.

A related development in some feminist-"progressive" circles is the suggestion that the rosary might be readmitted to the strictly biblical orientation. Of course, there is the "problem" of the glorious but nonbiblical "Hail, Holy Queen" ("Salve Regina") prayer, which is traditionally recited at the end of each set of five Mysteries in the rosary. In a "rationalized" rosary, that would have to be deleted, as would the nonbiblical second half of the "Hail Mary" prayer. To meld this particular "popular devotion" with the more strictly biblical orientation, one feminist "progressive" has proposed redesigning the rosary to focus on biblical women. The creator of the "Feminist Rosary" offers it as a form of prayer "that feminists and reformers could embrace."[6]

(All Catholic feminists? Alas, I hope this book will demonstrate that the "progressive," strictly biblical view of Mary is not a monolithic position held by all Catholic feminists; hence, this proposed version of the rosary could more accurately be labeled a feminist-"progressive" rosary.)

Fortunately, three developments of the early twenty-first century are converging in ways that facilitate a new respect for the religious perception of Mary in her larger proportions. First, we now have enough distance to assess the zeitgeist of the post-World War II era, a time when modern, "tough-minded," rationalist, rather macho thinking was aggressively applied to all our institutions, hacking away anything perceived to be sentimental, soft, or old-fashioned. In some respects the effects of "modernizing" our collective consciousness were salutary, but in many respects a ham-fisted denial of subtle yet profoundly relational aspects of life contributed to the increasing sense of alienation among the post-war generations. Second, the current mood of reassessment is joined today with a growing appreciation of the wisdom inherent in several premodern, or nonmodern, systems of knowledge, such as herbal medicine and Chinese acupuncture. Shedding the prejudices with which we moderns were taught to consider any nonmodern culture rather pathetic, we now recognize the wisdom of certain earlier delineations, however partial, of the mysteries of life, including the dynamic web of creativity infusing both the body and the cosmos. A third development is the discovery by contemporary science of a number of revelations about the nature of the universe that are relevant to the cosmological symbolism around Mary as Queen of Heaven and her mystical body of grace. To favor religious symbolism that reflects a profoundly relational universe — that is, the understanding of reality that has emerged from the sciences of cosmology and ecology — signals not a "regression" to the medieval worldview but, rather, a progression of religious doctrine to match the revelations of the Creation in our time.

The convergence of these three developments provides the ground from which this book arises. Together they make possible both a recognition of loss and a movement further into an expansive spirituality that is *simpatico* with the unfurling and profoundly relational universe. With this book, I hope to further a correction of Mary's fate —

although I gratefully acknowledge that numerous ethnic groups, some religious orders, and many entire countries have kept her full presence alive in their own ways. *Missing Mary* explores how and why official contemporary Catholicism, especially in North America and Western Europe, has become comparatively Maryless, particularly with regard to her larger, cosmological presence. (Remarkably, most Catholics today seem to be in the dark about what happened to her.) I also consider what is at stake if the loss continues and why a revitalized recognition of Mary is so relevant to the twenty-first century. In addition, I address the question of how Mary's full spiritual presence might be grasped anew without aiding the political agenda of the Catholic right. While this book challenges certain positions of both the ideological left and the ideological right within the Church, it is intended primarily for the large, nonideological middle range of the spectrum of Roman Catholics.

My critical message is that it was a mistake for the Church to have deleted official recognition of Mary's cosmological spiritual presence forty years ago and disallowed her grand symbolization as the Maternal Matrix in order to shrink her down to more "rational" proportions. That is, I believe that the post–World War II, macho, modernizing mentality common to many of the younger intellectual priests then was insensitive, or "tone deaf," to the cosmological "grand" dimensions of Mary's traditional, biblical*plus* mystical presence. My constructive — and perhaps wildly hopeful — message is not only that scientific cosmology now illuminates many of the cosmological characteristics that were traditionally symbolized by Mary but, quite simply, that we are beginning to grasp her meaning once again. Every single addition to Church doctrine through the centuries that enlarged official acknowledgment of Mary as the compassionate Great Mother of the faith and the cosmological Queen of Heaven was insisted upon by grassroots pressure and only eventually accepted by Church authorities. In view of contemporary discoveries in cosmology, the instincts of the laity through the centuries carried not only piety but a deeply grounded intimation of the cosmological Maternal Matrix and the rightness of such a symbolic figure at the heart of Christianity with Jesus.

What, really, has been the effect of Mary's being largely dethroned forty years ago and "disappeared"? ("Disappeared" is a term that emerged from Latin America in the 1970s and 1980s when right-wing political regimes eliminated hapless citizens suspected of being opponents.) Are Catholic children better off now, being raised with "lite Catholicism," free of the mystical dimension? Has the diminution of the bounteously compassionate Mother of God really improved the Catholic experience? Has the "rationalizing" and narrowing of the sacramental presence in Catholicism been a boon? Are Catholic women better off spiritually now that Mary has been deposed from her cosmological throne and made their strictly human sister? Did Catholic men benefit from her grand maternal presence as the Mother of the Church in their formative years and beyond? Surely the secular world has become more callous in the past four decades, but is there some corresponding barrenness and sterility within modernized Catholicism?

The dynamic promise of modernization infused all our institutions in the 1950s and early 1960s. Within the postwar context of sloughing off the outmoded and boldly embracing the new, a worldwide conference of Roman Catholic bishops, cardinals, and theologians was convened in Rome from 1962–1965. The gathering was called the Second Vatican Council or, more popularly, Vatican II. The accomplishments of the Council were monumental. The Council Fathers created and adopted several new decrees and constitutions in various areas that initiated countless positive changes in the rules and official attitudes of the Church. Their charge from Pope John XXIII was to achieve *aggiornamento* (to bring the Church "into the present day").

Among the scores of major decisions made at Vatican II, which threw open the long-sealed windows of the Church to admit fresh breezes of vitality from the laity, clergy, nuns and monks, and theologians, I take issue with only *one one-eighth of one* of the sixteen constitutions, declarations, and decrees issued by the Council. In sharing this view, I have been surprised to discover that even this proportionately small disagreement with the great accomplishments of Vatican II excites shock, disbelief, and sometimes even anger from "progressives" in the Church. In short, I have discovered that discussions about Vatican II, like those about Mary today, are mine fields.

I believe that Catholic "progressives" consider even a circumscribed criticism of one bit of the work of Vatican II to be unthinkable and possibly reactionary because they fear that the rejecting of even one decision made by the Council might open a flood gate to other challenges (by the Catholic right). I appreciate their vigilance, for I know that there are real threats to the liberalization of the Church that has been achieved so far. However, I cannot imagine a roll-back to the situation that existed prior to 1962 in which the entire florescence of participation by the laity; the increased freedom given to communities of nuns, monks, and priests; the improved attitudes toward other religions and other branches of Christianity; and countless other advances would be cancelled. All that is good about Vatican II — the 98 percent — is very good indeed. Yet to deny that certain decisions regarding even a small portion of the total number of complex subjects might have been caught up in internal politicking and, in the case of some topics, in the intellectual currents of the post-World War II period seems to me a curiously unrealistic position. Although the hotly contested decisions about Mary that were made at Vatican II are nearly always discussed as a clash of forward-thinking "progressives" versus backward "Marian traditionalists," I seek to bring into the discussion an awareness of the larger, postwar expressions of modernity that constitute a significant part of the historical context of the Council.

The key question, of course, is why — after 440 years of Protestantism — an almost Protestant perception of Mary was suddenly compelling for many young, Catholic European theologians and priests. A decade before "Ecumenism!" became the official rallying cry at Vatican II for shrinking Mary's significance and presence, a few prominent Catholic theologians in Germany had begun to profess increasingly Protestant views of the Blessed Virgin. Why then, in the early 1950s? And why did other Catholic men in that period suddenly agree with theological positions favoring a drastic diminution of Mary that previously would have been unthinkable?

In my view, the Council Fathers were right about nearly everything they did at Vatican II *except* for the profoundly wrong decision about demoting Mary and shrinking her officially recognized presence to primarily being an exemplary member of the Church and a "model" or cipher representing it in Scripture. Her traditional role as conduit and mediator of divine grace was firmly cancelled. In addition, the section in the "modernizing" constitution on the liturgy urges all Catholic churches to get rid of their statues of Mary and other saints, or at least move them to less noticeable locations, so that Protestants ("our separated brethren") will not be "confused" about the true nature of Catholic worship. *I'm not making this up!*

Like all books about Mary, this one has a point of view. Readers who are happy with the current reduced sense of Mary within Catholicism might be well advised to stick with the widely admired and beautifully written books on the Virgin that have no argument with the Church's "modernizing" of her since the mid-1960s: Marina Warner's literary study of Mary's role in the cultural history of the West, *Alone of All Her Sex* (1976); Jaroslav Pelikan's sweeping history of the Virgin in Church history and doctrine, *Mary Through the Centuries* (1996); or Sally Cunneen's impressive historical exploration, *In Search of Mary* (1996). These masterful overviews have been joined in the past couple of years by a small flood of new books on Mary, many of which I have cited in Related Resources. While I welcome all the appreciations of Mary from various perspectives, this book specifically challenges the Church's radical shift concerning Mary in the otherwise admirable work of Vatican II and proposes some new directions in the evolution of Catholic thought.

I am aware of the reasons cited to justify Mary's shrinkage. I realize that her radical diminution is widely applauded — and guarded against "slippage" — in the modernized Church today. In the following chapters I engage with (1) the theological defense offered by the Church for the coup (because much of Mary's accumulated theology rightfully belonged with the Holy Spirit, she had to be cut down to size); (2) the ecumenical imperative that Mary have little presence beyond the few bits of text that mention her in the gospels (so that Protestant sensibilities won't be offended); (3) the feminist-"progressive" assertion that women are better off without Mary's being set upon some unworldly pedestal of perfection, and that energies formerly focused on the Queen of Heaven should better be focused on convincing the Church to consider God itself female as well as male; and (4) the belief that the Church wins greater respect from the modern world by getting rid of its embarrassing "medieval vestiges." By the way, it is sometimes said that Vatican II merely cleared away the "excesses" in Marian spirituality, but the major debate about Mary at the Council, in

October 1963, was not at all about overzealous practices; it was about a sea change in Marian theology.

It may be that there are as many nuanced perceptions of Mary as there are people engaged with her spiritual presence. Perhaps, as Gandhi surmised, everyone has his or her own religion. He was not advocating a solipsistic dissolution of collective faith but meant only that everyone, no matter how orthodox or "by the book," necessarily experiences spiritual teachings in a unique way. Particularly during one's formative years, certain teachings, lines of Scripture, or ritual moments are felt with great impact, while other religious experiences seem more neutral. No two people have exactly the same internal responses, so the exact contours of each person's lived religion are solely his or her own, even within the collective consensus of belief and practice.

The imposition of the new minimalist version of Mary happened after Vatican II, but I happened before Vatican II, so I remember Mary whole. In fact, I am beginning to think, as I learn more of people's childhood complaints, that I may have come to know her in the best possible way. I never heard a priest or nun say that Mary is a model of female submission against whom all women should measure themselves, or that Mary's primary message to women is meekness and obedience, or that teenage girls would fall from Mary's good graces if we ever kissed a boy. Granted, the odds against my hearing such common misuses of Mary were favorably skewed since my sister and I did not attend parochial schools, but we did go to classes in religious instruction every Sunday after mass, at Saint Christopher Catholic Church, so we were not lacking the standard inculcation, beginning with the *Baltimore Catechism*. In the collective spiritual life I knew then, Our Blessed Mother was a cherished presence.

It was not from our parish priests and nuns, though, that I learned about Mary, except in a peripheral way. Their formal pronouncements of doctrine were never more than background material. I could see that those teachings were well intentioned, but they could not even come close to what I knew of Mary and the way I knew it. I learned about her ineffable spiritual presence in ways mostly unspoken — or, rather, the words told to me by my mother and her mother were a small part of the message. Everything — the powerful Marian compassion, her spiritual beauty and goodness, her place in the divine order, her presence in our hearts — was made clear by the sound their maternal voices took on, the soft gaze in their eyes, their gentle and knowing smiles, their breasts rising and falling slowly as their breathing turned deep with the bodily release of deliverance, and their infinitely loving desire that I might grasp the meaning of Mary.

Extending from that spiritual understanding of compassion and care was — quite obviously, it seemed to me — a sense of social responsibility. My parents were New Deal Democrats (I was even born on Franklin D. Roosevelt's birthday), and they donated a good deal of time and energy to various liberal causes and community organizations. My mother, for instance, co-founded the UNICEF center in our city, Columbus, Ohio. Both she and my father endorsed the ideal of the Christopher Movement: It is better to light a candle than to curse the darkness. So it would have been difficult for me to imagine during my coming of age that a family informed by the social gospel of Christ, plus Mary's compassion for the suffering of the world, could believe that the poor are merely moral failures, or that the hidden hand of the market gives everyone what he or she deserves according to innate talent, or that social stability depends on keeping women tightly constrained. Yet those are the values most "progressive" Catholics today associate with people who are spiritually engaged with the traditional version of Mary.

I hardly think I am singular among American Catholics in both supporting the attempted democratization of the Church and kindred corrective efforts *as well as* urging a recovery and revitalization of Marian spirituality in its fullness. Many of my friends and acquaintances would fit this description. Several would probably identify themselves as "progressives," but others would not be comfortable with the connotations of that label even though they are committed to social justice. Some of them are among the six million Catholic signatories of the Vox Populi (Voice of the People) petition to the Vatican, which requests that three of Mary's traditional titles be made "articles of faith" (that is, core beliefs, or dogmatic principles, of Roman Catholicism): *Advocate* for the people, especially the poor; *Mediator* of divine grace from God-the-Father and God-the-Son; and *Co-Redeemer* (not equal to Christ but uniquely *with* him in the salvific Incarnation). A number of my peers signed in spite of the fact that this Marian petition drive was initiated by a conservative theologian, not because of it. I believe that many of the people among the six million signatories are less concerned with Marian titles per se than with sending a worldwide *cri de coeur* to Church officials in Rome about Mary's fate in the stripped down, modernized version of the faith.

Looking back, I now recognize an early warning sign that I would not fit easily into the "progressive" wing of the Church that was emerging in the mid-1960s: If the truth be told, I hated the guitar masses that were introduced during those years at my Jesuit university. I liked folk music well enough but not as a substitute for what the dear Jesuits (the quality of the education was great) should have been offering us in the way of cultivating a deepening adult spiritual life. They and their seminarians partook daily of the contemplative exercises developed in 1534 by the founder of the Jesuit order, St. Ignatius of Loyola, but nothing similar was offered to the students then, other than a daily mass. All that changed later, as the spiritual awakening that began in the counterculture of the late 1960s gradually rippled through our post–World War II religious institutions. I am told that spiritual counseling and programs galore now abound on Catholic campuses.

Through a long questing period that began around the time of those guitar masses, Mary was always with me in some way. In the 1970s I discovered, as many Catholics have, the felicitous combination of mindfulness meditation and the Catholic practice of examination of conscience. The late Anthony de Mello, a Jesuit, wrote a popular book on this compatibility, *Sadhana,* and was frequently invited to lecture on Catholic campuses here and abroad in the 1980s.

It was during that decade that I drifted further from the "progressive" orientation, though no closer to the conservative camp. I began to become aware of the systemic problems of modernity, the tracks left by the lean, mean machine of efficiency and "rationalized" life as it had callously paved over the subtle mysteries that all nonmodern cultures wisely honor. Certainly I was a modern woman, cognizant of the benefits that condition can bestow, but I increasingly perceived that the fierce reaction against anything premodern during the formative stages of the modern era had denied or marginalized vast areas of human experience that are precious. I pondered the ways in which our modern lives are still shaped by the effects of the mechanistic worldview and its postspiritual assumptions. Eventually I was heartened, however, by the emergent recovery of spiritual and ecological wisdom that had been shunted aside. During the 1990s I wrote two books on this subject, *States of Grace: The Recovery of Meaning in the Postmodern Age* (1991) and *The Resurgence of the Real: Body, Nature, and Place in a Hypermodern World* (1997).

Given that we are now living through a time of reassessment and expansive possibilities for correcting certain denials imposed by modernity, the current debates within the Church over the meaning and status of Marian titles are focused far too narrowly. They are largely situated on the surface and are mired in power dynamics and political strategies, which tend to silence, if not strangle, the articulation of deeper issues. Moreover, media coverage of the "deep-seated conflict between wildly popular devotion to the Virgin Mary and the efforts of the established church to keep that devotion in check" (as the *New York Times* put it recently[7]) has yet to grasp the deeply corrective impulse behind the contemporary Marian renewal because the journalists are seemingly unaware, as good moderns, that a serious loss might have occurred by banishing certain nonmodern spiritual insights at Vatican II. All references to the work of Vatican II in the press are entirely positive since it was indeed the great modernizing force in the Church. The grassroots resurgence of Marian spirituality, however, challenges not the entirety of Vatican II's accomplishments but, rather, the Church's reductionist view of Mary, and it does so for good reason. *Missing Mary* seeks to clarify that reason, as I see it, and to extend the argument for the Marian renewal.

Mary's full spiritual presence is reflected in Church doctrine but also extends beyond that delineation. My aim in this book is to evoke a sense of all that will be lost — to millions of spiritual lives now and forever — should the "modernizers" have their way with Mary. In these pages I hope to convey four meanings of the key theme: *missing Mary*. I personally am missing Mary; the full spiritual presence of Mary is missing from the "modernized" Catholic Church; modernity has missed (as in "failed to grasp") the cosmological meaning of Mary; and almost an entire generation of Catholics under age forty-five, including many priests and nuns, have missed the opportunity for deep communion with the Blessed Mother.

What credentials do I bring to a consideration of the complex situation surrounding the Virgin Mary in the Catholic Church today? First, I am a professor in the philosophy and religion program at the California Institute of Integral Studies, a graduate institute in San Francisco. But can the academic focus alone truly grasp the multivalent presence of Mary in people's lives? Much as I respect and admire the rigor and hard work required for intellectual research and analysis, the *something more* looms large in this subject matter.

Second, in addition to several years of focused research that went into this book, many of my past interests and experiences turned out to be highly relevant to the project. Obviously a full grasp of what has been lost of Marian spirituality during the Church's modernization requires experiential knowledge of pre-Vatican II Catholicism. To have passed one's formative years in a loving family to whom Mary was important would be ideal for the gleaning of such knowledge — and to have had a grandmother who walked, as a girl, with her entire European village every year to the national Marian shrine in their country would be even better. In this second area, I was abundantly blessed.

Third, to understand the assumptions and dynamics of modernity that underpinned the decisions about Mary at Vatican II, one would need to be well versed in the historical and contemporary ideology of modernity, as well as the cultural history of the West, two subjects on which I have written in *States of Grace* and *The Resurgence of the Real*.

Fourth, to bring insights to the Goddess-like symbols and attributes traditionally associated with Mary's spiritual presence would require knowledge of the long stream of female images of the Divine and semidivine that preceded the Blessed Virgin of Christianity and merged with her in so many countries, a subject on which I first published in 1978 (*Lost Goddesses of Early Greece*) and subsequently.

Fifth, to reflect on the cosmological dimension of those symbols, it would be helpful to have familiarity with the contemporary renewal of interest in both scientific and cultural cosmology, which I have followed for the past fifteen years.

Sixth, to accumulate and pore over a large body of historical and contemporary Marian art, a pastime that has intrigued me for the past decade, would facilitate, or reinvigorate, a nonlinguistic sensitivity to the spiritual presence of the Virgin Mary, which this sort of project surely requires.

Seventh, to understand how a key vote on a *procedural* matter concerning a statement to be written at a convention can become entwined with debates over the proposed *content* of the statement, such that the crucial vote is won by only a scant majority and most people are left confused about the full meaning of the vote — as occurred at Vatican II with the key vote on a doctrinal statement about Mary — one needs to have witnessed similar confusing moments in the democratic process at various assemblies. Regrettably, I have such experience.

Finally, to understand the powerfully seductive pull of the ideology of modernity and its "sophisticated" analysis, which have caused so many "progressive" Catholics to lose contact with the full spiritual presence of Mary, a personal experience of that loss — followed by the deliverance of recovery — would be invaluable. It seems, then, that several major streams of my life have delivered me to the writing of this book — as a scholar, a pilgrim, and an advocate for Mary in her fullness.

In the following chapters, I sometimes mention the petition drive initiated by the Vox Populi movement, but the observations I make are merely my own and are in no way connected with that movement. A succinct presentation of Vox Populi's theological brief for making three of Mary's traditional titles articles of faith is available in their eighty-page booklet titled *Mary: Coredemptrix, Mediatrix, Advocate* (see Related Resources). I personally do not believe, however, that Mary requires any new dogma.

In chapter one, "The Virgin and the Dynamo: A Rematch," I consider the context of modernity, in which the Church's responses to Mary during the past two centuries are embedded. It is necessary to understand where modernity and the modern worldview came from in order to fully grasp what happened and why in the early 1960s in the Church. I propose a convergence of several influences in the late 1950s as the reason Mary was suddenly diminished at Vatican II, on the grounds that such a shrinkage was the rational response to new "scientific," semiotic methods of biblical exegesis. I also and relevant the influence of the modern mentality and its diminished capacity to symbolize and to honor poetic and spiritual evocations, which are viewed disdainfully by moderns as mere vestiges of an irrational past. I then offer a new interpretation of the great debate over Mary at Vatican II. As an overarching metaphor, I revisit the agonistic dynamic that Henry Adams suggested in 1906 would characterize the twentieth century: The fading power of the Virgin Mary would be replaced by the ascendant forces of industrialization and modernity. And so it was. He could not have guessed, however, that by the early twenty-first century spiritual renewal would be manifesting itself in many areas of modern life. In fact, from our current vantage point, several of the "tough-minded" fiats of modernity, especially in its muscular burst following World War II, are seen now to be anachronistic period pieces. We have entered a historic moment of reflection on the ideologies of modernity and a reassessment of their effects. Where they are found wanting, there is a hunger for more deeply grounded possibilities.

In chapter two, "The Quiet Rebellion against the Suppression of Mary," I trace the growth of the current grassroots resurgence of Marian spirituality, which began in the late 1970s. In particular, I focus on the unexpected clash that captured front-page media attention around the world in the 1990s when the Marian renewal was rebuffed by the Church hierarchy. I also respond to the objections raised by feminist-"progressive" Catholic theologians to once again honoring the larger dimensions of Mary's spiritual presence, which include but also exceed her textual delineations in the gospels. Finally, I consider the highly charged political situation within the Church today concerning Mary, and I suggest some possible options.

Chapter three, "Premodern Mary Meets Postmodern Cosmology," relates Mary's traditionally recognized more-than-human attributes to cosmological dynamics of the Creation. Such dynamics have long been expressed cross-culturally in religious symbols and metaphors. Although some "progressive" Catholic authors dismiss the current interest in cosmology as mere New Age pap, that modern dismissal of the larger context of the human is out of sync with the deeper perceptions of non-modern religions: All of the great spiritual traditions have sought to situate the human within the Earth community and the universe. Many of the mythopoetic expressions of that profound cosmological relationship, including those associated with Mary as Queen of Heaven, reflect dynamics that have been newly illuminated by recent discoveries in postmodern physics. Consequently, the renewed interest in the metaphors of Mary, Queen of Heaven may be seen as part of the contemporary re-engagement with the cosmos as the fecund matrix, or quantum plenum, of all life. From this perspective, the traditional cosmological associations of Mary, as well as the brilliant celebration of the entire Creation in medieval art and architecture, no longer look like mere premodern irrational foolishness. Rather, they can be seen to reflect a spiritual wisdom larger than the modern focus on the human species alone, which triumphantly regards itself as living apart from nature. More importantly, our new knowledge of the cosmological reality of the Creation makes it possible at this time to continue the evolution of theological doctrine. To be vital, religious symbols must reflect physical reality as closely as possible, incorporating humans' deepest, most comprehensive, current understanding of the Creation.

In chapter four, "Where Mary Still Reigns," I consider the ethnic traditions that have largely ignored the Church's post-Vatican II shrinkage of Mary. The ways in which she remains central in the spiritual lives of Mexicans and Mexican Americans — as well as Filipinos and many other peoples, particularly from Central, Southern, and Eastern Europe — provide an example for Maryless Catholics under age forty-five of a rich and vital Roman Catholicism. As a North American author, I focus mainly on the spreading presence of Our Lady of Guadalupe ("In Guad We Trust"), but all Marian cultures honor the Blessed Mother as an advocate of the people and a fount of compassion. She absorbs the sorrows put before her and radiates a healing grace. She has been credited with facilitating millions of cures and transformations. She has always had a special association with the poor and oppressed. To all who approach her with an open heart, Mary bestows an inner peace. I believe that the strongly pro-Mary "holdouts" in the ethnic enclaves within the "modernized" post-Vatican II (or postconciliar) Church are bearers of deep spiritual renewal for that institution. It cannot be said that this large ethnic sector fits the equation often cited by "progressives": Love of the traditional, large version of Mary equals reactionary politics. On the contrary, many, if not most, ethnic U.S. Catholics support efforts for social justice and for making Church governance more accountable to the laity.

In chapter five, "Why the Church Deposed the Queen of Heaven," I trace the recurrence of efforts throughout the history of the Church to contain Mary and denigrate Marian devotion, which her opponents derisively call "Mariolatry." True, she was accorded a highly honored place in Catholic devotion, but there were always those who saw the Mother of God-the-Son as a looming problem. I also consider the compelling dynamics of modernity in the post-World War II period that affected the Second Vatican Council's decisions about Mary in ways that are generally not recognized. I then identify issues surrounding Mary that were underlying the extremely polarized positions at Vatican II over a Marian chapter in the new constitution on the Church. Many anxious males have tried to bring her down, yet far more men have honored her. Besides, her detractors all die off, but she does not. Finally, I assess the spin in the years since Vatican II that has been issued by popes and Vatican officials regarding the streamlined, minimized version of Mary.

In chapter six, "Mary's Biblical and Syncretic Roots," I propose that the Church shift its position on Mary's relationship to her regional predecessors: Numerous elements in the biblical story of the Nativity — as well as the historical grassroots' insistence that the story of Mary the Mother of God-the-Son logically include cosmological dimensions — demonstrate a continuity with the ancient religions of the Near East and Europe (and other continents as well) that symbolically honored the Maternal Matrix of life via female expressions of the Divine. Since those linking symbols and events are clearly stated in scriptural accounts of the Nativity, why does not the Church simply celebrate, rather than deny, its continuation through Mary of this impressive, extremely ancient spiritual stream? After all, the rich lineage of Western religious approaches to symbolizing an embodied Maternal Matrix stretches back 25,000 years. Moreover, Mary merges the Old World with the New in the figure of the indigenous Virgin of Guadalupe and other Latin American Marian forms, just as she merged with numerous indigenous goddesses in Europe. As the grand convergence of religions, cultures, and time, Mary is a "Co-Redeemer" in ways that extend beyond the Christian sense of sin and fallenness. She also redeems us from states of separation and loss: She is both the spiritual mother of particular nations *and* the Mother of All. Most instructively, she is a convergence of power and humility. Her allure emanates across deep divisions, as evidenced by Muslim as well as Christian pilgrims visiting shrines to Mary the Hebrew village woman. Her more-than-human "Goddess" attributes express her cosmological dimension. Those aspects cannot be lopped off for the sake of "rationalizing" her image to suit modern tastes. What is left is not the full Mary.

In chapter seven, "Her Mystical Body of Grace," I consider the ways in which Mary's function as mediator of grace is embedded in her entire person, the bountiful body of the compassionate mother. The grassroots perception of Mary through the ages has been that of a woman who became the God-Bearer and, consequently, acquired more-than-human, cosmological proportions and capabilities as the Blessed Mother of all the faithful. Leaving behind first-century physiology, which assumed pregnant women to be mere incubators and which obviously influenced the men who wrote the gospels, I suggest that twenty-first-century biology indicates that Mary's pregnancy would have rendered her ontologically changed. Moreover, to limit her to the text-based version deprives the West of a corrective balance to its fixation on transcendence *above* body and nature: Mary radiantly *embodies* transcendent grace. In her, the bountiful cosmic body and the bountiful female body are merged to powerful effect. For women, in particular, a deep loss ensues when Mary's *mystical female body* is denied and replaced by a strictly text-bound version of her. In addition, Mary's presence conveys a sense of the deeply female consciousness that modernity has sought to neutralize and contain, just as it has devalued beauty itself. An insert of examples of vibrant contemporary art depicting "*big* Mary" is included in this chapter. (Most of the art works in the insert were created during the past decade, but one was painted in 1926.) To honor Mary's strength and relational compassion once again is to participate in a broad shift in values in the early twenty-first century.

In the epilogue, "Being Mary," I relate a personal experience I had a few years ago with Mary's spiritual presence.

As I neared completion of this manuscript, I showed it to a number of Catholic and non-Catholic readers. The latter often found it "fascinating," as did nonideological Catholics, but many "progressive" Catholics expressed far more intense reactions. A few publishers who were shown a preliminary version of the manuscript sent it to one or two "progressive" Catholic authors for a professional opinion; those "progressive" screeners urged that the book not be published. For example, an author with a Master of Arts degree in Catholic theology who has written a book on Mary found my manuscript to be "erudite," "extremely bold," and "interesting," but she concluded that my "unique voice" will displease both the left and the right within the Church and that, therefore, the book would have no audience. The right, she predicted, would "report the author to the Ratzinger doctrinal police force," while the "cause" for which I argue "won't gain sympathy among the [progressive/liberal] intellectual community," merely in such gatherings as "rosary sessions and Spanish masses." Actually, I would be happy to have an audience in rosary sessions and Spanish masses. Moreover, all my books have irritated both the ideological left and the ideological right, so I took her dismissive prediction as a sign that I am on the right track. What surprised me most in her largely aghast (but helpful) reaction was her concurring with the astounding observation made by a Dominican nun, which I cite in chapter one: The nun told me that she has never met a "pro-Mary progressive" and cannot imagine one. The "progressive" Catholic author wrote, "Until I read Spretnak's manuscript, I would have said the same thing." (I trust that they each meant they had never met a pro-Queen of Heaven "progressive"; many "progressives" are pro-biblical Mary, although many now disapprove of any attention to Mary whatsoever.) Even at this point in the work, I still find it difficult to believe how extreme the polarization over Mary has become.

On the other hand, a Jesuit priest who read the manuscript applauded my proposing a "legitimate development of doctrine," a phrase he cited from John Henry Cardinal Newman, and "not merely reasserting an old emphasis that perhaps has not been sufficiently emphasized . . . over the last forty years." He surmised that since there is development in the "cosmic enterprise," there will certainly be development in our understanding of the great Mystery. Exhibiting the intellectual curiosity common among Jesuits, he found the explication of modernity, the insights concerning the new cosmology, and even the ruminations about Mary's continuity with the ancient lineage of images of the sacred female to be intriguing. He concluded that "your insights offer a valid opening to what still needs to be said, pondered, embraced, and made our own as Catholics."[8]

Considering the range of thinking and feeling about Mary today, I had best state my expectations. I do not anticipate that this book will be of interest to ultraconservative Catholics who regard the Virgin Mary as emblematic of right-wing social positions. Likewise, I assume that *Missing Mary* will not hold any allure for those "progressive-left" Catholics who not only support such noble goals as democratizing the Church, ordaining women, and endorsing contraception so that humans do not overrun and destroy the Creation but who also fully embrace the "lite," modernized, deritualized, "rationalized," text-limited, noncosmological, "streamlined" version of Catholicism that was put into place forty years ago. Who does that leave? Quite a few people, as far as I can surmise from the positive reactions I have received whenever I have presented the analysis and vision of this book to audiences in the past couple of years. "When is this book going to be out?" has been a common reaction. "You're trying to start a revolution, aren't you, dear?" was the response from a smiling elderly nun who loves both Mary and ecosocial activism. I have not, in short, encountered bloc thinking but thoughtful people willing to consider the case I make and to reflect on their own experience.

I fully acknowledge that the "modernizers" at Vatican II acted with good intentions when they succeeded in "rationalizing" the Blessed Virgin: They sincerely felt that a radically minimized Mary was the best option for the Catholic Church in the modern age. The point I wish to make, however, is that the historic vote on the Marian chapter in the new constitution on the Church at Vatican II, in October 1963, was extremely close. It was won at a time when the ideology of modernity gripped the thinking of countless young, post–World War II intellectuals, including many priests at the Second Vatican Council. We have now arrived at the need to reassess several of the assumptions of that period. It is time to revisit the debate.

I have aspired in the following chapters to convey that which is nearly lost but might be saved if the Marian resurgence continues to gain strength. It was lost to me as well in the years following Vatican II, but I have been graced with a glimpse — through my immersion in Marian spiritual culture and practice — of the sustaining luminosity that four decades of reductionist "modernizing" could not extinguish. Mary's totality, the presence of all the hearts attuned with her through the ages, often enveloped me quite unexpectedly. I have threaded some of those personal experiences through this book, but the main story is hers.

Chapter One

The Virgin and the Dynamo: A Rematch

In 1898 Henry Adams, a professor of history at Harvard University, as well as the grandson and great-grandson of two American presidents, encountered the Virgin Mary in Chartres Cathedral. As a boy he had attended the Unitarian Church in Boston twice every Sunday and had reached adulthood, as he put it, "without knowing religion, and with the certainty that dogma, metaphysics, and abstract philosophy were not worth knowing."[1] Nonetheless, when he experienced, at age sixty, the shocking grace and majesty of Chartres, "the Palace of the Queen of Heaven," Adams threw himself into a study of the florescence of religious art and architecture in twelfth- and thirteenth-century France. The result was a passionate engagement with two medieval masterpieces: *Mont-Saint-Michel and Chartres* (1904). He then wrote an autobiography, *The Education of Henry Adams* (1906), which complements the earlier book and has long been regarded as one of the most compelling works of American literature. In the autobiography's most famous chapter — or, at least, most famous chapter title — "The Dynamo and the Virgin," Adams weighed what he had grasped of Mary at Chartres with what he had seen of the new, industrialized twentieth century at the Exposition Universelle of 1900 in Paris.

Adams noted that a friend of his, and all other artists of the day, constantly complained that the power embodied in a railway train could never be embodied in art — to which he responded simply, "All the steam in the world could not, like the Virgin, build Chartres."[2] He continued:

> Symbol or energy, the Virgin had acted as the greatest force the Western world ever felt, and had drawn man's activities to herself more strongly than any other power, natural or supernatural, had ever done; the historian's business was to follow the track of the energy, to find where it came from and where it went to; its complex source and shifting channels; its values, equivalents, conversions.[3]

Yet Adams was mesmerized by the huge dynamos in the Gallery of Machines in the Champs de Mars at the Exposition and by "the astonishing complexities of the new Daimler motor."[4] He wrote to a friend that he sat "by the hour over the great dynamos, watching them run noiselessly and as smoothly as the planets, and asking them — with infinite courtesy — where in Hell they are going. They are marvelous."[5] Eventually, as he recounts in "The Dynamo and the Virgin," he came "to feel the forty-foot dynamos as a moral force, much as the early Christians felt the Cross. . . . Before the end," he admitted, "one began to pray to it; inherited instinct taught the natural expression of man before silent and infinite force."[6]

Although Adams agreed with his friend that these new forces were somewhat "anarchical" and hence threatening, he was convinced that "man had translated himself into a new universe which had no common scale of measurement with the old." The future, indeed the present in 1900, was to be shaped by "the sudden irruption of forces totally new."[7] In contrast, Adams offered a rueful assessment in *Mont-Saint-Michel and Chartres* of "the Virgin in her majesty . . . looking down from a deserted heaven, into an empty church, on a dead faith."[8] Adams's passionately imaginative account of Mary's interaction with each designer and craftsman who shaped Chartres Cathedral explained, to his satisfaction, how her elegant "taste" found form, a glorious artistic achievement before which anyone possessing even "the soul of a shrimp" should experience awe.[9] He felt, however, that she reigned in 1900 with only a grandeur of resignation that her time had passed.

Adams was not wrong about the twentieth century. The driving force was faith in technological deliverance and economic expansion . . . by whatever means necessary. Some one hundred years later, however, both the ominous dimension of such an ungrounded trajectory as well as the surprising resilience of religion are shaping our reality. In our hypermodern age, both of these forces — the techno-economic and the spiritual — share the zeitgeist, along with a cacophony of others.

After decades of the aggressive promises of both communism and consumerism, attention toward the spiritual increased noticeably in the secular West shortly before the turning of the millennia. Throughout the 1990s, an interest in Eastern practices of yoga and meditation, as well as a deepening appreciation for the Western religious heritage, swept through the postcommunist societies of central Europe. Even in such bastions of the secular as New York, the spiritual dimension of various arts and endeavors was suddenly alluded to.

Conversely, we are unlikely to see technological prowess in itself as a moral force, as did Adams, for we now grapple with industrialism's destruction of the quality of our soil, air, and water; the ramifications of genetic engineering; the effects of the electronic childhood; the spread of biological and nuclear weapons; and the failure of the modern model of development in the "Third World." In fact, it can be said at the beginning of the twenty-first century that "the Virgin and the Dynamo" are now engaged in a rematch. This time the sterile values, spiritual emptiness, and devastating "trade-offs" of a technocratic wonderworld hold far less allure.

Mary herself has not escaped the modern fate of a fragmented existence. To many Catholics who call themselves "progressive," Mary is now a minor player — barely a grace note — in the modernized Church. They are relieved that her once ubiquitous images and novenas have been greatly reduced since the mid-1960s, that the "cult of the Virgin" has been replaced with a more reasonable and scaled-down focus on the ordinary woman mentioned a few times in the gospels. Several "progressive" authors, and many parish priests as well, openly declare that they would not be dismayed if Mary were barely ever mentioned again. The attention shown to her in the past, they explain somewhat impatiently, was simply a mistake.

Conservative groups within the Church, on the other hand, have politicized the Queen of Heaven. She is revered by them as emblematic of an older social order before liberalism had chipped away at all that is decent and right, not only in society but in the Church as well. Feminism, gay rights, social justice, women's ordination, birth control, democratizing the Church — the conservatives are absolutely certain that Mary loathes it all. Hence, the larger Our Blessed Mother's traditional presence the better.

In turn, some "progressives" on the ramparts now speak of Mary as a reactionary collaborator or a figure of ridicule. The generally admirable head of Catholics for Free Choice, for instance, wrote in 1998 that "Mary is the darling of the Catholic Right" and an icon against feminism: "Save us from new Marian dogmas — and the old ones as well."[10] In a similar vein, I came across an article in a "progressive" Catholic magazine in which a noted peace activist and Benedictine nun observed, in response to Pope John Paul II's asking for a Marian Year of devotions beginning on Pentecost in 1987, that the usual response would be to "roll our eyes and snicker about a Marian Year."[11] I have discovered that such sentiments are not rare. They are not even extreme when framed within the larger — and bleaker — context expressed to me by a forty-four-year-old Dominican nun in 1999: "I don't know any pro-Mary progressives. I've never met one, and I can't imagine one." She meant, of course, that "progressives" tend to accept the modern, "humanized" version of Mary but disdain what they consider the antiquated sense of the Virgin's larger, mystical presence — connoted by rosaries, votive candles, and the entire premodern spectacle.

In the final decade of the past millennium, however, the certainty of modernity lost its grip in unexpected ways, as we began to question some of its dazzling assertions. Was the "tough-minded," streamlined rationalism of the modern worldview a beacon of truth or was it perhaps a particular, circumscribed perspective? In several fields — such as science, medicine, governance, philosophy, art, and religion — core tenets of modern thought were challenged in the 1990s and sometimes replaced. In science, the new field of complexity studies showed nature to be far more dynamic and creative in its self-organizing capacities than the modern, mechanistic model had asserted. In medicine, the rigorously mechanistic model of the body-mind split yielded, after 350 years, to a more realistic recognition of the bodymind as a dynamic system with self-healing capabilities — demonstrated at the grassroots level as several alternative therapies were found to be efficacious. In governance, the absolute sovereignty of the modern state, a concept in place since the Treaty of Westphalia in 1648, was widely challenged by the independence efforts of ancient nations (or "captive nations") that had been absorbed and nearly erased by the boundaries of the modern state. In philosophy, which had been largely antithetical to spiritual concerns throughout the modern era, expressions of "postsecular philosophy" began to appear. In art history and criticism, many of the great works of the modern movements were suddenly seen in the late 1990s to be infused with spiritual content, a possibility that had been denied for decades by the formalist perspective, which dominated the interpretation of modern art. In this larger context, the resurgence of Marian spirituality and other acts of revitalizing "modernized" religion can be seen as yet another quiet but forceful confrontation with the reigning ideologies of modernity.

I use the term *modernity* here not in the sense of the new or up-to-date but in the larger sense of the cultural history of the West. The values and assumptions that provide the framework of our modern worldview today were put into place by the succession of four foundational movements, beginning in the fifteenth century: Renaissance humanism, the Reformation, the Scientific Revolution, and the Enlightenment. Their constructive achievements are well known to anyone raised in modern schooling. The aspect I wish to focus on here, however, is that none of the four protomodern movements was favorably disposed toward the glorified, cosmological version of Mary, which had inspired the cultural flowering in medieval art and religion.

The first flickering of modernity, Renaissance humanism, sought freedom from the domination of church and king, who together had a lock on power of all sorts. To establish an alternative system of values, the humanists orchestrated a rebirth of the secular philosophy of ancient Greece. They championed "the ancients" as a more primary touchstone of Western thought than the subsequent Christianity of the Middle Ages. Unfortunately, "the ancients" in classical Greece had turned away from the earlier holistic orientation of the neolithic era and had perceived stark discontinuities that were to haunt the West:

the belief that there is a radical break between body and mind, between humans and nature, between self and the rest of the world, and between immanent and transcendent. No other culture had ever experienced life as so fragmented and dualistic. Neither native peoples nor Eastern philosophy perceived those radical discontinuities; only in early Europe did such a disjointed orientation arise.

The Renaissance humanists' assertion of (classical Greek) reason led to their tactical goal of dethroning the figurehead of the medieval church: Mary, Queen of Heaven. Unlike medieval artists, Renaissance painters generally limited Mary to domestic scenes and often painted her looking rather dim-witted or even coquettish (in the latter case, the mistress of the painter's patron frequently served as the model). Conveniently, the Renaissance humanists' heroes — that is, the humanists of ancient Greece — had themselves banished symbolic female spiritual presence in various forms of the Goddess. Another parallel between classical and Renaissance (neoclassical) humanism was that both championed a type of rationalism that denigrated traits traditionally associated with the female as being insufficiently tough-minded.

The second movement that contributed to the birth of modernity was the Protestant Reformation, in the sixteenth century. Its focus on the individual — that is, the sacrosanct, unmediated relationship between the individual and God (to the exclusion of a community of saints, nuns, priests, and bishops) — eventually became central to the emergent modern worldview, albeit as a secularized version. The Reformation also sought to "rationalize" Christianity by disavowing most of the sacraments (that is, ritual honoring of mystical transformative events such as baptism, confirmation, matrimony, and the approach of death) and focusing instead on the text alone. In keeping with this more "rational" Christianity, the Fathers of the Reformation emphatically rejected Mary as "Advocate for the People" and "Queen of Heaven," her most popular medieval title. They insisted that Mary was nothing but a Nazarene housewife, not to be glorified in any way but merely honored for her piety and obedience to God's will.

The third movement in the emergence of modernity was the Scientific Revolution, in the sixteenth and seventeenth centuries. A new priesthood, scientists of the Newtonian and Cartesian mechanistic worldview, replaced the religious priesthood as the fount of truth. Although the leaders of the Scientific Revolution were Christian, they championed a "tougher" type of truth about reality — with military metaphors for God and Christianity — that had no use for the relational *caritas* and compassion of Marian piety or any other.

The fourth foundational movement, the Enlightenment, recast all our institutions on the model of scientism. That is, eighteenth-century enthusiasts of the Enlightenment vigorously applied "the new mechanical philosophy" from the Scientific Revolution to all our social structures and institutions. Their grand contribution was the legal concept of human rights. Above all, however, they championed the notion of the Autonomous Individual, liberated from all "constraints" such as religion, tradition, family, and place. They considered the medieval apogee of Marian spirituality to be an embarrassing detour in Europe's grand march of rationalism from classical Greece to the French Revolution — during which, by the way, countless medieval and baroque statues of Mary were vandalized or destroyed entirely.

The ideologies of modernity shaped the nineteenth century in every way. Social theory absorbed the notion of atomism, which Newton adopted from the classical Greek philosophers Democritus, Leucippus, and Epicurus, via the Renaissance humanists. Atomism was the theory that all material reality consists of compound forms of tiny bits of inert matter, which have no connection to the cosmological whole (that is, they were believed to be entirely "locally situated"). Even though Newton had no empirical evidence for making this idea the cornerstone of modern science, it was universally accepted in the newly modern West. (In the twentieth century, atoms were found to consist of elementary particles of matter/energy, each with its quantum wave interpenetrating, ultimately, the universe as a whole.) Adam Smith then applied the Newtonian acceptance of atomism to his social analysis: Society is inherently atomized (composed of individuals with no organic connection), yet some sort of force seems to organize these random bits. What could it be? Smith concluded that order is supplied to social atomism by the invisible "hidden hand" of the capitalist market (working in tandem with individual initiative, which was an influential concept in Calvinist Scotland). Later, Darwin considered Smith's metaphor of a "hidden hand" as he pondered the problem of how species change over time. Darwin eventually concluded that evolution is guided by the dynamic of "natural selection," which may be seen as the "hidden hand" in nature.

To gain respect from the new secular culture, many religions in the nineteenth century tried to appear as modern and rational as possible. Various branches of Protestantism dropped mention of their medieval mystics and, instead, churned out books on the historical Jesus and the rational application of Christian ethics. (Luther, for instance, said he had gotten one-third of his theology from the mystical writings of Meister Eckhart, but that connection is not emphasized in Protestant teachings.) In Judaism, the Reform branch was founded as a modernized version that eschewed most rituals.

The Catholic Church, which had been targeted so violently in France by the champions of the new secular age, made a very different response to modernity, however. European Catholicism intensified its embrace of its mystical, nonmodern elements as a means of resistance against forces that would destroy its meaning and its existence. After all, the Enlightenment *philosophe* Diderot had reputedly declared during the Revolution that the French champions of *liberté, egalité, fraternité* should not rest until the last priest had been murdered.

Certain features of the modern worldview combined to make the Virgin Mary in particular, and religion in general, decidedly unmodern and problematic for the nineteenth-century forces of economic progressivism and a narrowly conceived rationalism — both of which were at war with nature, spirit, and the female. Modern thought is sometimes said to be hypermasculine because it values the persona of rationalism far more highly than that of empathy. In spite of modernity's muscular opposition to the Great Mother of the West, however, Marian spirituality experienced a stunning revival involving millions of people over more than a century.

Some thirty years after the final stages of the French Revolution and violent civil war had subsided, the modern-day visitations of Mary in France began to occur: at the Daughters of Charity convent in Paris in 1830, at La Salette in 1846, at Lourdes in 1858, and at Pontmain in 1870. That is, these are the sightings that finally received official acceptance, joined by those in Portugal (at Fatima in 1917) and in Belgium (at Beauraing in 1932 and Banneux in 1933). When twenty-

four-year-old Catherine Labouré saw the luminous Virgin in the chapel
of her Daughters of Charity convent in 1830, Mary appeared framed in
an oval inside which golden lettering read "O Mary, conceived without
sin, pray for us who have recourse to thee." That image was subsequently cast as the Miraculous Medal. Within seven years, ten million
copies had circulated worldwide, and numerous cures were reported.
Its circulation reached over one billion within Labouré's lifetime.
(Labouré kept secret her own role in the origin of the Miraculous
Medal, working humbly in the laundry and the kitchen of her convent
and speaking of the Marian visitation with no one except her father
confessor and, once early on, with the Archbishop of Paris, who had
sent for her. Only at the end of her life did Labouré reveal her
experiences to her mother superior and the other nuns around her.)

Throughout the nineteenth century, the Catholic Church felt itself,
with some justification, to be under siege by secular modernity. Just as
Mary had been the focal point of the medieval florescence of the faith
and, later, had been the target of anticlerical revolutionaries in France,
so she became the rallying symbol around which the Church declared
its identity and strength in the second half of the nineteenth century.
Again and again, even into our own time, the meaning of Mary is
viewed as the line in the sand when deep-seated confrontations
take shape.

In the midst of secular *fin-de-siècle* currents in Europe, a movement
for Catholic renewal found expression in the arts. In Milan, Mary's
spiritual story was depicted in Lodovico Pogliaghi's extraordinary
sculptures on the large bronze doors that were installed as the new
main entrance to the cathedral in 1895. In Paris, Mary was the subject
of numerous Symbolist paintings from the late 1890s until the early
1920s by such artists as Maurice Denis and his colleagues. In Barce-
lona, the brilliantly organic architect Antoni Gaudi designed Casa Milá,
an apartment block characterized by curvilinear lines and undulating
volumes that he conceived as an homage to Mary, the Virgin of the
Rosary, who was to be depicted in a very large statue to be installed at
the top of the dramatic façade. He was often satirized in political
cartoons in secular, Republican newspapers at the time, one of which
showed him as a tiny figure struggling absurdly to carry the huge statue
of Mary to the top of his new building.[12] After anticlerical riots in July

1909 resulted in some fifty religious establishments being burned down, the owners of Casa Milá cancelled the idea of the Marian sculpture. In response, Gaudí lost interest in the project and turned his attention to a commission that became his best known work: the Templo Expiatorio de la Sagrada Familia (Church of the Holy Family).

Preceding this Catholic renewal in artistic circles, Pope Pius IX had responded in the mid-nineteenth century to the grassroots enthusiasm that extended through two decades following Labouré's visitation. He himself had a deep personal devotion to Mary, and he eventually decided to declare as an "article of faith" for Roman Catholics (that is, as dogma) the Immaculate Conception. This doctrine held that Mary had been conceived without Original Sin, unlike all other humans, in preparation for her role as mother of the Savior. Prior to his declaration, Pius IX convened a consultation of theologians, who voted affirmatively on his proposal (17–3). In 1854 he issued an apostolic constitution, *Ineffabilis Deus,* that defined the Immaculate Conception as a dogmatic teaching of the Church.

The papal definition was a defiant gesture against the rising tide of aggressive secularization. In addition, Pope Pius IX made it even stronger by adding an unfortunate, or at least questionable, dimension to the declaration: He asserted, for the first time in Church history, that the new dogma was an *infallible* papal teaching. The First Vatican Council, now referred to as Vatican I, was called some years later to clarify the meaning of this new concept, papal infallibility, but was interrupted by the outbreak of the Franco-Prussian War in 1870.

Almost immediately after the "people's victory" regarding the dogma of the Immaculate Conception, grassroots pressure on the Vatican began to urge a second papal Marian definition: the Assumption of the Mary into Heaven, that is, the belief that Mary was taken, body and soul, to heaven by Christ upon completion of her earthly life. This event in Mary's spiritual story had been celebrated by the faithful since at least the sixth century, when the Feast of the Assumption was placed on August 15, where it remains to this day. In response to eight million petitions received by the Vatican over the ensuing decades, Pope Pius XII sent an encyclical, *Deiparae Virginis,* to bishops around the world in 1946, asking whether they thought that the Church should define the doctrine of the Assumption as being dogmatic. Nearly all the 1,181 bishops, except for 22, agreed with the proposed change. Consequently, the doctrine of the Assumption was proclaimed infallibly by Pope Pius XII in 1950 to be an article of faith for all Roman Catholics. This definition was only the second instance of framing a Church teaching in papal infallibility. In 1954 Pope Pius XII declared the first "Marian Year" and made official Mary's long-standing title *Queen of Heaven.*

Throughout the twentieth century, both modernity and its discontents continued to gain strength. From 1914 to 1918, the grand promise of Enlightenment — the perfectibility of the human through rational social engineering — collapsed as Europeans watched almost an entire generation of their young men be fed into the trenches of the Great War, there to be poisoned by mustard gas or sent over the top to be cut down by enemy machine guns. The grand illusion of Enlightenment rationalism was blown apart by the modern endpoint: technological devastation. In the years that followed, a mood of bleak pessimism settled over Europe. Still, the call for regeneration in the early 1920s situated all hope, once again, in the modern. The new priest and prophet was believed to be the engineer and the modernist architect. For three decades, design was dominated by the machine aesthetic.

World War II brought extensive aerial fire bombing, the gas chambers, and, finally, the atom bomb. The postwar period, as is often the case, was shaped by the extension to civilian society of military values — or, at least, a macho imperative that fueled an aggressive burst of modernity in the 1950s and early 1960s. The mechanistic worldview was intensified in medicine as well as most areas of science, while all our institutions were reengineered to produce efficient, "rational" policies and products. Anything considered to be insufficiently tough, streamlined, and rigorous was swept aside by the new ideological chain of command, which instituted a "freedom" that was reputedly wide open but, in reality, had fixed boundaries and a cold sterility. It was a dynamic, expansive time — but it was also rigid, conformist, and materialist.

A reaction to this aggressive denial of anything nonmodern arose in the second half of the 1960s. In the United States and Europe, the counterculture rejected the narrow assumptions of the modern worldview and championed, instead, the relational values of ecology, community, and sexuality — all within a context of loving kindness rather than the selfish "ego-tripping" of the modern icon, the free-wheeling Autonomous Individual who supposedly needs no one and no web of relations, ecological or otherwise, to exist . . . and to triumph.

A different sort of critique of modernity emerged in the 1970s from academic circles, beginning in Paris. Deconstructive postmodernism (also known as constructionism, constructivism, or post-structuralism) rejected the overarching concepts of the modern worldview such as "rationalism," "civilization," "progress," "Marxism," and "God." It called these core concepts "metanarratives" because they were seen to be fabricated stories about reality that conceal power plays which crush the particular, or the individual. Deconstructive postmodernism, a French critique, insists that there is nothing in human experience but "social construction," by which is meant the invention of concepts such as language, systems of knowledge, and culture. According to this critique, humans have *no* experiences or sensations that are not shaped by or even created by "social construction." Moreover, deconstructionists insist that all concepts and relationships are created to gain and maintain power over others. Consequently, they see all relationships as inherently power-laden, or "political." The possibility of truth is a casualty of this viewpoint, for everything in human experience is believed to be merely made up, or "culturally constructed," at a certain time and place. Since the results are, then, entirely relative and contingent, the notion of "truth" is seen to be impossible.

I have critiqued the extreme relativism and "cultural determinism" of the deconstructionist perspective in two of my books, *States of Grace* and *The Resurgence of the Real,* by pointing out a range of ecological and biological realities that inform the myriad versions of culture and other human experience. In *States of Grace* I also considered the vast number of revelatory experiences reported by people cross-culturally, in which language and cultural expectations are replaced suddenly, and shockingly, by something quite other. I believe such surprising states of consciousness are moments in which people experience the unitive dimension of the cosmos. One may consider them cosmological revelations of the sacred whole — or moments of grace.

Unlike the deconstructionists, my gripe with modernity is not that it contains power structures. All societies do, preferably in democratic, transparent, and accountable versions. Moreover, feminist and other activists were astutely analyzing the political dimension of numerous social concepts long before deconstructionism set foot in this country. The larger problem is that modernity intensified the received perception of the core discontinuities asserted by classical Greek philosophers. Not only did modernity assert a radical break between humans and nature, but its champions convinced the West for the past four centuries that modern humans live as if in a glass box on top of nature. The natural world is regarded as mere raw material for human projects, as inert matter that operates in mechanistic modes, which we can predict and control for human ends. The blinders of the modern, mechanistic worldview prevented us from seeing what had been so obvious to premodern cultures and what is now attested to by complexity science and postmodern physics: that the nature of reality — the natural world, the Creation — is dynamic, creative, and profoundly interrelated at very subtle levels. The postmechanistic sense of reality began to emerge in the early twentieth century with relativity theory, quantum physics, and the beginnings of general systems theory. The emergent perspective expanded rapidly through various discoveries in new areas of science after World War II. Today it is increasingly understood that the life forms we see, as well as their development and behavior, are the result of myriad nonlinear relationships in a vast cosmological field of being.

One might think, then, that the Catholic Church would have a lot to congratulate itself about by the late 1980s, by which time both the discoveries of postmechanistic science and the critiques of the ideologies of modernity had percolated into the general culture. After all, the Church had preserved its recognition of a nonmechanistic sense of the Creation (a world suffused with divine goodness!) through 440 years of attacks by the ideology of modernity, specifically the more literal, "rational" version of Christianity declared by the Fathers of the Reformation. It had stayed the course, even when the modern, mechanistic worldview had aggressively rejected as "medieval superstition" the sense of an unbroken field of being that unites Christ on the cross with the bread and wine of the sacrament of communion. For what the Church calls *transubstantiation* is not at all unthinkable within the quantum field explored by postmodern physics, in which subatomic relationships are both constitutive and "nonlocal" (that is, various subatomic events have effect over great distances simultaneously). Indeed, one could well imagine the Church patting itself on the back for hanging in there and finally being proven right — or at least *simpatico* with — the postmechanistic understanding of reality.

There was one problem, however, preventing that postmechanistic triumph from occurring. After steadfastly acknowledging and honoring many nonmechanistic mysteries throughout 440 years of modern attacks, the Church capitulated only twenty years before the rising critiques of modernity and the dramatic discoveries of the new postmodern sciences. Specifically, the Church cut a huge deal with philosophical modernity in the early 1960s. In addition to its admirable liberalizing at that time of its attitudes toward other religions and its own rules for nuns, monks, priests, and the laity, Roman Catholicism took a huge step that was unnecessary for that internal and attitudinal liberalization: The Church disavowed much of its premodern (and now postmodern) spiritual brilliance in order to become more strictly text-based, rational, and — in a word — modern. Bending to the ideologies of modernity that dominated intellectual circles in that period, the Church suddenly and radically reconstituted its theology and liturgy, as well as phased out most devotional practices, in order to make Roman Catholicism more acceptable to the postmystical, postsacramental age.

The Roman Catholic Church sought to modernize itself via the Second Vatican Council, also known as Vatican II, a worldwide convocation of bishops and cardinals called to Rome from 1962-1965 to bring the Church into the modern age and "renew" it. Because Vatican II accomplished numerous positive changes in the Church, most Catholics — and nearly all liberal Catholics, myself included — hold its work in high regard. It established a greatly expanded role of the laity in the spiritual life of Catholic parishes, announced the beginning of a more respectful attitude toward other religions, allowed the mass to be celebrated in vernacular languages, and freed nuns' communities to self-govern (which resulted in many communities eventually sloughing off the hierarchical structure that had been forced on them and devising more democratic alternatives). These are but a few of the scores of liberating results of the great Vatican Council. In both the Catholic and secular press today, passing references to Vatican II routinely identify it as the historic gathering that liberalized the Church and improved its relations with other religions. All true. Never mentioned, or even associated with the admirable legacy of Vatican II, however, is the "disappearing" of Mary. Yet that is where the deed was done, the beginning of the end of her full spiritual presence — or so hoped the "modernizers."

For the previous four and a half centuries, the opposing views of the Virgin Mary in Roman Catholic and in Protestant doctrine were as firmly fixed as any touchstone of Western thought. The extreme polarity of these two views seemed, if not eternal, utterly immovable, for Protestant leaders made clear that they would never budge from their minimalist version of Mary's role. Why should they? A "rational" reading of Scripture allows nothing more.

As I recall from my childhood in the 1950s in Ohio, no one at the grassroots level was bothered much by the difference between Catholic and Protestant versions of Mary, transubstantiation, grace, or the symbol of the cross (which in Catholicism is occupied by the body of Christ to denote the divine sacrifice of the Crucifixion and in Protestantism is empty to denote the Resurrection). It was all part of the mix that gave form and diversity to our society's religious life. Although each side found the other's beliefs largely unfathomable, there was no push to force a change in the status quo. At least, that was how it seemed to most grassroots Catholics.

Throughout the 1950s, however, dissatisfaction was brewing in certain quarters of the Catholic laity about the passivity expected of them by the Church, often summarized as the imperative to "Pray, pay, and obey." These Catholics wanted all lay members of the Church to be allowed fuller participation in the collective spiritual and activist life of the Church. Many religious communities of nuns and priests also felt that a liberalization was badly needed in order to enliven the ministry of the Church. In addition, some Catholics wanted to hear the mass celebrated in their own language instead of Latin. All of these currents were swirling quietly by the end of the decade.

Unbeknownst to the grassroots, though, a decision was made — and was made central — at that time in influential circles of the Roman Catholic clergy: Ecumenical rapprochement with the Protestants and the Orthodox was suddenly a top priority. In service to this new focus, the modernizing of the Church had to include not only a widespread liberalization but also radical theological and liturgical changes that would make Catholicism more acceptable to the "separated brethren." (In chapter five, I suggest several reasons for this sudden shift.) To achieve this end, Pope John XXIII, only ninety days into his tenure, unexpectedly announced that he would convoke the Second Vatican Council (the first having been held in 1869–1870). The theme of the Council was to be *aggiornamento*: bringing the Church up to date, or "into the present day." The Council Fathers from around the world were to compose a Dogmatic Constitution on the Church plus fifteen other constitutions, declarations, and decrees, which together would achieve the "renewal" of the Roman Catholicism in the modern age. In January 1959 the pope established various preparatory commissions, which labored for three years to bring draft proposals to the Council. However, in the invitation to all the bishops and cardinals, the pope also invited them to suggest topics that would be addressed by the Church's Twenty-First Ecumenical Council (Vatican II).

The focus of this book is not the hugely complex workings of Vatican II but, rather, its decisions about Mary. These are found in only one chapter of one of the sixteen major documents that were produced by the Council. This one chapter — "The Role of the Blessed Virgin Mary, Mother of God, in the Mystery of Christ and the Church" in the constitution on the Church, *Lumen Gentium* (The Light of Humankind) — is a small portion of the total output of the Council but has reverberated through four decades with huge repercussions.

Several intellectual currents of the post–World War II period flowed into the debates over Mary at Vatican II. Throughout the 1950s and early 1960s, young intellectual priests in Europe and elsewhere were influenced by supposedly tough-minded modern thought: Marxism was accepted by many European intellectuals as the "scientific" theory of history, the social sciences were skewed in the direction of econometric analysis, and the Freudian assertion that religion was an infantile regression cast a particularly critical light on the notion of Mary, Mother of God. If an intellectual in that period felt compelled to digress from materialist rationalism in order to participate in religion, it was thought best that the religious activity be kept compartmentalized and involve as little irrationalism as possible.

In this zeitgeist, the "Mary problem" began to bother some of the modern priests more than ever. Most Protestants and even some Catholics (who were part of the "biblical movement" within the Church) considered Marian spirituality nonbiblical and nearly idolatrous, while the materialist intellectuals found it absurdly irrational. What happened next — although never ever admitted but too obvious to overlook — was an iteration of the process whereby various guardians of patriarchal culture decide to clamp down now and then. Imagine a cardinal's inner circle or a clubby group deep within the Vatican. One of the members saunters in looking glum and peevish. He stares at the floor and reports dejectedly what his peers know but do not want to hear: "Those other guys are making fun of us for having a giant mother in the middle of our religion."

When the cardinals, archbishops, bishops, theologians, and others arrived in Rome in October 1962, a few naifs still held out hope that the pope would, at some point in the near future, issue a papal definition of Mary as having participated uniquely with Jesus in the Redemption, that is, as a Co-Redeemer. Most of the summoned Council Fathers, however, did not expect Mariology to be a focus of the reforming convocation. They anticipated debates in areas related to theology and the liturgy, relations with other denominations and religions, church structure, role of the laity, various issues for religious orders and communities, and what became known at the Council as "the five particular issues": marriage, culture, economics, politics, and peace. On arrival, the Council Fathers were faced with a vast amount of material to be considered. During the second month, they were given a draft of a rather traditional document about Mary, "The Blessed Virgin Mary, Mother of God and Mother of the People," which the pope had approved and which the Marian preparatory theological commission intended to be a separate declaration celebrating the full spiritual presence of Mary in the modern era. Although the Marian commission had gone back and forth on whether or not their draft should be a free-standing document, they finally opted for that designation before submitting it. Because of the huge crush of topics to be addressed, the matter of Mary was not taken up until nearly a year later, when seven bishops proposed that any statement about Mary should be included in the new constitution on the Church.

As soon as the word spread, in September 1963, that some of the Council Fathers wanted to abandon the separate and traditional document on Mary in order to address Marian issues as a chapter in the reforming constitution, tempers flared. Why include a chapter about Mary in a constitution instituting fundamental change? Marian traditionalists correctly suspected that any changes the "progressives" had in mind would result in a radically reduced recognition of the spiritual presence of the Blessed Mother and a severe pruning of devotions in her honor.

Indeed, the Marian "progressives" argued that Mariology should "progress" and "develop" in line with modern, "scientific" methods of biblical exegesis, which supposedly demonstrate that the Madonna should correctly be considered merely a *member* of the Church, having a status equal to all other Christians but being notable for her piety. This view had been articulated by a few prominent Catholic theologians in Europe in the years prior to Vatican II. Citing modern hermeneutical theory, the "progressives" maintained that the sophisticated interpretation of Mary's role in Scripture views her solely as a "type," or "archetype," or microcosm, of the Church: Rather than being Mother of the Church and the faithful, she is strictly a cipher, or sign, meant to represent the Church in Scripture. Fending off any claims that Mary had a unique and central role in the Redemption, they argued that her role was the same as that of the Church: to respond and cooperate. This position was known as the "ecclesio-typical" view of Mary, interpreting her as essentially a type, or model, of and for the Church. Although there were variations of the "progressive" Marian position among Council Fathers, the "progressives" all agreed that the Marian presence in the Catholicism must be made more strictly biblical and ecclesio-typical and that Marian devotions had become "isolated" from the Mystery of Christ. It was even argued that the list of traditional Marian titles called the Litany of Loreto actually refers to the Church rather than to Mary! The new "scientific," semiotic hermeneutics of Mary in Scripture, they asserted, would not result in a new Marian dogma; it would merely clear away all the nonbiblical elements in Mariology, which would make her more recognizable and acceptable to other Christian churches, as well.[13]

The Marian traditionalists, both liberal and conservative, were beside themselves with disbelief that such a radical (and nearly Protestant) demotion of Mary might well displace more than 1,600 years of spiritual practice. They felt that the modern world was desperately in need of the full spiritual presence of Mary in her mystical dimensions — which the Church had correctly defended and protected through the centuries. Moreover, they argued that a theologically sophisticated analysis perceives Mary as having shared in the Redemption in ways that were clearly unique and are the source of her great dignity and expansive spiritual presence.

In order to prepare for a vote on the issue, a debate was called from the floor, the only one of its kind at Vatican II. The Marian traditionalists were represented by Rufino Cardinal Santos of Manila, who spoke first. He presented ten arguments for keeping a doctrinal statement about Mary separate from the constitution on the Church. Primarily, he asserted that the historical moment of both renewal for the Church and engagement with the other branches of Christianity called for a complete explication of Catholicism's doctrines on the Blessed Mother; the necessary full treatment could not be accomplished if the doctrinal statement on Mary were to be merely a chapter in the constitution on the Church. Moreover, the subject of the other chapters in the proposed constitution on the Church (such as the laity; the hierarchical structure of the Church; the "call to holiness in the Church"; and the religious professions of priests, nuns, and monks) were not parallel to the subject of Mary because her call to holiness and her belonging to the People of God were different in nature from the callings of the laity and the clergy. To reduce the Council's doctrinal treatment of Mary to a chapter in the new delineation of the Church would give the impression, Santos warned, that the Church now favors an "ecclesio-typical" Mariology rather than the traditional "Christo-typical" perception of her (her essential meaning being Christ-centered and Redemption-centered, so that she watches over the Church and is called its Mother). Giving the impression of such a shift would spark divisiveness. Cardinal Santos also argued for doctrinal recognition of Mary's unique participation in the Redemption: She alone was the God-Bearer, who was intimately and singularly with Christ from the beginning to the end, as she suffered at the foot of the Cross.[14]

Representing the other side of the debate was Franz Cardinal König of Vienna. Cardinal König — who was well known by then for favoring a correction to the "isolation" of Marian devotions and for championing the "scientific" methods of biblical exegesis that reveal Mary's meaning in Scripture to be "ecclesio-typical" — opened with a warm response to Cardinal Santos. He began by saying that he did not wish to contradict the traditionalists' position as it had just been articulated. (Some apologists today cite this opening statement as evidence that the "modernizers" had no downgrading of Mary in mind![15]) König then went on to present four types of reasons why the schema on Mary should be inserted into the constitution on the Church. The theological reason was that including Marian issues as a chapter would save the constitution from appearing, to some, to portray an excessively institutional conception of the Church — and that an assimilated chapter would convey the message that the Council's pronouncements on the place of Mary were consistent with the purposes of Vatican II. The historical reason was that attention to Mary had reached the doctrinal level solely because of the mediation of Mother Church, so further mediation now through the new constitution on the Church would be historically consistent. The pastoral reason was that the faithful were being encouraged to "purify" their devotion to Mary and focus on what was essential to it. Lastly, the ecumenical reason was that an ecclesio-typical Mariology makes possible a convergence with Protestants and the Orthodox.[16]

It is often said by "progressives" that the argument presented at Vatican II to "modernize" Mariology, by Cardinal König and others, was "more nuanced" than was the traditionalist position, presented by Cardinal Santos and others.[17] The situation seems to me to be the opposite. As the *History of Vatican II,* the definitive presentation of the "progressive" perspective on the Council, notes disdainfully, "the defenders of the 'privileges' of our Lady . . . mainly analyzed the glorious titles of the Virgin as described in the encyclicals of the recent popes."[18] That is, these Council Fathers cited Mary's titles and doctrinally recognized attributes, hoping that the ineffable resonance of these spiritual responses to the maternal source of the Incarnation would be acknowledged. They noted the beauty of the devotions to her and spoke passionately of her presence in lived Catholicism. Because a religious Mystery, such as that of the God-Bearer, cannot be captured in words, the traditionalists alluded to the entire spiritual banquet of rich and historically layered perceptions of the Blessed Mother in the Mystery of her profound presence in the Redemption and the inner lives of the People of God. A draft schema submitted by some of the Marian traditionalists was titled *De Mysterio Mariae in Ecclesia* (On the Mystery of Mary in the Church); it did not get circulated. The Marianists appealed not solely to any one part of Catholic communion with Mary but to the immeasurable, nonlinguistic totality. This perception is *nothing but* nuanced, as it is so spiritually subtle that words violate the wholeness of the Mystery.

But what is all that to the modern mentality? It could not even hear the language, let alone the depth, of the traditionalist side, dismissing it as sentimental nonmodern gibberish. The "rationalizing" position came down like a fist on the poetic, mystical perception, declaring that the traditional view of Mary is disallowed because much of it lies outside the text, because Mary must be seen to exist solely in service to the institution of the modern Church rather than being theologically superior to it in any way, and because the Protestants — with their more rational type of Christianity — would not like it. Many of the "progressives" at Vatican II also asserted that the Early Church Fathers had considered Mary to be essentially "ecclesio-typical," a model or type representing the Church, but in the subsequent decades it has become generally agreed that only a very few of the Early Church Fathers viewed her in that way.

It is doubtful that all of the bishops who supported bringing in the new hermeneutical methods of interpreting Scripture and pruning some excesses in Marian devotions realized that draconian results would follow from a victory for the leaders of the "Marian modernization." It is evident, in fact, that a far more innocent spin was put on the issues: The options were framed by both sides in terms of what would most please Our Lady, a loving term for the Blessed Mother that, ironically, would not survive the Marian modernizing. A Council Father from South Africa recalled, in 2001, the solicitous concern for Mary in those days that shaped much of the discussion among the bishops themselves: "The question of our Lady in the documents of the Council was keenly debated. Those who wanted a special schema for our Lady felt it would be a derogation from the honour due to her to merely include her in the schema of the Church. The other side was convinced that Mary would want nothing better than to be closely associated with the Church."[19]

On the day of the vote, October 29, 1963, and the weeks leading up to it, the atmosphere was charged with intense lobbying. Ordinarily the Council voted with a unanimity higher than 90 percent, but over Mary they were almost evenly divided. By less than a 2 percent majority (40 votes) of the 2,193 votes cast, the "modernizers" carried the day: A chapter on the Virgin Mary employing new "scientific" methods of biblical exegesis, depicting her as primarily ecclesio-typical, and correcting her "isolation" would be written and added to the reforming constitution on the Church. (It is often claimed by "progressive" historians of Vatican II that this vote was merely about a procedural matter — that is, whether a Marian statement should be free-standing or included in the constitution on the Church — but the debate, lobbying, and vote were clearly about the content of the proposed statement as well.) A shift of only twenty-one votes would have saved the Roman Catholic Church from moving in a profoundly unwise direction, for the target of the "modernizers" was not merely "excessive" degrees of Marian devotion but the very heart of Marian spirituality itself. Many of the men left the hall in tears.

Mary, Queen of Heaven was scaled down to her new role as Mary, Just a Housewife, albeit a pious forerunner of the Church. So much more rational!

Because so much welcome change emerged from Vatican II, attention was focused, with great celebration, on the constructive results. An exciting current of new possibility flowed through grassroots Catholicism as we heard that the Church would soon be opening respectful dialogue with other faiths, enlarging the role of the laity, emphasizing the dignity of the person as a core value in modern institutions, and dropping the embarrassing insistence that non-Catholics are destined for hell. Protests did arise immediately among many Catholics over the loss of the beautiful Latin mass, but only slowly, over many years, did the laity absorb the full significance of the radical shrinking and deemphasizing of Mary.

In the new constitution of the Church composed at the Second Vatican Council, *Lumen Gentium* (The Light of Humankind), Mary is limited to such roles as "Helper" or "Associate of the Redeemer." Her title "Mother of the Church" is notably missing. Moreover, the Council Fathers argued against three aspects of Mary's spiritual presence. First, they decreed that the traditional titles "Mediator" (Mary shares and bestows, in a uniquely maternal way, Christ's mediation of divine grace) and "Advocate" (since the third century, Mary has been considered "Advocate for the People of God," especially the poor) may be used solely in a lesser sense: Christ is the one and only Mediator, but Mary "by her maternal charity, cares for the brethren of her Son who still journey on the earth." Second, while it is understandable that the controversial title "Co-Redeemer" (Mary was uniquely and inherently *with,* but not equal to, Christ in the bringing of salvation) is not mentioned, the entire theological perception that Mary's role in the Redemption was extra-ordinary and that the she, as the God-Bearer and prime disciple, is a site of Mystery was firmly set aside. Henceforth Mary is to be "hailed as a pre-eminent and altogether singular member of the Church, and as the Church's model and excellent exemplar in faith and charity."[20] *That* is a demotion of vast proportion.

The Council's decree on liturgical reforms, *Sacrosanctum Concilium* (Constitution on the Sacred Liturgy), urges in chapter seven that statues (of Mary and the saints) be minimized to more "moderate" quantities and displayed more discreetly (to "reflect right order") so that they do not "create confusion" among Christians, both Catholics and our modern, rational, Protestant "separated brethren," who might otherwise get the wrong idea about Catholics and conclude that we have a giant mother fixation. It simply does not *look right* to the modern world.

In tandem with the "modernized" Marian doctrines, Vatican II initiated "modernizing" liturgical reforms that eradicated Mary from the Sunday mass, except for the one-second reference to her when the Nicene Creed is recited. All prayers to her were deleted, except in special Marian masses celebrated on her few remaining holy days in the liturgical calendar or on Saturday, Mary's day. The Marian feast day commemorating Mary's maternal dignity, October 11, on which Pope John XXIII had opened the Second Vatican Council with a masterful speech, by the way, did not survive the "modernizing" of the Marian calendar. (The pope noted in that speech that he, like the "progressive" theologians, favored studying and expounding the Church's "authentic doctrine" "through the methods of research and through the literary forms of modern thought" as well as working to attain "the unity of the Christian family,"[21] so it is likely that he would have been pleased with both the Marian vote and the "modernized" Marian chapter, had he lived to see them.)

Following the conclusion of Vatican II, a great silence about Mary descended from the hierarchy and most clergy, as statues of her were removed from many Catholic churches and churchyards. The Marian Library, the world's largest collection of printed materials on Mary, located at the University of Dayton, was ordered to suspend three of its publications and to vacate its new, two-story wing adjoining the main campus library for less high-profile housing on the seventh floor so as not to "impede ecumenical dialogue."[22] Rosary devotions and novenas were largely phased out in parishes, as were nearly all the hymns honoring Mary. An entire generation of Catholics born after 1960 — including many nuns and priests — has almost no connection with "that old-time Mary stuff," which is commonly regarded with a shrug of hip disdain.

For many of us whose spiritual lives straddle the great divide — before and after Vatican II — the extreme reduction of liturgical and devotional practices is felt as an inestimable loss. Thomas Lanigan-Schmidt, an artist in New York who continues the tradition of Catholic peasant folk art by creating beautiful mosaic icons from common (urban-industrialized) materials, compares the "streamlining" of the liturgy at Vatican II to the Cultural Revolution in China: "An entire spiritual, aesthetic culture was betrayed and destroyed. They went into an iconoclastic frenzy of image-smashing. Just as everyone else was starting to see the limitations of modernity, the Church opted for a Bauhaus-type liturgy, a huge process of uglification!"[23] Another well-known creator of contemporary Marian icons, Robert Lentz, agrees:

"The aesthetic is the vehicle for the mystery; when that's gone, there's nothing left but the power structure."[24]

For some time, it seemed to the triumphant modernizers that the medieval vestiges had been successfully cleared away so that a more "rational," streamlined Church could sail into the coming millennium, winning greater respect from the modern world in general and from the Protestant denominations in particular. There were significant areas of hold-outs—the ethnic parishes in the United States, as one might expect—as well as most of the Spanish-speaking world, South Asia and Southeast Asia, plus Southern, Central, and Eastern Europe. However, the "progressives" believed that the premodern insistence in those cultures on inserting traditional Marian hymns into the modernized mass would surely die out eventually.

What the Church did not count on was a vast grassroots rejection of this type of "modernizing" at Mary's expense. By the late 1970s a growing sense of loss had spread among large portions of the laity as Mary slipped further from practice and memory, especially among young people. The prospect of a barren future in a "modernized" Catholic Church that has vigorously lopped off the Maternal Matrix, the Great Mother of Catholic spiritual life, was literally pathetic—full of the pathos of modernity's relegating poetic expressions of subtle but profound relatedness and spiritual beauty to the scrapheap of premodern sentimentality. There was uncertainty and confusion about what could be done because the "modernizers" of Mary were firmly in control. Yet a grassroots resurgence of Marian spirituality slowly took hold.

This spontaneous challenging of the excessive "rationalizing" of Catholic theology and practice is embedded, as we have seen, in the larger questioning of the ideologies of modernity, which began in the late twentieth century. We are, in fact, living through a historical moment of far-reaching transition that is parallel to what Henry Adams observed in his autobiography at the dawn of the fully industrialized age: "Every generalization that we settled forty years ago is abandoned."[25]

The hope of our time resides in our finding pathways to wisdom. Certain premodern perceptions of the cosmos are now seen anew through the discoveries of contemporary science. Every entity in the universe, for instance, is now known to be kin (that is, related at the molecular level) with everything else, so the metaphor of a cosmological Maternal Matrix, so beloved to medieval Christians, fits well. In chapter three, "Premodern Mary Meets Postmodern Cosmology," I consider several of these parallels.

Even without recourse to science, though, one can observe numerous areas today in which modernity's long-standing disdain for the nonmodern is giving way. During the past thirty years a new appreciation has emerged for the ecological communion inherent in traditional native cultures, for instance; the effects of prayer on healing are increasingly acknowledged; and women's relational ways of knowing and being are now studied and respected a bit more. This shift is part of a historic questioning of the failed or destructive aspects of modernity's narrowly defined yet aggressively imposed rationalism. Such questioning became widespread in the 1980s and 1990s. A relevant example is the British study *Losing the Sacred: Ritual, Modernity, and Liturgical Reform* (2001) by David Torevell. Another example is the recent restoration in many Reform congregations of Judaism of some of the previously eschewed rituals, such as the proscriptions for mourning after a death in the family. Modernity, in short, need not be accepted as a "package deal." Discernment is called for.

Although the results of Vatican II have been positive in nearly all areas except Marian spirituality, the Church's unfortunate timing in denying the mystical and cosmological sense of Mary has left them out of step with the rising tide of organic and cosmological sensibilities in the twenty-first century. Mary's human origins and larger-than-human spiritual presence — that is, the religious perception of "*big* Mary" the Maternal Matrix — are an organically symbolic link between humans and the larger reality, the sacred whole. Her cosmological nature, expressed symbolically in the all-encompassing title "Queen of Heaven," reflects the unitive dimension of all life forms and processes in the cosmos. All are inherently related, all tracing their lineage back to the birth of the universe in the primordial fireball.

The modern worldview, however, is blind to the essential correction Mary's cosmological dimension brings to the modern Western error of framing the human story in tragic alienation from the unfolding story of the cosmos. Seen through the lens of modernity, the millions of people in communion with Mary are simply afflicted with an immature fixation on a mother figure writ large, a need exploited by the Catholic Church to keep its followers childlike, suppliant, and obedient. I am heartened that such an interpretation is increasingly seen to be cosmologically barren. It reflects the shrunken modern focus on the human in isolation from the larger context. That sense of isolation has deep roots in Western culture, but Mary's roots are deeper still.

Mary, the bountiful *body* of grace who is both fully human and is the fount of the Incarnation, unites that which is thought to be divided. While it is true that Mary is the product of Western yearnings, they are not the pitiable narcissism of the shrunken modern psyche dissected by modern psychology. I believe that her particular attributes emerged through the devotion of the laity over time so that the collective Western psyche, within Christianity, could forge a way beyond the radical discontinuities bequeathed to the West by much of Greek philosophy and could be reunited with cosmological wholeness. Mary is thoroughly of the Earth and of the sacred whole. That is our nature as well. She is the mother of spiritual salvation in the West, not only bringing forth the Incarnation but also embodying the correction to so much that is otherwise unbalanced, incomplete, and ill conceived — not the least of which is all-male religion. Containing her has always been a problem for Church authorities, and these days they are nervous once again. Mary looms so large in such unexpected ways.

From inside the Marian resurgence, one can easily see what is apparently not visible from the viewpoint of modernity: Many of the elements in Mary's spiritual presence — her attention to those who are suffering, her female ethic of care, her cosmological dimension, her combination of power with humility, and her ability to instill hope — are essential elements in a new awareness that is taking root. The question is not whether we "go back to the Middle Ages" *or* remain in thrall to the ideologies of modernity but whether a new synthesis can draw deeply of enough wisdom to match our current knowledge of the Creation. Marian spirituality makes a crucial contribution by making available much of the spiritual richness that modernity disallowed. Mary's gifts are powers that are necessary to nurture the new possibilities at this fertile moment in human history.

We entered the new millennium with all the optimism we could muster, even though we realized that the modern trade-offs have degraded human experience in many ways with respect to community, nature, and our awareness of the sacred whole. Increasingly, the stripped down, "rationalized" version of religion required by modernity feels inadequate for the task of recovering that which has been lost. In recent years, however, spirituality that is multivalent and evocative in its symbols, metaphors, and rituals began to gain honor and respect once again. The all-embracing, poetic approach to the ineffable is compelling because it reflects the cosmological magnificence of which we are a part. The Marian rebellion is part of that recovery.

Seat of Wisdom

Eternal Genetrix

Our Lady of Good Counsel

Chapter Two

The Quiet Rebellion against the Suppression of Mary

Where is the Virgin Mary in the modernized Roman Catholic Church of the third millennium? She is not in the mass: The widely beloved "Salve Regina" prayer, which had been recited at the close of every mass around the world for centuries, was yanked by liturgical "reforms" forty years ago. She is often not even mentioned during the sermon on her few remaining holy days. She is not in the churchyards: Most of her statues are long gone or relegated to marginal locations. In many of the weekly parish bulletins, she is nowhere to be found: No group recitations of the rosary or novenas or other contemplative practices that further spiritual communion with her are included in the schedule. She is barely covered at all in the education that most young nuns and priests receive. Her image was even deleted from the commemorative rosary issued by the Vatican to pilgrims during the Jubilee Year 2000 in Rome. Since the rosary is the central contemplative device in Marian spirituality, a rosary without Mary is nearly unthinkable, yet this one was produced as a symbol of the Roman Catholic Church at the dawn of the new millennium.

To Protestant eyes these developments seem perfectly reasonable and were long overdue, for the Protestant acknowledgement of Mary is strictly text-based, limited to her few appearances in the New Testament.[1] Mary is to be honored as a pious housewife and an obedient servant of God, even a saint in some denominations. In contrast to this text-based (that is, strictly biblical) version of Mary, Catholics have traditionally acknowledged a mystical, cosmological sense of Mary as well (that is, a biblical*plus* sense of her). She is the Great Mother of the faith, a compassionate presence, and a confidant of the ages. She is the mediator between humans and the Divine, being more than the former and less than the latter. She is symbolically linked with the moon, for she reflects the glorious light of the Son while belonging to both heaven and Earth. She is a spiritual figure not only personal and cosmological but also cultural, bearing the heart of many a nation's deepest identity in their own vision of her.

The meaning of the Blessed Virgin extends beyond the two millennia of Church history and the delineation of Church doctrine. Mary moves backward and forward in time. Her lineage is far older than Christian or Jew. Her mystery is unbounded. How is it possible that Mar-yam (or Miriam), a simple Hebrew peasant girl, became the Mother of Nations, the Queen of Heaven, and the tender locus of spiritual hope in the hearts of millions? What moves so many to consecrate their lives to her — in liberation struggles, in daily gifts of service, in silent communion with the sacred? What compelling allure in her spiritual presence has inspired such great art and music? By what means do appeals to her heal the suffering of body and mind? Through what sort of communion does she evoke the courage and perseverance that propel a life to the level of the heroic, in both personal and public spheres? How can it be that she is rooted so deeply in so many different lands, bearing within her each culture's deepest memories? What is the source of her poignant dignity, infusing all who come to her with the radiance of grace? How is it that she makes clear the wholeness of heart-body-mind as no mere text can do?

For two thousand years, one of the great mysteries of Western spirituality has been the transformation of a teenage girl from Nazareth — who is mentioned only briefly in three of the four gospels — into the Queen of Heaven, the maternal conduit of divine grace, and the subject of two-thirds of all the pilgrimage sites in Christendom (more than 75 percent in some countries).[2] Every stage of that spiritual transformation was driven by the demands of the lay people. In response, the bishops and popes always found, or created, a rationalization by which they could incorporate the various expressions of powerful Marian devotion into official Roman Catholic theology.

Today, however, a different dynamic is in play. During the past four decades, the two thousand-year trajectory has been reversed, driven this time by the Church hierarchy. The rationalization they have come up with to justify their shrinking of Mary? They assert that much of the theology properly belonging to the Holy Spirit, the third aspect of God as Holy Trinity, had come to be associated over time with Mary. To correct that theological error, the Holy Spirit had to be elevated in importance, they explain, while she had to be drastically diminished. The Queen of Heaven was deemed problematic by a hierarchy of powerful men who then "disappeared" her former presence.

In the modernized Church, the Holy Spirit is now situated in (triumphant) competition with Mary, invoked to trump her at every possible opportunity. Even though I have seen this sleight-of-hand executed scores of times in recent years — when, for instance, speakers at Marian conferences are advertised as skilled teachers on Marian devotion who "bring people to the experience of the Holy Spirit" — I was shocked when I opened a velvet pouch containing a commemorative Jubilee Year rosary. It was a gift brought back from Rome by my friend Judith in February 2000. At first I was stunned by her generosity, for the entire rosary was made of heavy silver with intricate rosebuds as the beads. I held the silver beads in my hands, marveling at the beauty of the details. Suddenly I noticed something strange and felt a tightening in my solar plexus. At the spot where an image of Mary is always found, she was not there. I stared in disbelief. There was something odd in her place, some sort of logo . . . of swirling flames? Eventually I perceived that the design was a circle of four stylized, swirling doves: the symbol of the Holy Spirit. Banishing Mary even from the rosary? Could this be? Using the Holy Spirit to displace her? Could the "modernizers" actually have gone that far?

Surprisingly, many Catholics seem unaware of just how far the coup has advanced. If they have attended mass regularly, they are by now accustomed to the extremely minimized Marian presence. However, many of the twenty million Catholics who have "lapsed" in recent decades, myself included, have enjoyed the acute perception of a Rip Van Winkle when we have returned, even sporadically. The lovely surprise of seeing altar girls paled beside the shock of perceiving that Mary is missing — or nearly so. The contrast with her former presence is so severe and yet so largely unnoticed at the parish level after all this time that the situation feels slightly eerie. Countless intelligent Catholics immersed in an almost totally Maryless liturgy have responded to various of my comments with blank surprise: "Oh, has Mary been diminished in recent decades?"

Repression so successful as to have become invisible is unnerving indeed. Yet a large and growing segment of Catholics worldwide are quietly challenging the excessive pruning of Marian spirituality. Since the mid-1990s more than six million Catholics around the world have stormed the Vatican, by mail, to petition for the reversal of Mary's diminution. Specifically, they have appealed to the pope to make three of Mary's pre-Vatican II titles "articles of faith." Their petition drive is merely one expression of the current Marian resurgence. Other indications include the following: Attendance at Marian shrines is now far higher than ever before; Marian devotions are being reintroduced in many Catholic schools and churches; a new wave of Marian art is appearing; and recordings of traditional Marian music are selling briskly. In short, the "modern" rejection of Mary is itself being rejected all over the world. During the past two decades, millions of people have found their way back to her — or have arrived for the first time — constituting one of the major religious events of our time.

By 1999 the Marian renewal was manifesting itself in academic journals that had rarely featured articles on her in the past. At least three such journals, in fact, published entire issues on Mary that year: *Christos: Revue de Formation Spirituelle* and *Croire Aujourd'hui,* two French theological journals; and *Theology Today,* a predominantly Protestant journal from Princeton Theological Seminary. An article in the Marian issue of *Christos* (no. 183), titled "The Return of the Virgin Mary," opens by declaring, "After a long absence, Mary has come back." It advocates a vital Marian spirituality that is free of both the old excesses and the post-Vatican II "desiccated rationalism": "'The Marian dimension of the Church precedes the Petrine one,' John Paul II reminds us. In other words, the Church is more charismatic than hierarchical. Mary reveals to us that the identity of the Church, the heart of the alliance, is feminine."[3]

In August 2002 I presented the themes of this book at a national conference of the *actual* feminine in the Church, Catholic nuns. Many of them took me aside during the following two days to share their experiences, which, as I discovered, reflect the larger Marian awakening within the Church — particularly at the personal level. A sixty-two-year-old Dominican sister told me, "For the past few years I've been saying the 'Hail, Holy Queen' [the 'Salve Regina' prayer] before I fall asleep. When it first came up in my mind, I thought, 'What's going on?' — but I've kept it up because it feels right." Another, a white-haired Sister of St. Joseph, said laughingly, "I was one of the teachers who taught theology to the young nuns after Vatican II. You're right that Mary just seemed to fade away. Now I realize the loss. It feels as if I lost a dear friend." A third told me, "I was raised with Mary in a general sort of way, but then I put her on the shelf. Now I understand her in a different way that's deeper." Finally, a fifty-two-year-old sister told me she hadn't been to mass in years because she is so angry at the Church but added passionately, "I was in tears after your presentation. You've given Mary back to me. Nothing can stop me now from going to church and praying with her." Good luck finding her there, I thought. Better take a picture.

The fact that that organization of nuns is neither politically reactionary nor even very conservative illustrates the complex mix of orientations that constitutes the Marian renewal. Although the Catholic Church is now split over the issue of Marian spirituality — the traditional biblical*plus* version versus the "modernized," biblical*only* version — the old alignments of liberal versus conservative are crisscrossed or blurred in this rebellion, as is the case in many other grassroots struggles today. "Progressives" often assert that Catholics who favor the traditional, mystical sense of Mary are categorically right-wing reactionaries, or at least "social conservatives." Yet countless liberal Catholics feel that the "modernizers" at Vatican II, and in the years afterward, erred profoundly when they targeted Mary. Increasingly, Catholics who do not identify themselves with either right or left factions politely confront their parish priest to ask *why* the Church has downplayed Mary since the Second Vatican Council. Through countless acts grand and small, this quiet rebellion continues to grow.

No doubt some of the Marian resurgence can be attributed to the mood of spiritual renewal that accompanied the turning of the millennia as the year 2000 approached. Millennial fever aside, however, I surmise that the second half of the 1990s saw the Marian recovery balloon in size because it took some thirty years for the Catholic laity to absorb the far-reaching effects of the Virgin's shrunken presence in the wake of Vatican II. There was never any overt campaign against Mary by the Church hierarchy, merely the triumphant assertion of the new Church in which, it was understood, she would play a far more modest role.

Even had there been no resurgence of Marian spirituality in the 1990s, however, Mary still would have been inherent in the millennial moment. The dawning of New Year's Day in the year 2000 was merely another spin of the Earth in the range of the sun's beneficence. The moment was special to us only because Christianity — and now the entire modern world — marks time in a certain way: Two thousand years ago Mary assented to give birth to a miracle. In short, no Mary, no millennium.

In fact, Mary's inherent relationship with the millennial moment made all the more jarring her absence from the Church's sequence of dedicated years leading up to the "Great Jubilee of the Redemptive Incarnation in the Year 2000." In the Great Jubilee commemoration, the Church declared that 1997 was the Year of Christ, 1998 was the Year of the Holy Spirit, and 1999 was the Year of God the Father. *Where's Mary?* "Oh, we did her back in 1987" was the official response. Mary's symbolic birth year was celebrated then because she was thirteen when she became pregnant with Jesus. Even so, there can be no doubt that the current pope never intended his declaration of 1987 as the Year of the Blessed Virgin Mary to be used later by the "modernizers" as justification for the heavy silence about her during the Great Jubilee year. Defenders of the fullness of Mary's spiritual presence remind her censors that the divine plan for salvation via the Incarnation intimately and essentially involved maternal mediation and cooperation — "the heart of a woman" — which guided the unfolding of the life of Jesus, beginning with the Annunciation. No Mary, no Jubliee.

The Marian resurgence began not with a head-on confrontation but with a silent surge in the late 1970s of millions of people making pilgrimages to the great Marian shrines, both the medieval holy sites in Europe and the more recent additions in the New World. Perhaps they were encouraged when they heard that the new pope, the Cardinal of Kracow, who took the name John Paul II, was so devoted to the Mother of God that he had insisted on including a large "M" in his papal seal, over the objections of the "progressives" in the Vatican. Moreover, he had chosen for his papal slogan his life-long vow to Mary: *Totus Tuus* (My Entire Self Is Yours). On many other issues, this pope has proven to be exasperating, but repeatedly he has held the line against the erasure of Mary in her fullness.

Throughout the 1980s and 1990s, attendance at the major Marian shrines continued to increase annually. By the turn of the millennium, the number of Marian pilgrims surely surprised, if not alarmed, the "modernizers." This was not supposed to have happened in the aftermath of Vatican II. During 1999, for instance, 5.2 million people visited Lourdes, in France; 5.3 million visited Fatima, in Portugal; 4.8 million visited Czestochowa, in Poland; and 10 million visited Compostella, in Spain. In Mexico 14.8 million people visited the basilica dedicated to Our Lady of Guadalupe. In the United States the forty-three Marian shrines have drawn sharply increasing numbers of pilgrims since the early 1990s. More than a half million people annually, for instance, now visit the National Shrine Grotto of Our Lady of Lourdes, in Maryland.[4]

Moreover, a surprising number of visitations, or sightings, of the Blessed Virgin Mary have occurred during the past twenty years. Mary has reportedly appeared to individuals in churches and shrines from Nicaragua to Ukraine, most famously to six Croatian children in Medjugorje, Bosnia-Hercegovina, beginning in 1981. There have even been sightings of Mary in the bark of trees in California and weeping statues of her in Italy and elsewhere. What can it all mean? I believe that a sincere and unpremeditated correction of the denial of so great a spirituality is welling up from the grassroots.

Among Catholic women who had long since turned away from the Church entirely because they had suffered the misuse of Mary — such as priests or nuns insisting to girls that Mary is primarily a measure of perfect obedience against which they must constantly measure them-selves — many are now reconsidering the meaning of the Blessed Mother in their lives. Some of these women applaud the new "progres-sive" view of Mary, focused solely on the biblical stories of her as a real woman, without wealth or influence, who had to cope with a series of extremely difficult situations. Other women, and men as well, have become reacquainted with the full biblical*plus* spiritual presence of Mary and have discovered the richness of her mystical dimension.

Once again Mary is inspiring artists in large numbers. Several regional art galleries in the United States, especially in the west and southwest, have mounted juried exhibitions of new Marian paintings, most frequently featuring Our Lady of Guadalupe. From the beginning, this artistic wave has attracted painters and sculptors both within and outside of Catholicism. In late 1998 the Episcopal cathedral of the diocese of California, Grace Cathedral in San Francisco, held an exhibition of new Marian art on its premises. Much of this art is energetic, striking, and highly personal, expressing spiritual depth in ways that escape somber formulas.

Cutting across traditional alignments of left and right, two grass-roots movements have emerged in recent years that link conservatives, moderates, and even some "progressives" in opposing the Church's diminution of Mary. The first, a movement called Vox Populi Mariae Mediatrici (Voice of the People for Mary the Mediatrix), has inspired six million Catholics from 155 countries since the mid-1990s to petition the Vatican to declare three of Mary's traditional titles "articles of faith" for all Catholics: Advocate for the people, Mediator of God-the-Son's and God-the-Father's divine grace, and Co-Redeemer (not equal to Christ but uniquely *with* him). The Vox Populi movement includes approximately 550 bishops and 42 cardinals (12 of whom are in Rome) — plus numerous other clergy who have privately expressed agreement but fear for their career advancement within the "modernized" Church. I believe that many of the six million petitioners are less concerned about the fate of those particular titles, especially that of Co-Redeemer, than with registering dissatisfaction with the extreme demotion and disappearing of Mary since Vatican II, a suppression that extends far beyond the matter of titles.

From late 1996 through the summer of 1997, media around the world picked up the scent of a struggle and ran prominent articles about the petition drive for a papal (dogmatic) "definition" of the three Marian titles and the Vatican's response to the request. A cover story in *Life* called Mary "more beloved, powerful, and controversial than ever."[5] The cover of *Newsweek* proclaimed "A Struggle over Her Role Grows within the Church,"[6] while the religion writer for *Time* predicted that "Protestants and the Orthodox would go into orbit" if the three Marian titles were officially defined as dogma.[7] Actually, the Orthodox would object on grounds that are quite different from those of the Protestants. The Orthodox churches — principally in Greece, Russia and environs, and the eastern Mediterranean basin — include a strong biblical*plus* Marian component in their worship. They agree with the Vox Populi movement that Mary was enabled by her divine Son to act as advocate and intercessor, but they disagree that any further dogmatic definitions are necessary.

It was too tough to call the odds on this fight, the journalists conceded. On one side were (then) five million people and — at least initially — the pope, whose Polish devotion to Mary is strong. On the other side stood Joseph Cardinal Ratzinger, prefect of the Sacred Congregation for the Doctrine of the Faith, within the Vatican, who was joined by a battalion of male theologians and functionaries ostensibly protecting the progress of ecumenism. A theological commission of the Pontifical International Marian Academy, consisting of fifteen Mariologists and additional non-Catholic theologians (an Anglican, a Lutheran, and three Orthodox), was established and was asked by the Holy See to study the possibility and opportuneness of a definition of the Marian titles of Mediatrix, Coredemptrix, and Advocate. The opinion of this papal consultation was published in *L'Osservatore Romano* on June 4, 1997. The commission concluded by a unanimous vote that any doctrinal elevation of Mary would be contrary to the direction established by Vatican II and would be distasteful to Protestants and the Eastern Orthodox. Following the commission's report, the Vox Populi movement was emphatically rebuffed by Vatican operatives — but otherwise unharmed. It immediately issued a rebuttal of the commission's report to the pope.[8]

The second instance of grassroots rebellion is broader in scope and, as yet, embryonic. Unlike the Vox Populi movement, which was initiated by a conservative theologian, Mark Miravalle of the Franciscan University of Steubenville (Ohio), this more recent effort — sometimes called "Recovering the Catholic Heritage" — draws on the recent work of Andrew Greeley, a priest and sociologist who is associated with the "progressive" democratizing of the Church. (He likes to jokingly say, however, "Most of the progressives wouldn't want me!"[9]) After the publication of his book *The Catholic Imagination* (2000), which explicates Catholicism's "sacramental view of life," Greeley's emphasis shifted from an informational stance to an energetic denouncement that so little of the Catholic "sacramental culture" has survived the excessive pruning in recent decades. (The Catholic sacramental "imagination" connotes a deep response to God's blessings; "sacramental culture" is the cohesive totality of those responses.) In well-attended lectures around the country, he decried "pretending we are not Catholics" simply because a few "elites" decided to censor the rich metaphors of our sacramental religion. The main example he cites of this spiritual loss is the vastly reduced meaning and presence of the Virgin Mary.[10]

In an article published in the national Catholic magazine *Commonweal* in November 9, 2001, Greeley called for a long overdue national discussion among Catholics of our minimalized "beige Catholicism."[11] I happened to see not only the published version of the article but also the original manuscript, which reiterated the message of his lectures and which Greeley was graciously circulating via e-mail to interested people who contacted him, in the months prior to publication, about his call to "recover our Catholic heritage." The manuscript was a passionate and well-argued challenge to "Catholic elites" who "are only too eager to denude our rain forest of metaphors because, particularly in our Calvinist American society, they are more than a little ashamed of them." Greeley's position is that the constitutions and decrees of Vatican II have been intentionally misinterpreted by "false prophets" in order to arrive at a more acceptable "Calvinized Catholicism." He asserts, "If something is beautiful and hints of God's loving presence in the world, the question is not why we should recover it but why we abandoned it in the first place."

When the published version of the article arrived in the mail, I was shocked by the nature and extent of the editing and editorializing imposed by the staff at that "progressive" magazine. *Commonweal* has a well-earned reputation for publishing noteworthy articles on culture, politics, and religion. The submission of an article from a prominent liberal priest advocating the recovery much of the Marian devotions, as well as other spiritual practices, that had been discarded by Vatican II, however, set off a flurry of editorial activity, as a staff member later told me. Exactly what those well-intentioned "progressive" editors deleted from the article — and added to it — constitutes a snapshot of how deeply entrenched the attitudes toward the Virgin Mary have become in the Church today. Clearly, the "progressive" position — demonstrated not only by *Commonweal* but by other leading "progressive" Catholic publications as well — is that talk of restoring Mary's full spiritual presence, beyond the level of décor, is thoroughly unacceptable, a dangerous flirtation that would drag the Church backward into everything that was wrong with it prior to Vatican II. In fact, I have no doubt that an entire dissertation could be written on the fascinating "progressive" editing job done on Greeley's article as a case study of contemporary positions on Mary. Whether Greeley was as surprised as I about the difference between his manuscript and the published version of his article, I do not know. The contrast between the two versions, though, is striking and illustrative.

In the manuscript Greeley had mentioned Mary in several places and had written:

> Perhaps the most powerful of all our metaphors is that of the Madonna, the story of the One who is behind the Cosmos; the one who ignited the big bang is something like the love of a mother for her newborn child. . . . Could not the Mary symbol be rearticulated as representing the maternal Love of God for the creatures, the children, the crying babies to whom God has given life and nurturance? Indeed, is this not the *prima facie* meaning of the symbol? Why do we need to pretend that Mary isn't part of our heritage? Why do contemporary Catholic theologians ignore her like the Victorian novelists ignored sex? Why does she embarrass us? Why have we left her to those who wish to multiply titles or those who pursue gnostic interpretations in private revelations? Beats me!

Greeley's passionate call for a renewal of Marian spirituality appeared one-third of the way into his manuscript and continued beyond the excerpt cited above. The editors at *Commonweal,* however, moved the first (and only) mention of Mary in their edited version farther back into the article and reduced it to one paragraph; they deleted all of

Greeley's other mentions of Mary. Their Marian paragraph is based on parts of the one above, but they created and inserted a sentence into the middle of it that is based closely on a passage about liturgical reform in one of the constitutions from Vatican II. Just after they allow Greeley to note that we hear little about Mary today, they editorialize as follows: "This may be for fear that Marian devotion might offend our separated brothers and sisters." Zounds! Greeley's main point in the manuscript is the exact opposite:

> When I am asked how the Catholic imagination differs from the Protestant, I reply that we have angels and saints and souls in purgatory and statues and stations of the cross and votive candles and religious medals and crucifixes and rosaries and Mary the Mother of Jesus and First Communions and Candlemas and Ash Wednesday and May Crownings and midnight Masses and pilgrimages and relics — and they don't. These days I realize that we don't have most of them any more either. Our elite, our teachers, our experts, our professorate have banished them so that we can be more like everyone else, more Protestant, that is. It is a peculiarly one-sided notion of ecumenism in which we are asked to abandon the riches of our heritage to keep other people happy. If some Protestants are offended by the statues in our churches, and even today many of them are, they don't have to enter them or at least should be prepared to listen to our explanation of our statues as an explanation and not a defense.

In addition, *Commonweal* changed the title of Greeley's article from "Recovering the Catholic Heritage" to "A Cloak of Many Colors" — which frames Greeley's argument as if it were merely asking for a bit of space for regressive thinking among the more rational, advanced positions. In the manuscript Greeley was quite explicit in naming the problem: enthusiasts in the Church who lack "a mature understanding of Catholicism and its heritage, which sees that God's grace is everywhere and that indeed everything is grace." Taking aim directly at modernizers who insist that all "medieval vestiges" — the magnificent florescence of spiritual beauty in art, architecture, song, and prayer — must be banished in favor of premedieval austerity, Greeley wrote: "The sacramental imagination cannot be replaced by a mix of pseudo fourth-century liturgy and politically correct social attitudes. Whatever might emerge from such a melange, it is not Catholicism." Need I add that the "progressive" editors at *Commonweal* deleted that entire passage?

In the manuscript Greeley wrote of the need to "represent our sacramentality in ways that emphasize and celebrate its beauty." He explained, "By beautiful I do not mean cute or pretty or sweet but the kind of hint of the transcendent that tears a hole in the fabric of ordinary life and lets grace pour in. Yet there is little in the way of beauty in current American Catholic life. Quite the contrary, the minimalism of beige Catholicism desires only the commonplace, the functional." In yet another aikido reversal of Greeley's meaning, the editors printed this version: "We need to elevate the functional with the kind of transcendent beauty that tears a hole in the fabric of ordinary life and allows grace to pour in." Elevate the functional? The problem named in Greeley's passage is that our "Calvinized Catholicism," as he calls it elsewhere, respects *only* the functional. Remaining within that orientation while making some "elevating" changes is not what he advocates. The editors did, however, allow the article to end with Greeley's sadly noting that no program for the recovery of the sacramental heritage exists in American Catholicism. Instead, he observes, "the inertial energy of 'beige Catholicism' continues to plod unabated."

I encountered another example of "progressive" disapproval of the biblical*plus* sense of Mary when the editor-in-chief of a major "progressive" Catholic publishing house expressed disbelief and dismay during a telephone conversation after he asked what I was currently working on and was told about the material in this book. "But all that clearing away the Church did at Vatican II regarding the Virgin Mary was a *good* thing," he explained with polite exasperation. They went too far, I maintained, far too far. He countered coldly, "It was necessary for ecumenical progress!"

Was it? The goal of ecumenical rapprochement and interfaith understanding has always been desirable. In our fragmented and violent times, it has become imperative. On what assumptions, however, should such a confluence be constructed? The position expressed by the papal consultation in 1997 — that ecumenical reunion, of even a partial nature, can proceed only by denying the fullness of Mary's spiritual presence and shrinking it to the boundaries of the biblical text for all parties involved — is not endorsed by all grassroots Protestant and Orthodox women and men. Rather than viewing Mary as a divisive symbol, increasing numbers of people committed to interfaith dialogue are beginning to recognize her as a unique locus of *convergence* — among the branches within Christianity; among the Abrahamic traditions (Jews, Christians, and Muslims); and with all Asian and indigenous religions that include a compassionate Mother who manifests cosmological attributes. In the Quran, an entire chapter, or *sura,* is devoted to Mary, who is regarded with great esteem. No other women are mentioned by name in the Quran, but Mary's name appears forty-five times. Jesus is identified solely as the prophet who is "Son of Mary." For Muslims, Mary is full of God-consciousness and the same divine inspiration that touched male prophets.

With regard to Christian efforts at ecumenism, even if agreement on Mary cannot be achieved, why cannot reconciliation proceed with mutual respect for the vastly different perspectives in the strictly biblical view (Protestant) and the biblical*plus* view (Orthodox and traditional Roman Catholic)?

More will be said on the ever unamusing assumption that rapprochement among denominations and religions must be based on the flight from any powerful female embodiment of spiritual presence in the world. As for the worldwide effort by the Vox Populi movement, an iron curtain was drawn around the controversy by the Vatican after 1997, at which time the matter was largely dropped from mention in both the Catholic and secular press. The pope did issue a statement in May (Mary's month) of 1998, but it was not the grand declaration awaited by the Vox Populi movement. Instead, it was merely an apostolic letter addressing the importance of Sunday, one section of which tried to put the best spin on the great silence about Mary during the Sunday mass since Vatican II. The pope asserted that the Virgin Mary is present in every mass as the exemplar of those attitudes necessary for divine worship and that the faithful join with her in the eucharist and throughout the week with her "maternal intercession."

In August 1998 the pontifical Marianum college in Rome (Pontificia Facolta Teologica Marianium) organized a "serious discussion" of the Vox Populi movement's request for the papal definition of the three

Marian titles as articles of faith. The college subsequently published the preliminary statement from their faculty in their journal, *Marianum*. They concluded that the proposed dogmatic definition is unnecessary because "the doctrine of Mary's cooperation in the work of salvation" is formally taught by the Church and not contested or denied by Catholic theologians.[12]

Then why the eradication of her presence during the Sunday mass? Why the disappearance of so many of her statues? Why the downplaying of her devotions? Why does one hear from Catholic pulpits on the Feast of the Assumption (August 15) these days, as did a friend of mine at a university church in 2000, that there is "nothing special about the Assumption of Mary," that she was merely the "first of us to get into heaven"! This post-Vatican II spin — contradicting the 1950 papal definition of the Assumption, which is still in effect — is commonly preached repeatedly (and sometimes quite disdainfully) during the sermon on August 15 in parishes around the country.

In my own parish, the assistant pastor always seemed somewhat put upon to have to be discussing the Virgin Mary at all that day (or any other). He would mention her Assumption only as a point of departure, moving quickly into a rumination on other subjects: in 2000 it was Catholic respect for the body, and in 2001 it was the Feast of the Assumption's original identity in mid-August as a harvest festival of grapes! Surely the pontifical Marianum college and everyone else close to the Vatican must realize that the worldwide support for Vox Populi's petition drive is merely part of a much greater contextual problem: Millions of Catholics reject the suppression of Mary that is expressed in these sermons and in countless other ways. I am pleased to report, by the way, that the Feast of the Assumption mass in our parish in 2002 was quite memorable, both visually and spiritually beautiful, thanks to the arrival of a new assistant pastor and "parochial vicar," who is Mexican.[13] Such a celebratory effort is unusual in parishes today, however. More common is the response noted in the bulletin at a suburban church attended by a friend of mine: The priest writes that the Marian holy days seem to be occasions for parishioners to ask him on their way out of mass why Mary has been so minimized in recent decades.

The time is ripe to reexamine the "modernizing" agenda that influenced the decisions about Mary at the Second Vatican Council. As we have seen in the previous chapter, several of the assumptions in the ideology of modernity, which are now seen to be reductionist by many, figured largely in the decisions about Mary at Vatican II. As yet, however, Vatican II is not widely associated with its partially problematic legacy. Most Christians feel that it simply breathed fresh air into the Roman Catholic Church and invigorated it for the modern age. In fact, the very mention of Vatican II is often used as a synonym for irrefutably reasonable thought, which made possible the modernizing of the Church. Consequently, the very first item in the 1997 report issued by the papal consultation, the International Mariological Commission — in which they rejected the request by the Vox Populi movement to have the pope officially define Mary as Co-Redeemer, Mediator, and Advocate — was simply a flat statement: The current movement for a definition is not in line with the direction of Vatican II.[14] Well, yes, that *would* be the point.

A friend of mine expressed even more telegraphically the common attitude that the Second Vatican Council was entirely correct in all their scores of votes and other decisions. When I opined that the current groundswell of Marian spirituality is a reaction to the excessive pruning imposed by Vatican II, she stared at me in amazement. Following my critical analysis of the Council on this point, she responded with a tone of incredulity: "*Charlene!* Vatican *II!*" I had to laugh a bit because she is an intellectually sophisticated Catholic professor of religious studies at a secular liberal arts college who is well aware of the problematic assumptions embedded in the historical emergence of modernity. Yet when it comes to sorting out the destructive assumptions at work in the modern worldview, including the "modernizing" of Mary at Vatican II, criticizing modernity lumps one with the reactionaries.

Some "progressive" Catholics feel that Vatican II did not even go far enough in "rationalizing" Mary. The distinguished historian Garry Wills, for instance, adamantly rejects the "cult of the Virgin" because it is nonbiblical and did not make its way into official Church doctrine until the bishops approved it in 431. Unlike many men who hold that position, however, he finds the desire for a feminine expression of the Divine (or semi-Divine) to be quite reasonable. In *Papal Sin: Structures of Deceit* he suggests that the problem be solved through feminizing the Holy Spirit by calling it "She" and simultaneously minimizing the presence of Mary.[15]

At very least, the current debate within the Church over the Virgin Mary needs to recognize the existence of "pro-Mary progressives," but even that option would not address the problem identified by Fr. Greeley: The diminution of Mary's spiritual presence since Vatican II is one among many denials of the sacramental orientation of our Catholic heritage. To accept modernization as a "package deal" means absorbing the modern prejudices against acknowledging that which cannot be quantified; that which exists outside of texts and the rationalist, mechanistic worldview; that which reflects the subtle, interrelated field of existence. While it can be said that most "progressives" in the Church favor the democratization of its governance, the ordination of women, the approval of birth control, and other liberal stances, Greeley believes that only a small portion are committed to the eradication of our sacramental heritage. I agree, but I feel that the embedding context must be addressed: The options that are possible for "prosacramental progressives," as Greeley might call them — people who are politically liberal or "progressive" but cherish the full sacramental heritage of Catholicism — have never been presented clearly. Nor is it widely understood among liberals who feel that "modernized" Catholicism is a bit lacking that it was shaped by certain ideological forces. The assumptions in the ideology of modernity go largely unexamined in our modern culture. In fact, modernity is very good at some things and very poor at others. A ham-fisted denial of everything that cannot be contained in a text and limited to a literal interpretation (preferably not involving multivalent symbols or metaphors) is, indeed, highly modern, but it is also overkill.

Once in a great while, this critical perspective on the "modernized" Church is preached from the pulpit by a priest whose order is identified with social justice and kindred "progressive" goals. A striking example was the sermon delivered by Fr. Walter Burghardt, a Jesuit, on the Feast of the Blessed Virgin Mary (April 22) in the 500 anniversary year of the birth of St. Ignatius of Loyola, 1991. Noting the Jesuits' commitment to "promote justice to the unfortunates of earth," he traced their founder's profound spiritual engagement with Mary (see endnote 15 for this chapter) and then asked, "Four centuries later, in our rough-and-tumble 1960s, what happened to Our Lady? Put bluntly, we lost her. Not only American Catholics at large, but unnumbered religious as well. The reasons were complex; the result was patent: Mary faded into the background of Catholic devotion. . . . 'Lovely Lady dressed in blue' became a fun line for sophisticates." He then addressed the gravity of the error he sees within the larger, admirable work of Vatican II:

> In the process, all too many rushed all too hastily to an un-Catholic extreme. They forgot, if they ever knew, that Catholicism, for all its stress on intelligence, is not a cult of cold reason; that knowledge, even grace-full, is not identical with holiness; that a saving spirituality, oneness with God, must link heart to mind, emotion to understanding, passion to purpose. In the process of purification, too many unwittingly betrayed God's Word, the Church's theology, and a Catholic art.[16]

Most "progressives" in the modernized Church, however, firmly believe that the traditional, cosmological sense of Mary as Queen of Heaven and "our mother, even into eternity," as Fr. Burghardt put it, is situated on the wrong side of a vast chasm — theologically, historically, and politically. The term "pro-Mary progressives," then, would most logically denote Catholics who may feel that the role played by Mary the Nazarene woman in salvific history has been inadequately appreciated in recent decades but who approve solely of the biblical, noncosmological, nonmystical, post-Vatican II (or postconciliar) version of Mary. Consequently, a different term — and indeed a different orientation — is needed to denote Catholics who are committed to "progressive" democratic change in both the Church and society but who are equally committed to the full, mystical, cosmological spiritual presence of Mary.

Surely we could embrace the "progressive" goals — democracy, accountability, and female priests, as well as birth control and other care for the Creation — without sacrificing the spiritual richness of our sacramental heritage. In the following chapter I will explore the ways in which such a development is not a mere return to pre1960 decades but a dynamic progression. First, however, I would like to consider the objections raised by many feminist-"progressive" Catholics to any recovery of Mary's pre-Vatican II spiritual presence. I trust that they will welcome the opening of a dialogue, since for years they have been hailing the dethroning and shrinking of Mary as a great advance. I see the situation differently, as a liberal Catholic feminist who likes — nay, cherishes — "*big* Mary."

The main arguments I have encountered from my feminist-"progressive" sisters against expanding the biblical*only,* post-Vatican II version of Mary to her larger, biblical*plus* spiritual presence are that (1) the ethereal version of Mary on a pedestal is an insult to the dignity of women and their very real bodies; (2) women can relate better to the Mary who is solely a Nazarene woman, especially one committed to the social-activist values she declared in the Magnificat (Luke 1:46-55); (3) efforts to restore Mary's more-than-human, quasidivine status would be better focused on getting the Church to recognize God as being female as well as male; and (4) the mystical version of Mary is essentially a pagan hold-over and, therefore, irrelevant to Christianity.

I would like to respond first to the objection one hears most often from feminist-"progressives" regarding Mary: that the "glorified" Mary is ethereal and is honored as being beyond the physical realities of the female body, hence denigrating actual female bodies by comparison. This perception reflects two streams of thought: the feminist and the modern. Quite rightly, feminists are alert to the ubiquitous expressions in Western culture that demean female physicality, such as the misogynist insistence by a few key theologians in the fourth century that Mary's hymen was not ruptured in giving birth so Jesus experienced none of the usual "contagion" suffered by all others who were born of a woman.[17] The other reason Mary's ethereal characteristics are rejected, however, derives from the modern insistence that the material and the historical must replace the symbolic and the mystical. Most Catholic seminarians, for instance, have been taught since Vatican II to avoid mysticism entirely and stay glued safely to the biblical text. The modern mindset is generally "tone deaf" to symbolization of the subtle, invisible forces and processes that constitute the universe and give it an inherently relational, unitive dimension.

As we have seen in the previous chapter, the mechanistic worldview eventually achieved a tenacious grip on Western thought, so much so that Newton's work on an invisible force called *gravity* was initially dismissed as preposterously mystical "action at a distance." If one agrees that the ineffable, the more-than-human, the sacred whole can be approached only through poetic symbols that evoke a greater field of meaning than that circumscribed by human languages and concepts, then the question becomes one of *which* symbols and metaphors to use. In my view, symbolizing the cosmological life-supporting dynamics — which can be seen metaphorically as the Maternal Matrix of the universe — through the human maternal matrix who brought forth the Incarnation and is honored as the Queen of the Universe is an utterly grand choice. She is at once cosmological and human and mystical. No other honoring of the female in Western culture since the rise of Christianity is even remotely as colossal in its meaning and scope. Granted, "queen" is a premodern honorific title, but surely we can appreciate it for its poetic aura.

As for dismissing Mary's cosmological dimensions in order to focus feminist efforts on getting the Church to call God "She" as well as "He," why must we apply a gender, even both human genders, to the Divine, to the ineffable, to ultimate creativity in the cosmos? It seems small-minded to stamp our species' reality onto the profound dynamics of the sacred whole. Moreover, even if one prefers to call the Divine *She,* or *He,* instead of *It,* why should that interfere with appreciating that we have, in Mary, a symbolization of *a human* who has cosmological dimensions, as do we all. She coexists and coparticipates with the Divine, as do we all.

Moreover, this spiritual symbol that is human plus cosmological — *and,* not least, female-honoring — is deeply associated with myriad landforms, flowing waters, and roadside shrines. Mary most certainly is on Earth with the faithful, just as "progressive" theologians advocate. Far from being "remote," as the moderns charge, Mary's presence has been felt so deeply by Catholics through the centuries that they made that felt connection central in their cultures, both the official and the grassroots versions. In Mary the fecundity of the universe and the Earth community is symbolized not as an abstract concept of form manifesting from the subatomic field but as the Maternal Matrix. Indeed a complex web of processes "care for," that is, support, life forms of all sort. Mary as a religious symbol that is fully human, cosmological, and female — in particular, a caring, compassionate, and powerful female — is irreplaceable.

What of the "progressive"-feminist charge that Mary in her grand proportions is more pagan than Christian and, hence, inappropriate for the Christian era? On this issue the Bible itself bears witness. Whether one approves or not, the Nativity story in the gospels contains several events and associations that link Mary with the long stream of female spiritual figures that preceded her, as I discuss in chapter six. The pre-Christian goddesses, however, were conceived of as depictions of the Divine. Mary, with her fully human embodiment and experiences, carries forth the lineage of the symbolic sacred female into the Christian era but does so in a new, material dimension. Once God was perceived as having entered human history through the covenant with the Jewish people, Western religious history took a turn toward the material. Mary fits that Western development perfectly. She is not solely mystical. She is not God. She is both fully material as well as more than material. She has a "small self" (which has cosmological dimensions, as do all humans), a grand-scale cosmological self, and an honored role in the spiritual symbol system of Catholicism. How could one possibly invent a more fitting spiritual symbol for the Great Mother of the West? She reflects who we are, where we are, what we are, and what we might become if we bring our consciousness into attunement with divine grace.

What of the charge that Mary has always been considered the maternal face of God, a role that is merely a pagan borrowing that was useful in helping Christianity to spread? Is it not logical, within the sacred narrative, that Mary, having grown the Divine from her very flesh, would acquire quasidivine attributes? Surely it is likely that Mary's experience of growing God-the-Son in her body, from her body, as part of her body, *changed* her. Though never officially acknowledged in Church doctrine, it has seemed entirely plausible to most Catholics that the Mother of God-the-Son would partake of a semi-divine status.

Catholic theologians are certainly accurate in calling this aspect of "lived Catholicism" out of bounds in terms of official Church teachings, but it is a logical element in the sacred narrative surrounding the Incarnation.

As for the Protestant — and the "modernized Catholic" — interpretation that Mary's role as an intercessor and conduit of divine grace is insulting to God because it makes Him (It) seem unapproachable, I sense a straw-man argument. In truth, Catholics, unlike Protestants, were always traditionally fairly ignorant of the Old Testament, as compared to the New Testament. Consequently, Yaweh, with his wrathful, vindictive dramas — which caused the Israelites to identify themselves as a people who "wrestle with God" — is not the God-the-Father who, for Catholics, occupies the head of the Trinity. There is ample evidence that Catholics have always communed in their prayer lives with God-the-Father, Christ, and Mary — or any of the three at various times. Mary was not honored through the centuries because God-the-Father and God-the-Son were considered by Catholics to be bullies or unapproachable or ineffectual. Rather, she was honored because she had assented to the messenger (the Archangel Gabriel) of God-the-Holy-Spirit to allow the Incarnation to happen in her very body, had raised Jesus presumably with the values she espoused in the Magnificat when she was pregnant, and had supported and born witness to his ministry and his sacrifice on the cross, and was named by Jesus (when he spoke to John during the Crucifixion) as the Mother of the apostles and disciples. The spiritual beauty of honoring the Maternal Matrix as Advocate, Mediator, and Intercessor — as well as the spiritual beauty of Mary herself — has always been self-evident to Catholics. Why is it suddenly twisted into something inappropriate for the Church? Quite simply, modernity cannot bear to honor a grand female symbol of power and presence, especially one so deeply embedded in both the contours of the Earth and the events of the Redemption.

Regarding the argument that contemporary women can "relate" to Mary only if she is shrunken down to the proportions of a socially committed Nazarene village woman, one sees here another pitfall in the reductionist ideology of modernity: the narrow modern focus on the individual self at the expense of realizing the larger context in which individuals exist. Modernity reduces the ineffable to its own proportions rather than stretching to meet, even partially, the boundless mystery of life with symbol and metaphor. It makes sense to think of Mary as a human "companion" only if one refrains from slipping into the mechanistic understanding of what a human is: As Mary walked the streets of Nazareth, as she did the daily work of a wife and mother, as she observed the practices of Jewish worship, she was also a cosmological being, one linked — as are we all — with every other manifestation of the universe, one held in the gravitational embrace, one constituted from one nanosecond to the next by the unimaginable range of subtle relationships that form and inform a living entity. In fact, the cosmological dimension provides a solution to the central problem in Marian spirituality: the seeming discontinuity between the domestic version of Mary and the "glorified" version of her as Queen of Heaven. Continuity between the two phases of Mary's symbolic life exists because her grand cosmological proportions are present all along: in the smaller cosmological proportions of the human and, later, as the ubiquitous Blessed Mother of the faithful.

The disappearing of "grand Mary" in the modernized Catholic Church is saddening for many reasons, but I am particularly struck, from a feminist perspective, by the pathos of seeing women themselves deny profound female power, even in symbolic form. That is, many feminist-"progressive" psyches today have been so "modernized" as to support the erasure of the elemental power of Mary's maternal body, her *mystical body of grace*. When "progressive" nuns and feminist theologians in the Church accept the modern (and Protestant, or "ecumenical") delineation of religion as text, they limit themselves. Clearly the disembodied, text-based version of "rationalized" religion is more comfortable to the male psyche, in general, than were earlier religions with their colossal female forms. Consequently, "progressive" feminists fight the good fight against patriarchal forces within the Catholic "biblical movement" — but only within the tightly circumscribed arena of biblical hermeneutics, a turf more comfortable to the male psyche and, therefore, the one declared to be the main arena of action and importance in modernized religion. The modern "progressive" female theologians argue courageously for feminist insights and reflections on biblical texts and are grudgingly accepted by many male theologians today, but have not those competent, intelligent women given up far too much to win acceptance on that turf? Have they not lost something precious in abandoning an engagement with the larger Maternal Matrix that is their birthright? In the final chapter, "Her Mystical Body of Grace," I aspire to illuminate the spiritual treasures of the female heritage.

Alas, that perspective is, I admit, quite remote from the theological positions put forth today by leading feminist-"progressive" theologians and activists. An example is "The Madeleva Manifesto: A Message of Hope and Courage,"[18] a one-page statement on women in the Church composed by sixteen prominent "progressive" Catholic feminists, each of whom had been chosen in past years to give the annual Madeleva Lecture at St. Mary's College in Notre Dame, Indiana. They gathered at a conference there in April 2000 to declare, as the prologue of their statement notes, "a message of hope and courage to women in the Church." Their declaration suggests many ways in which women might live their lives with Christ and the entire trinitarian God but contains not even the slightest mention of Mary in Catholic women's spiritual lives! A manifesto composed at *St. Mary's* College in *Notre Dame!* In fact, their position is curiously indistinguishable whatsoever from a Protestant perspective. These are impressive women poised to move up in the Church, and rightfully so, but they have apparently absorbed all too well the message that their advancement depends on presenting themselves as "rationalized," modernized Catholics with no retrograde "weakness" for the full spiritual presence of Mary, no collapsing backward into "that old Mary stuff." The ordaining of female Catholic priests who would enforce the disappearing of Mary in her cosmological proportions would contribute to a grim and fallen future in which the repressed have become the repressors.

One of the signatories of the Madeleva Manifesto, Elizabeth A. Johnson, wrote an influential article in June 2000 expressing the feminist-"progressive" approach to Mary. Johnson, who is a Distinguished Professor of Theology at Fordham University and also a Sister of St. Joseph, suggests in "Mary of Nazareth: Friend of God and Prophet,"[19] that we interpret and honor Mary in our time by inviting her "down from the pedestal where she has been honored in the past to join us on the ground." Johnson then explains, "The ladder enabling her to reach the ground has four steps," which form the structure of the article. First, Mary must be brought into the community of saints, where the nonbiblical "patron-client" relationship with regard to of her intercessory role must be replaced with a "companionship model." Second, divine qualities migrated to Mary in the past because of a deficiency in the theology of God and because of the "baptizing" of pagan images as a missionary strategy; today women must "deconstruct the Marian symbol as the maternal face of God" so that every woman's — and man's — face is seen as an *imago Dei*. Johnson also proposes that God should be directly considered "Mother of Mercy," among other titles: "Let God have her own maternal face." The third step in ushering Mary down from her pedestal is the rejection of her as an idealized woman or an expression of the eternal feminine; such a notion is "an obstacle to personal growth" for women. (In this section Johnson faults Mary at the wedding at Cana for exhibiting feminine passivity: "She noticed the lack of wine and, rather than deal with the lack on her own initiative, performed an act of self-emptying by turning to Jesus for help.") The final step focuses on the gospels, "the primary source for remembering Mary." Here Johnson reflects on the actual Nazarene woman behind the texts: a Jewish woman, a village woman, and a woman of faith. By defining Mary as a "friend of God and prophet," Johnson feels we arrive, through the four steps, at "a theologically sound, spiritually empowering and ethically challenging view of Mary, mother of Jesus the Christ, for the twenty-first century."

While I appreciate the spiritual reflection that Johnson and her colleagues in the "progressive" orientation have developed within the post-Vatican II, text-bound parameters, it seems to me a tragic and unnecessary reduction, one that blocks perception of the lived richness of the fuller sense of Mary. This article, so strong and confident, reflects the common assumption among "progressives" that everything before Vatican II in Catholicism was pathetically bad. I welcome the attention to Mary's life as a village woman, but I prefer the inclusive view of her that also acknowledges her traditionally perceived cosmological dimensions. In truth, I can think of nothing *less* empowering — and more depressing — than to see the grand Marian spiritual expression of the profound human *connection* among Earth, cosmos, and the Divine (for Mary both takes on cosmological dimensions *and* is felt to abide in countless springs, hills, and grottos of Earth *and* in the hearts of all of us) reduced to being solely a politically engaged friend who is no better than we are — except for the fact that she got to pal around with God a while back.

All of the "progressive" feminist objections cited in the preceding pages, and more, are drawn together in *Hail Mary?: The Struggle for Ultimate Womanhood in Catholicism* (1995), a book by Maurice Hamington, a "progressive" Catholic professor who identifies himself as "a profeminist male." He concludes that "deconstructing" the traditional imagery of "the Cult of Mary" is a "moral" imperative for Catholic feminists today, in fact, an "inevitable" ethical quest. Hamington, who also reviews books for the *National Catholic Reporter,* states repeatedly in *Hail Mary?* that Mary is "a model of the Church's moral control over Catholic women" and "the ultimate model of alienation for Catholic women."[20] I am stunned. Can he seriously believe that the millions of Catholics engaged with Marian devotion, past and present, see Mary as the patriarchal bludgeoning tool he describes in chapter after chapter? It feels as if my entire lifetime experience of Mary took place on a planet very different from Hamington's. He makes anthropological pokings at the Marian spiritual culture and maintains negative assumptions about it, but he does not comprehend its essence. Is all this animus among "progressive" theologians toward Mary's traditional presence merely a problem of the intelligentsia, rather than the grassroots? While I appreciate that he is motivated by the liberatory impulse (and, of course, one wishes there were more "profeminist males" in the world), I can only surmise that he came of age after Vatican II.

Still, I was heartened to arrive at the final chapter of *Hail Mary?*,[21] in which Hamington draws not only on arguments by such prominent "Marian minimalists" as Rosemary Radford Ruether (who coined the term "Liberation Mariology") and Elizabeth Johnson, as he has throughout the book, but also brings in other theological voices who ask whether a large and multivalent Mary, yet to be fully defined, might not be key to a "rebirth of Catholic feminist spirituality." Hamington finally notes that deep below the surface of patriarchal religion, there is a "subversive power" in Mary. He quotes the distinguished German Protestant theologian Dorothee Solle's refusal as a Christian in "the liberation movement" to "surrender Mary to our opponents."[22] He cites the Latin American theologians Ivone Gebara and Maria Clara Bingemer, who assert that Mary has evolved into "an empowering religious symbol in each age" and that a pluralist understanding of her meaning should be "rooted in popular experience, not hierarchical need."[23] Amen!

At the end of Hamington's final chapter, he titles a section "What's Missing?"[24] I noticed recently that I had written in the margin next to that question "Cosmology!" While Hamington calls for "reinterpreting" Marian images, I would call, rather, for "reclaiming" the full, spiritually rich meaning therein, expanding the implications of her cosmological dimension from a twelfth-century perspective to that of the twenty-first century, instead of denying it altogether. I am encouraged by the sense of openness to possibilities and by a hint of anticipation in the voices of the theologians featured in Hamington's last chapter. They seem to suggest that something great — for women and the Church — might emerge in our time regarding Mary. To their various reflections, I add the proposal that there is an alternative to the dualistic stalemate that runs through post-Vatican II thinking about Mary, the belief that if Mary is not reduced to being strictly "ecclesio-typical" (a symbol for the Church) she then erroneously becomes a figure in competition with Christ. In fact, Mary is neither "ecclesio-typical" nor a competitive threat to Christ. Rather, everything about Mary's symbolic and spiritual presence is "Matrix-typical" — that is, a symbol of the Maternal Matrix, from the womb of a Nazarene village woman to the cosmological matrix of all life. She does not need to be changed, merely comprehended.

A final issue in this chapter on the Quiet Rebellion is the *realpolitik* within the Church today regarding Mary. A white-haired nun from Boston, after hearing my presentation of the material in this book at the Sisters of Earth conference in August 2002, said to me, "I think you're right about so much you said about Mary and what has happened. It's a great loss. But — do you understand that if I were to go home and teach my students in my religion classes about the glorified, cosmological sense of Mary as Queen of Heaven, who is the compassionate mediator of divine grace, the 'progressive' parents would immediately report me to the Archdiocese of Boston for sneaking in right-wing material favored by conservatives and reactionaries?" Indeed, the situation in several predominantly Catholic cities, especially on the East Coast, is severely polarized and increasingly tense. Activist conservative groups such as Catholics United for the Faith (CUF), for instance, have reportedly adopted confrontational tactics to intimidate those who support liberal positions within the Church.

The question, then, for pro-Mary Catholics who agree with "progressive" goals is how to take part in the Marian renewal without seeming to feed the ranks, or at least the cause, of the Catholic right. Not much is possible, of course, without first unraveling the "progressives'" acquiescence to the right's claiming of Mary as their own. It is as if the left and right have agreed on one thing: the meaning of Mary as the emblem of support for right-wing positions. In contrast, it is accepted by both camps that when the entire political spectrum within the Church shows up on Sunday for worship in parishes across the country, disparate associations arise in the minds of the laity as they gaze at the sculpture of Jesus on the cross. Conservatives may feel in their hearts that he suffered for and stands against sins that liberals condone, while "progressives" may feel in their hearts that Jesus stands for the social gospel, that is, the gospel of love, which challenges injustice in all its guises. Everyone accepts that these different associations with Christ, and other variations as well, are careening around the sanctuary throughout the mass. So why should the "progressives" assume that everyone who spiritually communes with Mary sees her as an emblem for conservative causes? Perhaps this is primarily a North American problem since "big Mary" is widely associated throughout Latin America, the Philippines, Poland, and elsewhere with movements for social justice and liberation from tyranny. The "progressives'" desertion of Mary in her full spiritual presence is deeply entangled with the ideologies of modernity, as we have seen. Only a reexamination of those assumptions can provide a possible opening in the deadlock.

If that opening were to manifest itself, aided perhaps by the observations in this book, pro-Mary liberals would then have to break the great silence about her in their circles. Just as she is openly associated in so many cultures with movements for social justice — having been called since the third century "Advocate for the People" — so might Mary be regarded by liberal activists in the American Catholic Church as central to the spiritual dimension of their efforts for social change. After all, spiritually based activism is primarily distinguished from its secular twin in its commitment to combining action with contemplation. A rich contemplative practice by itself would not achieve any gains for justice, while an action-oriented program that lacks self-examination and deep reflection has often resulted in aggressive errors that damaged the final outcome for a long while, even when a victory was won. The quality of the process, in short, affects the quality of the result, no matter how admirable the cause. Certainly the Marian qualities of compassion, patience, and humility would serve group dynamics well in activist efforts.

On a deeper level, the contemplative opportunities afforded by spiritual communion with Mary are boundless. The many beautiful prayers to her deliver one to a mental space of spiritual calm and groundedness. Throughout the centuries Catholics have spoken silently with Mary at random moments in their day. Particularly when situations become difficult, as they often do in political actions and meetings, a quick check-in with Mary is valuable, for she knows well the range of human suffering but also contains the "big picture" dimension of reality — and she expresses maternal compassion for even the most obnoxious of the well-meaning. All that should be sufficient to demonstrate her relevance to social-change activists in the Church, but there is still more: the rosary. As I discuss in chapter four, the rosary is the multilevel, multivalent contemplative device *par excellence* in the West. While praying the rosary is not relevant solely to political activism, its contemplative dimension is steeped in the experience of suffering and the transformation of suffering. It is Mary's luminous treasure, available to us all.

With regard to the content, rather than the process, of political efforts, the spiritual presence of Mary, so rooted in myriad places on this earth, might logically be invoked in ecological efforts in parishes, colleges, or retreat centers — and not only those whose name celebrates her association with the natural world, such as St. Mary of the Springs, St. Mary of the Woods, Mount St. Mary, and Our Lady of the Plains. Lest this possibility seem too obvious to deserve mention, I offer yet another example of how thoroughly the association between Mary and nature has been severed: A couple of years ago, a bright, creative nun showed me a design she had completed for a mostly glass, round chapel to be set in a beautiful natural setting at a college named for Mary — in which absolutely none of the ecological or cosmological expressions she had included were connected with Mary in any way. In fact, Mary was to be missing entirely from the cosmological chapel!

As for issues of social justice, no leap of the imagination is required to grasp why Mary, who expressed a rallying cry when she spoke the Magnificat, might logically be held high as the standard bearer of liberal causes, a case that has been made by my feminist-"progressive" sisters. In fact, I would think "progressives" in general might enjoy confounding the conservatives at this point by doing so. Why not have a little fun?

In spite of severe disapproval from the "progressives," the renewal of Marian spirituality has certainly gone further in the past two decades than anyone could have predicted. As recently as twenty-eight years ago, Marina Warner's classic study, *Alone of All Her Sex: The Myth and the Cult of the Virgin Mary* (1976), concluded that "the reality her myth describes is over; the moral code she affirms has been exhausted."[25] Warner could not have known, writing in the mid-1970s, that within a very few years Mary, far from "receding into legend," would be the subject of a vast grassroots affirmation: new sightings, pilgrimages by the millions, rosaries by the billions, and, finally, a postal storming of the Vatican with the Vox Populi petition.

Yet I am concerned for the Quiet Rebellion. Might not a diffuse movement, consisting largely of grey-haired people who came of age before Vatican II, be crushed over time by a highly organized global institution, the modernized Church? Have the rebels already been rendered too quiet? As for the petition drive launched by Vox Populi, I understand that some strategic particulars had to be chosen as a focus out of the huge field of imperiled Marian spirituality, but I am unconvinced that citing historical theological doctrines about Mary will carry the day or that fighting for the elevation of various Marian titles is a broad enough approach. What is at stake is so much more than titles.

This book attempts to sketch the larger context and, in doing so, to aid and expand the defense of the Blessed Mother. In the following chapters I consider her resilience, her cosmological depth, her impressive lineage, her bountiful body of grace, her advocacy for the poor, and her ineffable effect in the lives of countries, clans, and persons. I have called on the witness of the centuries that it may speak to the careless, hypermodern impulse of the past forty years. It is not too late.

It often seems I can *feel* the millions of silent prayers and conversations held with Mary every hour, feel the passage of her beads through countless fingers calloused or soft, old or young. Each day this presence grows in the world. I am buoyed by the vital, healing spirit of this renewal. I know we have been imperiled before, at other moments when the West had swung too far from the wisdom of the heart. Then, as now, we turned to her, the Eternal Genetrix.

Queen of Heaven and Earth

Mother of Mercy

Our Lady of Peace

Chapter Three

Premodern Mary Meets Postmodern Cosmology

In the ecumenical struggles over the Virgin Mary, the Protestants have maintained the sensible course. They have paid a bit more attention to honoring the biblical Mary than in past times — noting that her "pondering" in her heart certain things Jesus did, for instance, was the first christological reflection — but they have hardly *expanded* their Mariology at all in the forty years since Vatican II because the chasm between their text-based (that is, strictly biblical) version of Mary and the mystical, cosmological (that is, biblical*plus*) sense of Mary is so vast that it should be left alone. Honor diversity.

The post–Vatican II period has demonstrated that it is possible (temporarily) to dismantle and repress vast areas of the Catholic biblical*plus* version of Marian spirituality, but it is not possible to add any of the *plus* to the strictly biblical Protestant version. As an Episcopalian divinity student explained to me recently, after I was pleased to note a few pro-Mary Episcopalian events at Grace Cathedral in San Francisco, "There's still a great deal of wariness in our church about acquiring *any* Mariology . . . and *praying* to the Virgin Mary is extremely unappealing, pretty much unthinkable." In short, the logical conclusion of Vatican II's "streamlining" — if the ecumenical impulse is to be fully satisfied one day — is the eventual disappearance within the Roman Catholic Church of Mary as Compassionate Advocate and cosmological Queen of Heaven.

Even now there are Catholic theologians calling for a reconsideration of the papal definitions of both Mary's Immaculate Conception and her Assumption as "articles of faith." Where will the roll-back stop? Will the entire extraordinary stream of art, poetry, and music inspired by the biblical*plus* aspects of Mary's full spiritual presence gradually be delegitimized as merely exuberant error? Too bad that Dante, Giotto, and Van Eyck, lacking the benefit of modern "scientific" biblical exegesis, failed to discern that *Mary is nearly nothing in the text*. So true — but the Roman Catholic faith, container of mysteries older than itself, escaped the limitations of the text early on.

It did so by honoring the cosmological context of the Incarnation and the Redemption and, indeed, of all life. When Christ was born, a stellar event in the night sky guided the three wise men to him. At the end of his life, while he slowly expired on the cross, the skies darkened from noon until three o'clock, followed by an earthquake at the moment of his death. Only then, when the cosmos had spoken, did the Roman soldiers realize that they had crucified the Messiah. This symbolic linking of the order of the cosmos with God and the Son (the *Logos*, or expression of God) — inadequately translated as "the Word" — is made explicit in the Prologue to the Gospel According to John: *In the beginning was the Word, and the Word was with God.* That is, *In the beginning was the Expression of the Divine, and the Expression of the Divine was with the Divine.*

All the great spiritual traditions situate the human drama within the larger context of the cosmos. All the primal cultures perceived, as does postmodern science, that a subtle interconnectedness suffuses the vast diversity of life forms. This unitive dimension of being is the relational ground from which all religious narratives are constructed: the perception of the sacred whole. A sacred story of a people, or a sacred metanarrative spanning many cultures, always involves interaction between the visible world and the dynamic creativity of the cosmos — called the Divine, God, Goddess, the Great Holy, the Great Mysterious, the Way, or other names. Awe and reverence for the grand communion of life were the touchstones of original religion. In Europe this coherence was eventually envisioned as a hierarchical "Great Chain of Being," topped by the Divine. With the emergence of the modern era after the Reformation and the Scientific Revolution, however, the Western sensibility absorbed the mechanistic worldview: The cosmos and the earthly world were henceforth seen as mere inert matter acted upon by Newton's laws of physics. From that time until the present, Christianity has deemphasized the cosmological grandeur of the Creation and emphasized the spiritual drama of the human individual. In fact, one of the major debates within the Reformation was over the nature of the Creation. Luther and Calvin argued, successfully, for the doctrine of "radical sovereignty," the belief that God's sovereignty excluded any contribution of lesser beings to his work. This position conveniently made it possible for the philosophers of the subsequent Scientific Revolution, in Protestant countries, to declare without danger of heresy that nature possesses no active, internal forces but is, rather, inert matter moved around by mechanistic forces — which have divine origin, of course. This movement toward the mechanistic worldview, though, was initially declared primarily to separate the new Protestant position on nature from that of the dominant "medieval synthesis," which had been framed by St. Thomas Aquinas in the thirteenth century.

Aquinas, a Dominican priest and scholar, had succeeded in melding Scholastic theology with the Aristotelian observation that the laws of nature are internal to nature itself. He thereby solved the problem for medieval Europe of the disjunction between the newly recovered Aristotelian texts on natural science (which had been "lost" to Europe but preserved by Islamic scholars) and the teachings of the Church. In Aquinas's "grand synthesis" the natural world is understood to unfold through dynamic cocreation involving divine sovereignty along with the patterns and processes of nature. In contrast, the Reformation asserted the passivity of nature in order to protect the glory of God, specifically his "radical sovereignty."

Moreover, the Reformers' insistence that that no "natural revelation" was possible through human apprehension of the Creation squarely refuted Aquinas's perception that the earthly world, and indeed the entire cosmos, are expressions and teachings of the Divine. In his extremely influential *Summa Theologiae*, which is dedicated "To the Blessed Virgin, Mary Immaculate, Seat of Wisdom," Aquinas asserted,

> Hence we must say that the distinction and multitude of things come from the intention of the first agent, who is God. For He brought

things into being in order that His goodness might be communicated to creatures, and be represented by them; and because His goodness could not be adequately represented by one creature alone, He produced many and diverse creatures, that what was wanting to one in the representation of the divine goodness might be supplied by another. For goodness, which in God is simple and uniform, in creatures is manifold and divided; and hence the whole universe together participates the divine goodness more perfectly, and represents it better than any single creature whatever.[1]

Aquinas's "grand synthesis," then, explicated a universe infused with the grace of "divine goodness" in which each creature, tree, and constellation of stars is to be recognized as a partial reflection of the Creator.

The Reformation Fathers' rejection of the Catholic Church's teachings about the Creation informed the subsequent design of Protestant churches and cathedrals, which display a far more austere aesthetic than the exuberant celebration of nature and cosmos found in the extraordinary stone carvings and stained glass of their medieval predecessors. Throughout *pre*modern Europe, the cosmological context of the human was central to religious thought and art, often expressed by the inclusion of the constellations or symbols of the zodiac. The latter can be seen, for instance, in the stained-glass windows of Chartres Cathedral. With regard to Mary in particular, her long-standing role as the Mother of God-the-Son — she who melds the human and the cosmic — acquired a rich array of cosmological symbolism and associations from the twelfth through the fifteenth centuries.

In medieval paintings the cosmological dimension of the Blessed Virgin is celebrated with aesthetic vitality, as it had been in earlier depictions of the Mediterranean and Near Eastern forms of the Goddess. Mary reigns from the heavens, adorned with a halo of twelve stars to represent the apostles. She is attended by angels and saints, patriarchs and prophets, all joyfully sharing in the grace she so generously conveys. Sometimes she is linked with Sophia, the figure in Hebrew Scripture who is a manifestation of divine wisdom. In that role, Mary is depicted as the Seat of Wisdom, Maria Sophia, at the center of the universe. She is often encased by a mandorla, a vertical almond shape that evokes her (vaginal) heavenly "gate" through which the Redeemer entered this world. Her womb is the symbolic Holy Grail. Sometimes, as Mother of Mercy, she looms as a huge cosmological figure holding open her cloak, under which are sheltered the multitudes.

Medieval hymns to the Virgin echoed this focus on her cosmic presence, such as this song for early morning:

> Like the glow of dawn she rises to heaven's heights;
> like the sun Mary shines, like the loveliest moon.

One of Mary's most popular cosmological titles was *Star of the Sea.* This association derives from St. Jerome's Latin gloss on *Maryam,* her Hebrew name, which carries the connotation, he felt, of *stilla maris* (a drop of the sea). It is widely accepted that this phrase was changed to *stella maris* (star of the sea) by some hapless medieval scribe who simply made an error. But did he? In the Goddess traditions, which thrived until the fifth century of the Christian era in Ephesus and elsewhere, the association of a goddess with the pole star or as guardian of the seas was common. Perhaps the scribe merely harmonized, even if not quite consciously, the "glorified" Mary (assumed into heaven and there enthroned) with the logical and long-standing stellar associations accompanying such a position.

In any case, the Great Mother of the new era inherited a symbolic connection with the "star of the sea," as this medieval processional hymn demonstrates:

> O bearer of the eternal word, Virgin Mary,
>   what voice, what human tongue can praise you well enough?
> You, new star of the sea, window to the lofty heavens, ladder
>   from earth
>   to heaven, from the lowest to the highest.
> You conceived eternity; you gave birth to your parent; the
>   maker came
>   from what he made, the creator from the creation.

In the twelfth century, an extraordinary Benedictine abbess in the Rhine Valley, St. Hildegard of Bingen, created a body of liturgical music, *Symphony of the Concord of Heavenly Revealings,* which is widely praised by musicologists today and is increasingly performed and recorded. Hildegard composed sixteen Marian pieces — mostly antiphons, hymns, and responsories — that complement her theological writings on the Virgin. She depicted Mary as both a verdant, fruitful branch and the source of primeval, pure light: "freshest, greenest bough"; "mediating stem"; and "serene glory of the sun." Using ecological and cosmological metaphors, plus the biblical style of the Psalms, Hildegard composed such lyrics as "Your blessed womb overcame death, and your womb illumined all creatures."

During the second century of the Renaissance, however, cosmology became yet another area of disagreement between the Reformation and the Catholic Church. Initial opposition to the new, Copernican cosmology had arisen not from the Vatican but from Luther and Calvin, who asserted that Copernicus's claim that the Earth moves around the Sun flagrantly contradicts the literal truth of the Bible. They condemned the Catholic Church's acceptance of such heresy as further evidence of the corruption of Christianity through the Church's rapprochement with Greek thought (primarily Aristotelian science). Proper Christian cosmology, the Fathers of the Reformation insisted, is delineated in a passage from Psalm 93: "The firmament is firmly fixed and will not be moved." Such muscular literalism from Protestant critics evoked a matching stance from the Renaissance Catholic Church, which eventually condemned the heliocentric hypothesis, at least officially. Not only the Reformers but also many Catholics felt that the meaning of the Incarnation would be diminished if, as the Copernican hypothesis indicated, the Earth no longer occupied a central place in the universe. Why would God-the-Son incarnate on an insignificant planet orbiting around a star, its sun?

On the level of practical applications, however, the Copernican breakthrough was absorbed in many quarters of the Church. On the very day he died in 1543, Copernicus was presented with one of the first copies of his published book, *On the Revolutions of the Heavenly Spheres*. Its calculations were the basis of the new Gregorian calendar and were used in astronomy classes at Catholic universities until the Curia opted to be publicly shocked — *shocked* — by the heliocentric hypothesis. Even after the official condemnation (in effect until 1712), the new astronomy was practiced and taught privately. In fact, several late Renaissance cathedrals, built between the mid-sixteenth and mid-eighteenth century, were designed to function secondarily as observatories. A small hole, called a "meridian," was carefully placed in the dome or high on a wall such that a beam of sunlight would fall across precise calibrations that were inlaid into the cathedral floor, marking the angle of the sun and the passage of the seasons. A commonly cited rationale for these observatory-cathedrals was found in Psalm 19: "The heavens declare the glory of God, and the firmament shows His handiwork."

The Renaissance mind studied the Creation with greater scientific precision but with less spiritual richness than had its medieval predecessor. Unlike the ancients, who had blended accurate astronomical calculations with symbolic representations of the ineffable, the emergent modern mentality was dominated by the ascendance of a mechanistic scientific worldview that aggressively imposed the "new mechanical philosophy." The only acknowledgement of nonmechanistic thought that the "priests" of the new science would grant to the priests of Christianity was the general accommodation that emerged in the seventeenth century: Henceforth, the truth of the physical world would be recognized as residing in Newtonian science, while the truth of faith would remain the province of religion. Once religion was dissociated from any true knowledge of the universe in the modern age, all symbolic approaches to Ultimate Mystery paled in significance before the expanding influence of secular science. Religious symbols and metaphors have since then floated as ghostly forms in marginalized institutions. To this day, we moderns struggle to grasp and absorb the spiritual meaning they hold.

The Catholic faith is an expression of mysteries far too vast to be contained in dogma, myth, or symbol. The mysteries it contains vitalize and sustain the institutional Church as it continues to make its way in the world with many admirable deeds and some colossal errors. We can wrap our minds around certain particulars of the mystical core, but we apprehend the totality of the sacred whole only at the nonlinguistic, noncognitive level, which resists the linguistic confines of our interior monologue . . . or any text, including a reified scripture.

Symbolic expressions of the Blessed Virgin Mary, the Creation, and the Incarnation are poetic approaches to Ultimate Mystery. The meaning of Christ's Ascension and Mary's Assumption is not that they are sitting together enthroned on a cloud somewhere but, rather, that they consist of cosmological dimensions. Like all religious forms, they stretch the conceptual in order to reach the ineffable. They resonate with the human psyche because they participate in the larger reality.

There is no dearth of psychological interpretations of religion, along with historical, sociological, philosophical, and anthropological analyses. It is the cosmological dimension that has been ignored during the modern era, as the cultural historian Thomas Berry has pointed out in numerous essays.[2] Modernity shrinks the focus of the human from the dynamics of the universe and the Earth to those of humans alone. Within that arena, the scope is narrowed even further in modern life — to a life-long project of consumption or "manipulating symbols" (letters, words, and numbers) in the Information Age. No culture in the history of humankind has been as alienated from the larger reality, the cosmological context, as is the modern world. Caught up in the ever-accelerating pace of change and the increasingly contingent sense of all meaning, the modern human feels adrift and disengaged from the universe.

Unfortunately, it was at the height of the post-World War II period, when modernity flexed its muscles so aggressively in so many fields, that the Catholic Church updated its thinking about Mary, through the deliberations at Vatican II. The majority of the Council Fathers — although it was a very slight majority — were gripped by an urgent need to jettison as many nonmodern elements of Catholicism as possible. Mary, Queen of Heaven and Earth, Star of the Sea, and Queen of the Universe may be premodern, nonmodern, or postmodern, but she is certainly not modern. She had to go.

Yet how differently we regard the effects of all that modern "rationalizing" forty years later. The monotonous grid embedded in the International style of modern architecture (the "dumb box"), the blanketing of the world with DDT and other toxic elements of industrial agriculture, and the mass addiction to television all seem far less enticing today. The larger problem, however, is not simply that the Council Fathers got caught up in the mood of the day and eagerly cut Mary down to (modern) size but that, in doing so, they capitulated to one of the most disastrous assumptions of the 500-year modern project: the denial of our cosmological fullness of being. To reconnect with our larger context, our larger being, is one of the central challenges of religion in the dawn of the third millennium.

In Christianity today, a growing movement seeks to honor the Creation by learning about the life forms and relational processes of Earth community and the entire cosmos. The cosmologically and ecologically informed spiritual orientation by now includes numerous authors and lecturers, the best known of whom are probably Fr. Thomas Berry and Dr. Brian Swimme.[3] Within Catholic circles, their work, as well as that of Sr. Miriam Therese MacGillis,[4] has been embraced in particular by several communities of nuns. Those "green sisters" hold spiritual retreats in which they reflect on the nature of the Creation as illuminated by the latest discoveries from the sciences of ecology and cosmology — and on our role in the unfolding story of the Earth community and the universe. I personally know nuns (a Dominican and a Franciscan, for example) who have placed on their personal altars NASA photos of glorious nebulae or other dramatic expressions of universe life to further their reflection on the nature and wonder of the Creation. Another nun (a Sister of Mercy) recently showed me the conceptual project I mentioned in the previous chapter: She had designed a chapel for a small, Catholic, liberal arts college that is named for Mary. Her design featured a domed, plexiglas sanctuary with a circle of supporting pillars shaped like tree trunks and incorporated several references to the manifestation of cosmological processes on Earth.

For these modern nuns and countless other Catholics inspired by the spiritual implications of cosmology, however, the possibility of the Virgin Mary as a symbol of profound cosmological relatedness never seems to enter their minds. That aspect of her has been largely relegated in the post-Vatican II era to the "scrap heap of history." How could such a pathetically nonmodern religious figure be relevant, these modern nuns wonder (if they ever think about Mary at all), to the latest news from contemporary science? How could the meaning of Mary, that tired old mom, possibly contain the cosmological magnificence of a Hubble deep-field photograph, delivered to their devotional altars via the Hubble Space Telescope?

Just as some Catholics today cannot see the point of Mary but celebrate the cosmological wonders of the Creation, others accept (a modernized) Mary but reject cosmology as being irrelevant to the faith. A typical example of the incompatibility assumed by many Catholic "progressives" between Mary's cosmological symbolism and various feminist causes appeared in an opinion piece recently in the *San Francisco Chronicle*. In the section advocating (rightly, in my view) the ordination of female clergy, the Catholic author made a surprising association. He wrote, "The current pope has made Mary almost an alternate deity. Why don't we allow her to step down off the crescent moon, roll up her sleeves, and manifest for us on a daily basis?"[5] The idea that she *is* manifesting in our daily lives *with* her cosmological symbolism, a concept that was easily grasped by nearly every Catholic prior to Vatican II, is apparently unthinkable to the modern sensibility. The "progressive" imperative is that she should be depicted as looking and being just like us — and get rid of that moon!

Is this literalism, as well as the stiff-arming of our cosmological context, really spiritual "progress"? Certainly it reflects the alienation of the modern mind from our embeddedness in the cosmos. With a disengagement that would astonish nonmodern cultures, modern people are educated to think of the universe only as something cold, dark, and remote — the subject of astronomy but nothing more. Consequently, all cosmological symbolism is disallowed as being pathetically nonmodern. Yet this assertive "clean sweep" is the tragic boosterism of a shrunken soul, whose cosmological proportions have been reduced to functional specifications.

I have often been told by "progressives," after I had declaimed on the spiritual richness of Mary's cosmological dimension in our tradition, that all such talk about the universe is merely "New Age." That very condemnation was also expressed by a conservative Catholic who wrote a letter to our weekly diocese newspaper complaining that a local publication called *Catholic Women's Network*, a fully admirable periodical to which I have subscribed for years, should remove the word *Catholic* from its title because, among other transgressions, it advocates "cosmos walks."[6] *Quel* horror! I assume the writer of the letter was referring to such contemplative and educational exercises as the "Walk through Time," in which participants quietly walk along a progression of posters or other displays that tell the story of the unfolding universe and the Earth community — that is, the biography of the Creation.

I shall argue in the following pages that it would be a very good thing indeed were the art and architecture of our Catholic churches today to celebrate the "big story" of the Creation. Suffice it to say, at this point, I find it disappointing that such a Calvinist disapproval of any Christian celebration of the Creation is entrenched in the modernized Catholic Church. I am not surprised when Evangelical Protestants tell me that they must spend a great deal of effort convincing parents that sending their children to a church camp that focuses on nature studies, as well as Bible studies, would not amount to exposing the little innocents to "devil worship" or other paganism. I am, however, surprised — in fact, appalled — when the contemporary heirs of the Catholic Church's grand stream of brilliant aesthetic celebrations of the cosmos have been so thoroughly wrenched from the heart of their tradition that they feel they must raise a finger in admonition against cosmological exuberance and cry, "Tut, tut! Nothing but the text!" After all, even Cardinal Ratzinger, when speaking in Paris recently of the need for liturgical reforms, advocated that the Church adopt the ancient custom of directing church altars toward the East as a "radical expression of the liturgy's cosmic dimension."[7]

Let us return to basics for a moment. To be vital, religious symbols and metaphors must be *simpatico* with the contemporary understanding of reality. In our day, then, they should reflect not the old, mechanistic worldview of modernity, which pushed aside all medieval organicism in the sixteenth and seventeenth centuries, but the latest, postmechanistic discoveries of the reformulated sciences that have been evolving since the Einsteinian revolution in the early twentieth century. Our perception of reality — in our bodies, the biosphere, and the entire universe — is gradually altering quite radically as recent discoveries in contemporary science make their way into general awareness. Ironically, today's postmodern findings in science (also called "post-classical" or postmechanistic) are so profoundly organic that a good deal of *pre*modern organic religious symbolism, far from being irrelevant vestiges from an abysmally ignorant past, once again makes imminent sense as poetic engagement with the actual nature of reality.

The cosmological matrix, in which the quantum level of existence arises and passes away trillions of times per second, is inherently supportive of life over time. The result is the unfolding story of universe life: galaxies, planets, and organic life forms. In our own species, like our close primate relatives, cooperation has always been key to survival. Without patient care and caring, usually from our mother, we humans would die at birth. So the recognition of a fecund and nurturing matrix — and the profound interrelatedness of all life forms that issue from it and return into it — evokes the image of a beautiful cosmic mother, a fount of the mercy and compassion that derive from inherent relationship, a mother whose arms are open to all, reminding us of the unitive dimension of our being, which human narcissism would have us forget.

In fact, Christian theologians currently calling for new religious metaphors to reflect the organicism of the Creation revealed by biological and cosmological science in recent years might well consider Mary in her depth. No doubt St. Thomas Aquinas, who valued so highly the knowledge about God's creation conveyed by (Aristotelian) science, would be thrilled to learn that twenty-first-century science seems to explicate various aspects of what the Blessed Virgin represents. The following examples of four concepts from contemporary science illustrate this complementarity: molecular kinship, omnicentricity, nonlocal causality, and the recognition of compassion as an evolutionary achievement. The first four concepts are from physics; the fourth is from biology.

Molecular kinship means that everything in the universe today is composed of elementary particles that have their common origin in the fireball at the birth of the cosmos 13.7 billion years ago. Through dynamic processes, the elementary particles, the stars and planets, the remarkable Gaian conditions that support life on Earth, the mountains and rivers, our animal relations, every one of us, and every blade of grass evolved from that singular event. When Mary the Maternal Matrix, the Mother of God-the-Son, looms large in medieval paintings, with her cloak spread open to shelter the multitudes in her care, we are reminded that everything in the Creation is literally kin.

Omnicentricity means that the universe is expanding outward away from every point within itself; each of those points is, therefore, a center of the universe. Just as the universe has countless centers, Mary, Queen of the Universe, is felt to be powerfully centered in myriad sites on the planet, not only in the cathedrals and churches dedicated to her throughout the Catholic world but in the thousands of shrines large and small. In Italy alone, there are 1,500 Marian shrines, or "centers" of her spiritual presence. Moreover, everyone is at the center of her heart and vice versa.

Nonlocal causality refers to the observation in quantum physics that occurrences in one region of space are inherently correlated with events taking place in other, distant regions. That is, when two subatomic particles whose spin is correlated are shot off in different directions, any change in the spin of either particle instantaneously occurs in the spin of the other as well. Therefore, the universe is seen to possess a quantum wholeness. Within that context the appeals to Mary that have resulted in hundreds of thousands of miraculous cures may be understood as prayer eliciting "action at a distance" through communion with the cosmological Matrix, who is a conduit for Divine grace.

Compassion as an evolutionary achievement can be traced in the story of life on Earth. The bond between mother and child, which first emerged, in mammals, some 200 million years ago, was a new power in the unfolding story. Natural selection favored this power, in that offspring that bonded with their mother had a better chance of survival. The bond of compassionate behavior then surfaced between animal siblings. Eventually it emerged within kin groups, although fighting still took place with other kin groups. All of these developments were favored by evolutionary dynamics and continued into the human species. Mary the Compassionate Mother may be seen as the culmination of this progression because no one is outside the embrace of her outstretched arms or beyond the reach of her bountiful grace, visited upon the whole world and the entire cosmos.

It can be seen from even this small sampling that to align oneself with the cosmological dimensions of Mary is to engage one's spirituality with the dynamics of the universe. The vast cosmological order and its extraordinary unity; the deft gravitational embrace that holds all forms of universe life; the self-organizing capabilities of galaxies, ecosystems, and cell clusters; the instantaneous correlation between subatomic particles at great distances; the astounding creativity and dynamism of the cosmological order — all these infuse the human species and emerge from the fecund matrix. Clearly, the universe creates the conditions for life and is biased toward it.

The cosmological sense of Mary can be understood to complement the cosmological sense of Christ that was expressed by the French Jesuit cosmologist Pierre Teilhard de Chardin. He posited that the eucharist transforms not only bread and wine but the totality of joys and pains engendered by "the convergence of the world" as cosmogenesis pursues its principal axis, the movement of the evolutionary cosmic drama into ever-increasing complexity and consciousness. Just as there is both a historical and a cosmic-transcendent Christ, so one can perceive that there is a historical and a cosmic-transcendent Mother of Christ. Or, as Thomas Berry puts it, *Mary is a cosmology*,[8] a grand context for our religious expressions of the human and the Divine.

In fact, the cosmological dimension of both Christ and Mary can be understood to have sacramental import as well. In the period shortly before and after Vatican II, a number of prominent Catholic theologians in Europe — such as Otto Semmelroth, Karl Rahner, and Edward Schillebeeckx — asserted that the seven sacraments of Catholicism should be viewed as derivative of two underlying, or embedding, sacraments. The more essential of these is the "primordial sacrament": Jesus in his humanity. The other is the "foundational sacrament": the Roman Catholic Church.[9] (As one might expect, the other branches of Christianity are decidedly unconvinced by this line of thought.) Anyone who is seriously engaging, either spiritually or theologically, with the cosmological dimension of Mary as the Maternal Matrix of the Incarnation and the Redemption, however, most probably sees a gap in the schema of these distinguished theologians. If the Church is to be granted sacramental status, then surely Mary must be seen as a fundamental sacramental presence as well.

Mary's sacramental nature is particularly apparent in light of recent theological thought that posits a sacrament as consisting of God's blessing action — including the entire cosmological Creation — *plus* a response to it. In other words, the nature of sacrament is both primary and relational. A ritual response to God's blessing is what completes the sacramental relationship. Mary, who responded with the fullness of her very being to the possibility of the Incarnation and the Redemption, is the Grand Respondent. When she agreed to grow God-the-Son from within her womb, the Maternal Matrix in her individual self was transformed to cosmological proportions, creating a field of sacramental presence.

The deepened and enlarged sense of sacrament and the "sacramental imagination" — that is, sensitivity to the sacramentality of every moment — has been rooted historically by contemporary theologians in the teaching of the Scholastic theologians of the Middle Ages, who expressed an integral view of all reality and its sacramental nature. Edward Kilmartin, for example, points out that the sacraments were valued in the medieval Church as "particular concentrations of the sacramental nature of all creation" and the highest manifestation of God's presence throughout the cosmos.[10] With the emergence of modernity, a secular sphere of philosophy developed that emphasized the power of human reason to construct reality and to manipulate and change it. This dominant perception resulted eventually in a profound disconnectedness within the Christian framework of sacramentality itself. Kilmartin notes, "In a word, with the loss of a sacramental understanding of all reality, the doctrine of analogy is deprived of its grounds."[11] After such a loss, Aquinas's teaching that the extraordinary diversity of the Creation as an analogous mode through which we may perceive divine magnificence falls on deaf ears. As was typical in other areas of modern thought, the premodern, more-than-human frame of reference was reduced to a focus on the human project.

One of the difficulties in understanding Mary's symbolic presence as the Maternal Matrix is modernity's atrophied ability to think symbolically with the subtlety and holism of religious consciousness in past times. The premodern mind had a subtle sense of religious symbols as being part of a larger, living context. With the emergence of modernity, the vast and deep engagement with symbolic presence was collapsed into the barren sense that a symbol is merely a sign, that which represents or points to something else. The resultant modern field of semiotics is the study of signs, signification, logic, and all patterned communication. Symbols might be considered psychologically to be "emotionally charged" but nothing more than that. In contrast, a nonmodern sensitivity to the multivalent nature of religious symbols is still alive among many traditional Native American peoples. They regard a symbol not as a sign representing some other and higher reality but as containing the reality, being part of it. There is an unbroken continuity among the larger presence and context of the symbol, the symbol itself, the process of symbolizing, and the person who views the symbol. With the emergence of modernity and its supposedly more "sophisticated" way of thinking, that entire vast and deep sensibility was lost, shrunken into the perception of symbols as mere signs.

Fortunately for our possibilities for recovery, the perception in *post*modern science of an unbroken field of space-time as the nature of reality illuminates the *pre*modern sense of religious symbols. An example within Catholicism is the mystery of transubstantiation. The meaning of this symbolic commemoration of Christ's sacrifice on the cross was one of the theological battle zones of the Reformation. The Church has always insisted that Christ is actually and substantially *present in* the communion host and the wine. As the *Catechism of the Catholic Church* puts it, Christ's presence in the eucharist in the fullest sense is a *substantial* presence by which God/Christ/man makes himself wholly and entirely present.[12] In contrast, Protestantism took a more modern, "rational" view, interpreting the communion ritual as *a sign that reminds us* of Christ's ultimate sacrifice. Luther himself proclaimed that Jesus is truly present in the eucharist, holding that "the bread and the wine in the Supper are the true body and blood of Christ."[13] Subsequent Protestant denominations, however, moved further into the modern, semiotic sense of the bread and wine as mere signs that *refer* to the Last Supper.

Not surprisingly, numerous "progressive" Catholic theologians have opted since Vatican II for a more modern replacement of the concept of transubstantiation: *transignification*. This interpretation posits that the meaning, or significance, of the bread and wine is changed by the words of consecration. According to John A. Hardon,

S.J., writing in *The Catholic Faith,* the consecrated elements are believed by those advocating transignification to signify all that Christians associate with the Last Supper, and the bread and wine have a higher value than merely food for the body. Fr. Hardon notes that this semiotic version of the meaning of the eucharist was condemned by Pope Paul VI in *Mysterium fidei* in 1965 and has never been accepted by the Magisterium (the teaching function) of the Church in Rome. It has, however, continued to gain adherents among "progressive" theologians and is taught in many courses on sacramental liturgy.

Hardon explains transubstantiation as follows:

> As understood by the Catholic Church, transubstantiation means that the whole substance of bread and wine cease to exist at the consecration at Mass. The whole substance of bread and wine becomes the whole humanity of Christ. It is not only that the substance of bread and wine becomes the whole humanity of Christ's body and blood. The substance of bread and wine becomes everything which makes Christ Christ. It becomes everything which Christ is.[14]

Transignification, in contrast, asserts that Christ is personally, but not locally (physically), present in the communion bread and wine.

Is there a physicist in the house? Local presence (also called "simple location"), like local causality, is now seen to be an assumption of the mechanistic worldview. That is, the Creation is now understood to be a dynamic complex of relationships. The ground of one's being is the ground of the entire universe. Consequently, each entity exists not only in its local manifestation but also exists in relationship throughout the universe, just as the entire relational universe exists in each entity. With the proof in recent years of nonlocal causality and the inherently relational field of being from which all phenomena in the universe emerge, the premodern perception that a spiritual figure exists in a field of cosmic holism, with its presence everywhere at once, is closer to the discoveries of postmodern physics than is an assumption of simple location or its absence.

Interpreting presence as being a matter of either substance *or* "personal presence," rather than the cosmological field of being, amounts to placing the modern blinders of the mechanistic worldview onto the deeper wisdom, which the Church has guarded in its mysteries throughout the modern era. The notion that the Savior is actually present in the eucharist appears in the gospels (for example, John 6:53-55) and is mentioned by theologians in the early centuries of the Church. The sense of the Divine being present in sacramental offerings of ritual food has an extremely long, pre-Christian history, of course, in the eastern Mediterranean basin. The Church protected this precious vestige of the subtle primal mind throughout the entire span of time from the attacks by the Reformation in the sixteenth century until the aftermath of Vatican II. Since then, modern, "progressive" thought has sought to brush it aside.

The unbroken field of space-time is also relevant to the cross-cultural sense of "participatory consciousness" in the *non*modern engagement with figurative symbols, that is, statues. Despite the "modernizing" decreed by Vatican II, the laity in all Catholic countries have continued to focus a great deal of spiritual attention on devotional statues of Mary. Viewed through the lens of modernity, this response is nonsensical. The "sophisticated" mind sees the statues only as primitive fetishes or infantile projections. Even a cultural historian I know who possesses a particularly wise and sensitive grasp of the ways in which symbols function told me a few years ago that he had recently been to a major Marian shrine (Einsiedeln in Switzerland) and was bemused to see all the fuss over . . . a dressed up doll! I was taken aback by the fact that his usually astute sensibilities regarding spiritual symbolism broke down when faced with a renowned medieval statue of Mary (even though he had had a Catholic childhood). He saw only a diminutive effigy clothed in an elaborate small gown embroidered with gold thread — plus a chapel full of people engaged in religious practice.

Why all the fuss? Because the statues of Mary are not dolls. They are not even mere "signs" representing something to us, as the modern theory of semiotics would have. The concentrated symbolic power possessed by these "small bodies" of the Great Mother can best be understood in the premodern and postmodern sense of "participatory consciousness": Our engagement with an expansive and multivalent symbol brings us into the unitive embrace of the sacred whole, into nonlinguistic awareness of the unbroken field of matter and energy arising and passing away trillions of times per second, constituting all things past and present. Mary is a gateway to our realization of that profound unity. That is why communion with her spiritual presence brings one to a peaceful state of mind. That is why 66 percent of all Catholic shrines in Europe are devoted to Mary the fecund Matrix (while 27 percent focus on a saint, and 7 percent focus on Jesus). In Italy, France, Spain, and Belgium, at least 75 percent of the shrines are Marian.[15] During processions once or twice a year in which the Marian statue is carried through the nearby streets, the stream of people walking, singing, and praying before and behind her often experience a palpable sense of deep continuity with Mary and with the surroundings — trees, buildings, other people.

For hundreds of years most Catholics throughout Europe made an annual pilgrimage to a Marian shrine, which often meant walking for more than a day. Entire villages would walk together, men, women, and children, singing and chanting. What drew them to the shrines — and continues to do so? It is an atmosphere that feels closer to the spiritual peace of Mary and Jesus than does the mundane world, not only because of the statue of her mystical body of grace but also because of the subtle ambiance. There one may rest in Mary's complexity and her oceanic peacefulness. In addition, a shrine, like a meditation hall or a church, accumulates hundreds of thousands of emanations of mental energy that constitute a thought field of spiritual harmony. If one doubts the existence of such emanations, the many recent double-blind studies proving the healing effect of prayer should be of interest. (See, for example, *The Faith Factor* by Dale Matthews, M.D., *Timeless Healing* by Herbert Benson, M.D., and *Prayer Is Good Medicine* by Larry Dossey, M.D.) Moreover, the hundreds of crutches that cover one or two walls of most shrines testify to the special presence.

The Marian statues are often linked to specific places in the natural world. Several of the black madonnas, for instance, are said to have been rooted literally in a particular spot; that is, it proved impossible to lift and move the small statue from the place where it came ashore or was otherwise discovered, so the shrine had to be built in the physical locus seemingly selected by the statue itself. A few of the shrines to Mary established on this continent are replicas of European shrines, but many reflect — less dramatically than in the medieval stories — the embeddedness of Marian spirituality in the physicality of the New World. She often dwells in place, bearing such titles as Our Lady of the Rockies and Our Lady of the Prairies. The latter carries a sheath of wheat in one crooked arm as she stands surrounded by still more of the staff of life, which represents the Communion Host, the Body of Christ. In both the Old World and the New, Mary is frequently linked with a form or a power of nature: Our Lady of the Rivers, Our Lady of the Grotto, Saint Mary of the Springs, Our Lady of the Dark Forest, Our Lady of the Brambles, and Our Lady of the Plain. Our Lady of Bistrica, the national Marian shrine of Croatia, for instance, is named for the stream near which her church was built. When my grandmother was a girl, she and her entire village made a pilgrimage every year to Marija Bistrica.

In traditional Catholicism the Virgin Mary is understood to be not only a conduit of divine immanence but a locus of it as well. (She is not, however, considered to be a source of divine immanence. Her elevated position derives from her ontological relationship with God-the-Son.) In mythological terms, the sacred narrative of Catholicism looks like this: The divine son of the sky-god visited Earth for thirty-three years and then returned to the heavenly abode of his father; eventually, he brought his earthly mother to the heavenly abode, but because she is of Earth and is the mediator between heaven and Earth, she simultaneously remained on our garden planet by inhabiting myriad local formations of nature. Mary is profoundly earthly *and* cosmological, as are we. She is at once the particular and the universal.

Her shrines, churches, and cathedrals throughout Europe — as on the hill called Tepeyac near Mexico City — were often built directly over natural sites formerly honored by earlier religions because those spots seemed to exude a concentrated field of vibratory energy in the land or the water. Chartres Cathedral, for instance, was built over a well, or spring, that was held sacred in pre-Christian times. There, as elsewhere, the Christian overlay retains traces of Goddess religion. In Ireland 86 percent of the shrines (that is, 104) center on a "well" that encloses a spring once held sacred to the goddess Brigid (who was transformed into St. Brigid) or other ancient expressions of Celtic or pre-Celtic religion.[16] St. Patrick reputedly Christianized these wells by thrusting his staff into each of them.

Sacred stories in all religions allude to the ultimate mystery of cosmic creativity, which we call the Divine. The cosmological vantage point affords a deeper comprehension of these mythic stories than do most modern and deconstructive-postmodern analyses. Both of the latter generally consider mythic narratives found in religions and elsewhere to be aggrandized, strategically skewed reflections of formative developments that shaped a culture and that are made to appear as if they had been profound events of nature. Through the lens of modernity, myths appear to be solely "political," meaning that they are expressions of control by the group that attained dominance. This view was famously expressed by the late Roland Barthes, a major theorist of semiotics, when he declared that myth transforms history into nature, that is, myth makes ancient power plays seem like natural events or outcomes. From a cosmological perspective, however, this conclusion is exactly backward: Mythic religious narratives are culturally specific expressions of the larger mythic drama of the cosmos and its subtle processes that compose the Earth community. In short, *myth transforms nature into history*. That is, "nature" writ large is transformed into a particular religion's or society's own cosmological epic. Better still, however, is a third view of myth, an ecosocial or cosmosocial perspective: Religious myth is the overlay of "political" stories (such as patriarchal religion) onto the very real cosmological drama of which we are a part and which shapes our physical and cultural existence.

Modernity, of course, has no use for any of that — not for a sense of the cosmos as primary, not for the Earth community of all our animal relations, not for any intimations of the sacred whole. Yet it is evident by now that our hypermodern culture has gone awry, that something dies in the human, in our families, and our societies when our sense of being is reduced to a relentlessly manipulated pursuit of consumption as self-definition and self-development. We need conduits to our larger context, the unfolding story of the universe and our role in the Earth community. We need spiritual symbols that evoke consciousness of our larger selves and the cosmic unity. We need to feel grounded in the matrix of being. We need to honor and emulate maternal compassion and be healed by it. We need Mary.

The very act of rallying to save that which is precious energizes our relationship with it. As word spread about the Marian petition drive and the spiritual experiences at Marian shrines, people began thinking and speaking of Mary again as if waking from a long dormancy, the post-Vatican II "dogmatic slumber" of acquiescence to the "rationalizing" ideologies of modernity. The Marian renewal has brought us back into contact with the vital, through a rich communion that cannot be replaced. We are grounded once again in an organic expression of the unity of the cosmos. We are embraced once again by the compassionate Great Mother, arms outstretched as always, for indeed the universe is beneficent: Through cataclysms, floods, and famine, life goes on. We had grown weary of a world without her, a world that sees her only as a bit player in a religious saga that has outgrown her, a world that is barren and deadly because it shunts aside the wisdom and compassion of maternal ethics, a world that sacrifices relational values such as compassion, protection, and peacemaking to more "tough-minded," macho proclivities in the modern era.

Certainly the "industrial" values of efficiency at all costs and unbounded material expansion shaped the past century, just as Henry Adams foresaw. Even though the Brave New World has ravaged the life support systems of our planet, leaving technoman alienated and incomplete, technology is still touted as the new transcendent, freeing us progressively from all "constraints" of body and nature. Our children are so "liberated" by virtual reality and other electronic saturation in their formative years that many of them have become more comfortable interacting with machines than with other humans, and they rarely play outdoors anymore. They are being socialized perfectly for a disembodied, disembedded dystopian future.

As contact with the rest of the Creation — that is, other humans and other species — has been replaced by television, video, and computer time, people feel increasingly shrunken into themselves. The first casualties are empathy, compassion, and even consideration. These are traits that all religions seek to instill in order to counter our species's problematic evolutionary inheritance: narcissism. The "default position" in the human, absent spiritual and ethical teachings, seems to be self-absorption, scant attention to our effects on others, and a solipsistic perception of the world. Although "taking care of Number One" may have been a key to survival during the past two hundred thousand years, that orientation, nestled deeply within us, requires wise cultural responses that are sufficiently potent to counter it. As modernity continues to shift respect away from religion, devaluing its crucial ability to illuminate our embeddedness in a sacred whole, modern societies enshrine the concept of the supposedly unbounded Autonomous Individual — but end up with unbounded narcissism.

During the past several years waves of violence, aggression, and disrespect have been reported in several "advanced" societies; the perpetrators were not only the usual demographic hot spot (males aged eighteen to twenty-five) or even high-school boys but, rather, children in middle schools and elementary schools. Their callousness and insensitivity may indeed suit them well for a world in which a relentlessly competitive, corporate-dominated market economy has gained ascendancy over civil governance and safeguards of all sorts, a world in which incivility and antagonism are taken for granted.

It would be difficult to imagine a situation in greater need of a numinous reminder that the sacred streams of Christian, Jew, and Muslim converge; that they converge with the deeper streams of native peoples and female forms of the Divine reaching back to the paleolithic era; that they meet in a bountiful maternal body of grace at once earthly and cosmic; that her compassion holds and heals them all; that it provides a model, a guide, and a teaching; that there is a way.

Perhaps our new century will be shaped not by the empty values of the electronic and biotech "dynamo" but by those of the Blessed Mother: empathy, compassion, kindness, forgiveness, and nonviolence. Mary is not the past but the future. More than merely a pathway to these values, Mary is a matrix, as are her surviving sisters, Kuan Yin, Tara, Yemaya, Durga, White Buffalo Woman, and many more. They are the sea, the earth, and the sky, fecund, resilient, and eternal. In their spiritual presence we are reminded of the inherent nature of compassion and its basis in the profound interrelatedness of all life. Just as the universe cherishes the empathic bond of mother and child wherever it exists and rewards it with life, the Earth community is now calling out to us for empathic bonding.

The feminine face of the Divine, including its semi-divine forms, has long been recognized and honored by men who were not afraid. She is respectfully called "the Mother Love of God," for instance, by Fr. Andrew Greeley. Perhaps such men are even somewhat embarrassed for their brothers who insist that the divine creativity of the cosmos must be depicted in all-male trinities or pantheons with preposterous all-male creation myths. The patriarchs have prevailed, ever vigilant lest the female go uncontained, but other men have celebrated the Mother of the Savior with a deep, if only implicit, awareness that Mary is the Mother of Salvation as well. These men have been able to comprehend the Blessed Virgin as both the merciful conduit of the grace of God-the-Father through God-the-Son — that is, the sky-god type of transcendent salvation — *and* the locus of earthly salvation from woundedness, loss of connection, and the truly deadly sins of atrophied compassion, habitual indifference, and rapacious self-absorption. Mary is the ground of such salvation, absorbing human suffering and radiating hope.

As in the past, the efforts to deny Mary have been washed over by waves of renewal. The Marian tide has been rising for more than two decades now, buoyantly carrying multitudes who have been dashed against the rocks of a sterile modern world that sees nothing beyond itself. At the heart of it all is personal communion with Mary in her full cosmological sense, through one's inner conversation with her or the felt connection that needs no words.

In the stable, in the cosmos, on the altars of cathedrals and mud shacks — the spiritual presence of Mary embodies even more than cosmic beneficence and profound unity. In her are merged a poignant array of pathways to the sacred whole. She is the collective soul of many cultures, each seeing in her its deepest roots. She brings into the present moment from our paleolithic past the unbroken stream of female forms of the Divine. She links the Old World with the New. She is invoked as the patron of seas, springs, and hills. She is called the Queen of Heaven yet dwells in the spiritual sanctuary of every heart attuned to her.

Mary most intimate, Mary most cosmic. May you return in full to our sterile modern churches. May our spiritual lives be nourished once again by the maternal ground of all. May we be infused and inspired by your healing compassion. May we never part.

Star of the Sea

Queen of the Universe

Singular Vessel of Devotion

Chapter Four

Where Mary Still Reigns

In the previous chapters I have sought to make the case that the Catholic Church's decision in the early 1960s to radically suppress Marian spirituality was a period piece, a sudden and sweeping allegiance to the ideology of modernity at a historical moment, the post–World War II period, when that worldview enjoyed an intensified burst of dominance. Only a decade after Vatican II met in Rome, however, critiques of the assumptions of modernity and its destructive results began to sprout in Europe, the United States, and the "developing" nations. Because of these disparate *post*modern critiques and because of the increasingly painful "trade-offs" demanded by the modern condition, it is now widely conceded that modernity brought significant losses along with its many benefits. Certainly it has changed our inner landscape as well as the outer.

Are Catholics who were raised after Mary was shrunken and suppressed different from those who came of age with Mary in her fullness? Most of the "modernizers" within the Church would respond with an enthusiastic *yes*: Catholics who have grown up knowing only the "rationalized" version of Mary have been "liberated" from all measure of medieval mysticism and hokum, freed to focus with clarity on the story of Jesus Christ in Scripture, where Mary is merely a minor character necessary to advance the plot. As one such Catholic nun proudly explained to me with regard to the radical "rationalizing" of Catholicism at Vatican II, "The Church finally responded to the Reformation! It just took 440 years."

Others of us would agree that the "minimalist Marian" Catholics (not only those who came of age after Vatican II but also those older "progressives" who are happily, even enthusiastically, accommodated to the drastically reduced presence of Mary) are somehow different in their spiritual sensibilities — different in ways that deliver them into the maw of modern reductionism with its emphasis on efficient, instrumental thinking and being. Some of my own encounters mirror the observation made in *Virgin Time* by the Catholic memoirist Patricia Hampl about the young "progressive" nuns she met on a tour of Assisi in 1990. They were intelligent problem-solvers and "on-the-mark analysts about the role of women in the Church" but lacked the "romantic quality — of a life lived from desire, not essentially from effort": "Romance, the engine that kept the whole Franciscan machine steaming down the centuries — this was absent from their intelligent, decent faces." Instead, it seemed to Hampl, these nuns gave off "an almost hygienic aura of good cheer and earnestness."[1] They are often motivated by a perfectly reasonable desire to attain leadership positions in the Church, but I would say that their spiritual center of gravity is different. It seems to be less infused with participatory consciousness, the subtle perception of being vibrantly kin to all life grounded in the mysteries of the Maternal Matrix and the divine Creation. What is Mary to these "progressive" nuns? In general, they do not think much about her at all — except as the annoying mascot of the Catholic right, or as embarrassing medieval baggage correctly jettisoned by Vatican II, or perhaps as an activist Nazarene village woman mentioned a few times in the gospels.

By the early 1990s it seemed in many quarters of the Church hierarchy, especially "progressive" circles, that the future of Catholicism would be largely post-Marian and successfully "rationalized." Rising evidence to the contrary was dismissed as right-wing fanaticism that would eventually die out. In truth, however, the millions of visitors to Marian shrines worldwide are liberal, conservative, and "none of the above" in their political persuasion. In the United States, in particular, the widely perceived gap between "progressives" and conservatives with regard to Mary has been tentatively bridged in recent years by a well-known priest many would consider "progressive." As I noted in chapter two, Fr. Andrew Greeley has called for a renewal of Marian spirituality as part of a larger recovery of "much of what was distinctive and precious in the Catholic sacramental heritage."[2] Since the late

1970s, in fact, Greeley has argued for a larger sense of Mary in the post-Vatican II Church.

In *The Catholic Imagination* (2001), Greeley cites a recent sociological study of young Catholics that found a high correlation between a positive sense of Mary — as "warm," "patient," "comforting," and/or "gentle" — and a commitment to social justice, frequency of prayer, concern for racial equality . . . and an expectation of sexual fulfillment in marriage.[3] This study would seem to belie the common assumption among many older Catholic "progressives" that only reactionaries cling to an interest in Mary. From my perspective, of course, a key question to put to young Catholics would be whether they have any sense of Mary as anything more than a nice lady mentioned in the Bible. Still, if even the pared down, "modernized" version of the Blessed Mother can inspire commitment to the social gospel among Catholic youth, the residual power of Our Lady, Mirror of Justice is evident.

Greeley himself, when lecturing on recovering our Catholic heritage, emphasizes the need to represent our sacramentality in ways that celebrate its beauty. Indeed, it was beauty that guided many of us back to Mary: Because so many Catholics my age experienced in our formative years the infusion of spiritual beauty emanating from the Blessed Mother, we have been able to reconnect with her spiritual presence at mid-life. For women the reunion has a poignant resonance with our lives. The novelist Mary Gordon, for instance, described this recovery process early on in the Marian resurgence. In an essay titled "Coming to Terms with Mary," Gordon reflected on sifting through "the nonsense that has characterized thought and writing about Mary" to come back to that figure who has "triumphed over the hatred of women and the fear of her, and abides shining, worthy of our love, compelling it." Gordon, who considers Mary both Mother and Queen, suggested that it is through painting, sculpture, and music that we can best find "the surest way back to the Mother of God."[4]

Most American Catholic women who grew up after Vatican II, in contrast, feel very little connection with Mary. I was shocked to read in the introduction to Sally Cunneen's *In Search of Mary* (1996) that when she surveyed and interviewed a number of Catholic women about the Virgin Mary, most of them described their mother's or grandmother's Marian spirituality because they had never experienced any of their own. An entire generation of Maryless Catholic girls! By acquiescing to the ideology of modernity, we are depriving our daughters of a deep psychological and spiritual communion with the female embodiment of grace, dignity, potency, and compassion . . . writ large in cosmological proportions.

Even the overflow crowds who turn out to hear Greeley speak about "recovering our Catholic heritage" at universities and conferences have little idea of *how* to recover a spirituality they have never known. For modernized Catholics trying to find their way beyond the stripped-down version of their faith, then, the ethnic communities who have never deserted Mary may provide inspiration. One can still hear Marian hymns sung in the dwindling number of parishes that are strongly identified with immigrant cultures from Eastern, Central, and Southern Europe, as well as the growing number of Latino and Filipino parishes. In fact, when Catholic college students from abroad enroll in a public university here and discover that there is usually a nearby Newman Center, a student-oriented Catholic church run by the Paulist Fathers, the foreigners are often puzzled by the nearly Maryless version of Catholicism they encounter in the hypermodern United States. At least one Newman Center, the one adjacent to Ohio State University, responded recently to the foreign students' strongly *missing Mary* by creating a Marian room adjacent to the sanctuary.[5]

From such incidences and from accounts given by nuns and priests returning from service in the "Third World" — where, as a Jesuit returning from Asia told me, "the anti-mystical bias is not a factor" — one might well conclude that post-Marian Catholicism, at least in its most intense forms, is essentially an Anglo-American problem. For instance, when the archdiocese of San Francisco ordained Fr. Ignatius Wang as the first native of China to become a bishop in the United States, the homily in the mass of ordination, on January 30, 2003, was delivered by his old friend from seminary days in Hong Kong, Auxiliary Bishop John Tong Hon of that city. In a statement that must have seemed thoroughly uncontroversial to the bishop from Asia, but no doubt made the American clergy at the gala event uncomfortable, Bishop Tong happily declared of his friend Bishop Wang and himself, "We are both Chinese and in service to the universal Church, and we both share a dedication to Our Lady."[6] Sounds right to me.

In North America the largest Marian presence by far is that of Our Lady of Guadalupe. In December 1995, I heard a feature on National Public Radio about the celebration of her feast day at the main church in the Mexican and Mexican American community of Los Angeles. The reporter noted that this event was much like the larger one at the basilica in Mexico City. At that moment I knew I would go to Los Angeles the following December.

When I placed a long-distance call in fall 1996 to Our Lady, Queen of the Angels Catholic Church in the old Mexican American section of Los Angeles, a man with a Spanish accent assured me that I would be welcome to attend the all-night celebration on the feast day of Our Lady of Guadalupe, December 12. Small groups and mariachi bands would be coming at various times throughout the night to sing their serenades *(las Mañanitas)* to Mary in the courtyard before and between the masses. Then he added, "Be sure to get here by two A.M. That's when the bars and nightclubs close."

Bars and nightclubs?

Sensing the puzzlement in my silence, he explained, "That's when all the waitresses and busboys and dishwashers come to the church. This is about the poor. This is all about the poor."

I flew to Los Angeles, rented a car, and headed to the barrio in the early hours of Guadalupe's day. I had first spent the day with my daughter. Because she had an exam the next morning at UCLA, she could not come to the all-night celebration. Consequently, both she and her roommate were very worried that I was heading out alone at that hour to an area known to have high levels of gang activity. I assured them that it was the safest night of the year, but they were unconvinced. In the end, those well-wired twenty-somethings insisted that I at least take along one of their cell phones in my purse.

It was unnecessary. As soon as I pulled into the parking lot near the church, I was greeted by a man who called out "Buenos Dias!" with a broad, welcoming smile as he directed me to an open spot between a beat-up black pick-up truck and a well-worn car. Walking to the church, I passed people setting up food stands and a sidewalk shrine to the Virgin of Guadalupe, a nine-foot-high structure with candles, flowers, and gauzy white drapery framing her image. Inside the courtyard of the church, which was strung with hundreds of tiny white lights in the overhead lattice, I saw that three more elaborate shrines had been constructed with large banks of votive candles and red roses. It was a joyful, if noisy, scene with two mariachi bands only a dozen yards apart playing and singing different songs to Mary. At times a third rhythm was added by a small group of young men in scant Aztec outfits and clacking rows of ankle bracelets who danced to pulsing drumbeats. Around the perimeter various groups sold food and drinks or an array of La Virgen de Guadalupe rosaries, medals, bookmarks, refrigerator magnets, and books. I bought a wooden rosary.

The crowd emitted a low buzz as people circulated among the attractions, stopping to listen to the music or to offer a prayer at the shrines. At one of the three shrines — the only permanent one, where Our Lady of Guadalupe's image was painted on tiles set into the wall of the church — the atmosphere was remarkable. Some forty people stood close together as they silently prayed or otherwise communed before a bank of tall votive candles, dozens of groupings of red roses, and the image itself. In that area, that small section in the middle of a high-decibel courtyard, it was quiet and palpably still.

At 3:15 A.M. the doors to the church were swung open as bells announced the first mass of the day. The sanctuary was starkly modern and far too brightly lit, but on the wall behind the altar the comforting figure of Our Lady of Guadalupe (a reproduction of the cactus-fiber *tilma* on which the image reportedly appeared in 1531) almost made one forget the sterile surroundings. To the left of the reproduction was a large mosaic depicting the Virgin of Guadalupe by a lake, to the right a large mosaic of Jesus dividing the fishes and loaves in Mexico, flanked by cactus and framed by distant mountains. In the center, the priest began by welcoming everyone with a vigorous sequence of call and response: "Viva La Virgen de Guadalupe!" "Viva!," the people roared back. "Viva Mexico!" "Viva!" "Viva Central America!" "Viva!" "Viva USA!" "Viva!" The entire set was repeated twice more, energizing everyone for spiritual engagement.

In front of the altar two young men held a large painting of La Virgen de Guadalupe featuring gold glitter on her gown, around the border, and over three words at the bottom: *La Zona Rosa*. Groups of other young men with an insignia on their matching sweatshirts stood on either side of the picture, while still others formed a procession to bring the communion bread and wine down the center aisle to the priest. The sea of adults in the pews was dotted with beautiful little children dressed in the traditional clothing of their parents' and grandparents' home district in Mexico or other Central American countries. During the mass, two mariachi bands and singers took the place of a choir and were often joined by the entire congregation in melodies that were obviously well known and much loved.

After the mass, everyone was directed to approach the altar, walk along its left or right side, and proceed toward the back wall. There each woman was given a red rose as the crowd passed through a doorway under the large picture of Our Lady of Guadalupe. That route delivered us into the adjacent baroque chapel, which features a dramatic painting of Mary over the altar in the style of seventeenth-century Spain. Since the chapel was dimly lit and very European, the short journey felt like walking out of garishly lit modernity into a past that was more sensitive to paradox and mystery. From there we were directed back outside to the courtyard, where a sequence of still more mariachi groups serenaded Guadalupe, this time broadcast far beyond the church by a local radio station. The next mass was at 5:00 A.M., followed by one every hour and a quarter all day long. (I ended up staying for two and a half masses, a one-day "personal best" in my lifetime stats.) The grand finale occurred at the 7:00 P.M. mass, when a long procession of little children in their diminutive regional attire — each child carrying a red rose to Nuestra Señora — accompanied the communion bread and wine down the center aisle to the altar.

The following year on the feast day of Our Lady of Guadalupe, December 12, 1997, I attended a more modest observation at our parish church in Half Moon Bay, a coastal town twenty-five miles south of San Francisco. The mass was held in the evening, but at 5:00 A.M. nearly every Mexican and Mexican American family in town, it seemed, was packed into the church for *las Mañanitas* (which literally means the songs sung in the "wee, small hours" of early morning). The parishoners sang the melodic serenades to Mary for an hour, led by a mariachi band with singers. Most of the people were agricultural workers who had migrated to our town during the past four decades from the Mexican states of Jalisco and Oaxaca. They had found work here in the fields and the many nurseries. Among these families, as I was soon to discover, were twelve Aztec princesses, or at least their symbolic descendents. For as I started to walk to my car after the hour of serenades, I saw that twelve high-school girls — dressed in white gowns and elaborate headdresses with tall white feathers — were performing Indian dances in front of the church. Our two priests circulated among the crowd inviting everyone to stay and watch. Later I learned that the dancers had probably been presented in infancy to Our Lady of Guadalupe at the basilica on Tepeyac hill in Mexico City, as are all the newborns whose parents can make the trip back home to her.

The celebration of Mary's compassion and spiritual beauty takes place in all Catholic parishes, albeit in sadly minimized form, on her few official feast days remaining in the post-Vatican II liturgical calendar. In response to the growing Latino population in the United States, however, the American bishops recently included in the new Spanish-language Sacramentary for the United States fifteen Marian feast days that honor Mary as the patroness of fifteen Latin American nations, plus Puerto Rico. These feast days celebrate Our Lady of Altagracia (Dominican Republic) on January 21, Our Lady of Copacabana (Bolivia) on February 2, Our Lady of Suyapa (Honduras) on February 3, Our Lady of Lujan (Argentina) on May 8, Our Lady of the Rosary of Chiquinquira (Columbia) on July 9, Our Lady of Carmel of Maipu (Chile) on July 16, Our Lady of the Angels (Costa Rica) on August 2, Our Lady of Charity of el Cobre (Cuba) on September 8, Our Lady of Coromoto (Venezuela) on September 11, Our Lady of the Eastern 33 (Uruguay) on the first Saturday in November, Our Lady of Divine Providence (Puerto Rico) on November 19, Our Lady of the El Quinche (Ecuador) on November 21, Our Lady of the Immaculate Conception (Nicaragua and Panama) on December 8, Our Lady of Caacupe (Paraguay) on December 8, and Our Lady of Guadalupe (Mexico) on December 12. Many observers predict that the Church in North America is evolving into two distinct halves: a modernized, Calvinized Catholic Church on the one hand, and a richly expressive, sacramental Latino Catholic Church on the other.

Perhaps because the aesthetic abundance of past celebrations of the Blessed Mother is no longer present in most Catholic churches, other than the ethnic parishes, an aesthetic grassroots devotional movement called "Mary's Gardens" has spread to hundreds of thousands of back yards and several church grounds. These gardens are living works of art in which contemplative prayer may flourish. The first Marian garden planted in the United States was the creation of Frances Crane Lillie on the grounds of St. Joseph Church in Woods Hole on Cape Cod in 1932. The Mary's Gardens movement grew from the vision of two men in Philadelphia, Ed McTague and John Stokes, Jr., who in 1951 sought to counter the aggressive thrust of modernity in the post–World War II years, which they correctly perceived was going to push aside the Virgin Mary as a medieval vestige from premodern times.

Indeed, the medieval era was shaped by an extraordinary burst of creativity that honored the Maternal Matrix. In addition to the new cycle of prayers called the rosary, the new music in polyphonic hymns, new architectural techniques allowing the Gothic cathedrals to rise toward the Queen of Heaven, and new shrines drawing a steady flow of pilgrims, the spiritual presence of the Blessed Mother was honored in everyday life by linking her story and attributes with various plants and flowers all over medieval Europe. To these were eventually added adaptations and additions in the New World.

The Mary's Gardens movement has discovered that some 500 plants were once considered "Flowers of Our Lady," the rose being merely the best known. A large number of these flowering plants are featured and explicated on the movement's website, which is itself an abundant garden of information.[7] There one can browse through a color-slide lecture on fifty Marian flowers, each with an accompanying paragraph of historical research. In addition, there are articles on "the Church and nature symbols of Mary," "the richness of medieval plant symbolism today," Mary's flowers in particular countries, and a review of the book *Mary's Flowers: Gardens, Legends, and Meditations* (1999).[8] A horticultural section gives advice on starting and maintaining a Mary's Garden at home or on one's parish grounds, as well as creating an indoor dish garden and installing a windowsill garden for classrooms.

The poignant tenderness of Marian sensibilities infuses every aspect of this practice, none more so than the section on "Garden Prayer and Meditation," where the recognition of the profound unity symbolized by Mary — matrix (the ground of all), mater (mother), and matter (soil) — comes to spiritual fruition. Catholics involved with the Mary's

Gardens movement feel that cultivating the living associations of the Blessed Mother furthers their own inner cultivation of communion with her. As Mary's presence dwells in their gardens, so it dwells in their hearts.

Older still than such medieval associations is the perception of Mary as Advocate, which dates from the third century and is today being invigorated through the resurgence of prayer and silent conversation. In all Catholic cultures, Mary's role as advocate of the people of God was seen as an extension of her unique sharing in the mediation of Christ's salvific grace. The Blessed Virgin is, therefore, acknowledged as a compassionate intercessor. This role of mediator, or instrument of union, was foreshadowed in Hebrew Scripture by the patriarchs, the prophets, and the queen mothers of the great Davidic kings. In the case of Mary's maternal sharing of Christ's salvific role, she not only mediates the flow of divine grace to humanity but also mediates the "petitions," or distress calls, from the human family to the Divine. The Church traditionally taught that praying to the Blessed Virgin Mary is not a matter of bypassing Jesus or God-the-Father because her central role and compassionate maternal presence are part of the divine plan for the salvation of all souls. For these reasons, Catholic theologians formerly asserted that Mary's role is profoundly significant not only in the Incarnation but also in its legacy, the Christian path to union with the Divine.

Even today certain medieval prayers honoring Mary's powers of intercession are held dear — at least by those old enough to have learned them before Vatican II. The famous "Memorare" prayer was composed in the twelfth century by St. Bernard of Clairvaux, who often celebrated her unfailing compassion:

Remember, O most gracious Virgin Mary,
   never is it heard that anyone
   who fled to your protection,
   implored your help, or
   sought your intercession was left unaided.
Inspired with this confidence, I fly to you,
   O virgin of virgins, my Mother.
To you do I come, before you I stand sinful and sorrowful.
O Mother of the Word Incarnate, do not ignore my petitions

But in your mercy hear and answer me. Amen.

Bernard, who detested the new Gothic style of architecture because he felt that its gargoyles and other dramatic flourishes must surely act as a distraction for those in prayer, preferred the austere form of Cistercian churches. Within their stark white walls and plain windows, he preached passionately about Mary the Intercessor. The following is an excerpt from one of his sermons:

> She, I tell you, is that splendid and wondrous star suspended as by necessity over this great wide sea, radiant with merit and brilliant in example. O you, whoever you are, who feel that in the tidal wave of this world you are nearer to being tossed about among the squalls and gales than treading on dry land, if you do not want to founder in the tempest, do not avert your eyes from the brightness of this star. When the wind of temptation rises within you, when you strike upon the rock of tribulation, gaze up at this star, call out to Mary. Whether you are being tossed about by the waves of pride or ambition or slander or jealousy, gaze up at this star, call out to Mary. When rage or greed or fleshly desires are battering the skiff of your soul, gaze up at Mary. When ... you begin to founder in the gulf of sadness and despair, think of Mary. In dangers, in hardships, in every doubt, think of Mary, call out to Mary. Keep her in your mouth, keep her in your heart. Follow the example of her life, and you will obtain the favor of her prayer. Following her, you will never go astray. Asking for her help, you will never despair. Keeping her in your thoughts, you will never wander away. With your hand in hers, you will never stumble. With her protecting you, you will not be afraid. With her leading you, you will never tire. Her kindness will see you through to the end.[9]

In the Middle Ages the emphasis on Mary as compassionate intercessor was also expressed in artistic forms so moving as to still be cherished in the twenty-first century. It is this aspect of her spiritual presence that inspired the conclusion of Dante's medieval masterpiece, *The Divine Comedy*. In the final canto of *Paradisio,* St. Bernard of Clairvaux offers this prayer to the Virgin Mary on behalf of the seeker (Dante), who aspires to attain "the ultimate salvation":

> Virgin Mother, daughter of your Son,
> more humble and sublime than any creature,

fixed goal decreed from all eternity,
   you are the one who gave to human nature
so much nobility that its Creator
did not disdain His being made its creature. . . .
   on earth, among the mortals,
you are a living spring of hope. Lady,
   you are so grand and can so intercede
that he who would have grace but does not seek
your aid may long to fly but has no wings.
   Your loving-kindness answers not only
the one who asks but is often ready
to respond freely long before the asking.
   In you compassion is, in you is pity,
in you is generosity, in you
is every goodness found in any creature.[10]

To the modern mind, so bereft of participatory consciousness, any such approach to a semi-divine spiritual figure or goddess or god is an infantile regression, excusable only in the most extreme conditions: "There are no atheists in foxholes," as the saying went in World War II. Religious engagement with a numinous symbol is illuminated, however, by the premodern and the postmodern sense of reality as a vast, unbroken field of subtle relatedness. When a person communes with divine creativity in the cosmos via a symbolic representation — whether in sadness and distress or in celebration and awe at the wonders of the universe — she or he is acknowledging the sense of interrelationship and balance in which all life forms are held, from subatomic particles to self-organizing galaxies. In times of danger or psychological agitation, the balance in and around one is shattered. To approach, through whatever metaphoric route, our larger context is a sensible effort to reconnect with the greater order, the *logos* of the universe. Expressing through prayer or "petition" the desire that everything might be made right, that harmony of all sorts might once again prevail, expands one's focus from the distressed ego to the larger scope of unfolding possibility. Spiritual "petitioning," like its more joyful twin, spiritual gratitude and delight, reactivates one's relationship to the Divine. Indeed, opening oneself to the sacred whole, the

Great Holy, through any means can alleviate the sense of alienation from one's vital self that is so common in the modern world.

It is with this deeper, cosmological understanding, rather than an attitude of condescension and barely respectful "political correctness" on the part of modernized Catholics, that the Vatican's *Directory on Popular Piety and Liturgy* should be received. Published in 2002 by the Congregation for Divine Worship and the Discipline of the Sacraments, the *Directory* is a 300-page discussion of many examples of "popular piety," that is, Catholic folk customs and spiritual practices such as Advent wreaths; re-enacting the Passion of Christ; offering of prayers for souls in purgatory; kissing sacred images; pilgrimages; and processions with statues of Jesus, Mary, or various saints. As Jorge Medina Cardinal Estevez, prefect of that congregation, or office, within the Vatican, explained at a press conference, the document has two aims. First, it seeks to inform modern Catholics that these spiritual practices, which have arisen over the centuries "from the culture and faith of particular peoples," have led to "a deepening of faith": "When, out of a desire for liturgical purity, expressions of popular piety are chased away, our faith is impoverished." Second, it seeks to "purify" the practices of popular piety of "any tendency toward superstition" by educating the faithful about the connection between the traditional practices and "the fundamentals of Christian faith": "The solution is not to throw it all out, but to purify it through evangelization and education."[11] Purify it, yes, but one hopes this is done with the recognition that the premodern spiritual holism from which the folk practices arose is now supported by the postmodern discoveries in physics and other sciences regarding the unbroken field of inherently relational existence of which human life is a part. The practices of "folk Catholicism" reach across the seeming divisions that separate material reality on Earth from the larger cosmological context, the sacred whole.

A related example of broaching those seeming divisions is the healing responses experienced by those in physical as well as psychological distress. The miraculous cures following spiritual appeals to Mary are, in fact, becoming less unfathomable as modern medicine is finally realizing that the body is far more a dynamic energy system than a mechanistic biomachine. The emergent field of energy medicine is based not on a simplistic claim of "mind over matter" but on the mountain of evidence from psychoneuroimmunology and other medical fields that the bodymind is an integral unit, not a graft of mind onto body. Mind itself is seen to be located throughout the body, with remarkable capabilities even at the cellular level to perceive problems and act to correct them. The evidence is irrefutable and finally widely accepted that psychological states generally influence health and healing. The healing power of prayer, for instance, has been found to elicit significant results. Studies of several thousand subjects at Johns Hopkins University, Duke University, and other research centers have determined in recent years that prayer often reduces high blood pressure, lowers the relative risk of dying, and strengthens the immune system.[12] Surely it is time to set aside the label "irrational" for the ill and infirm who "petition" or otherwise commune with spiritual figures of profound harmony and healing grace.

The number of miraculous cures attributed to Mary's grace and intercession is impossible to determine since most are not reported beyond family, friends, one's prayer circle, and perhaps the parish priest. The Marian shrine that keeps the most extensive medical records is Lourdes, in France, where 2,000 miraculous healings have been documented since 1848. Sixty-six of those reported healings have been accepted by Church authorities through a review process involving several levels of scrutiny of the medical evidence presented. While every Marian shrine is associated with healings, numerous miraculous, or otherwise inexplicable, cures have occurred without visits to a shrine. Communion with the spiritual presence of Mary was reportedly the key.[13]

In the scriptural sense, the Greek word for "advocate" (*parakletos*) literally means "called to help." That call from the heart reverberates in one of the most moving of the prayers to Mary the Advocate, the "Salve Regina" ("Hail, Holy Queen"), which all Catholics — prior to Vatican II — used to recite together as they rose to their feet near the close of every mass around the world. Although deleted from the mass by the modernizing Council Fathers, it survives as the final prayer in the recitation of the rosary. I had not heard "Hail, Holy Queen" aloud for a great many years until one day in September 1997 when I was listening to the National Public Radio program *Talk of the Nation* in my car. The person being interviewed was Sally Cunneen, author of the excellent historical study *In Search of Mary*. She did an edifying job of disabusing two male theologians, also featured on the program, of antifeminist projections about Mary the Nazarene woman and then began to take calls from listeners.

A middle-aged man telephoned to express the importance of Marian spirituality in his life. As soon as he mentioned "Hail, Holy Queen," Cunneen said, "Ah, yes," and began to recite it. The man on the phone joined in, I joined in, and I suddenly had the feeling that hundreds of thousands of listeners across the country joined in as well, our hearts swelling with the memory of Mary's presence in our communal life before Vatican II. Later I learned that a friend of mine, driving in his car with his wife at that time and listening to the same radio program, had had to pull off the highway, so moved was he to hear the long-lost affirmation:

Hail, Holy Queen!
Mother of Mercy, our life, our sweetness, and our hope!
To Thee do we cry, poor banished children of Eve;
To Thee do we send up our sighs, mourning and weeping
    in this valley of tears.
Turn then, most gracious Advocate, thine eyes of mercy toward us;
And after this our exile, show unto us the blessed fruit of thy
    womb, Jesus.
O clement, O loving, O sweet virgin Mary!

Many Catholics who have come of age after the mid-1960s have no idea that of all the gods, goddesses, and semi-divine figures ever embraced by the Western spiritual imagination there once was one we called not Zeus the Thunderbolt God; or God Almighty, Our Mighty Fortress; or even Athena, Gaia, or Bau but this: *our life, our sweetness, and our hope*. There she stood, arms outstretched to all, on our dressers, in our churches, and wherever this valley of tears became too much to bear. *Because* she is so cosmological — and not *Mary, Just a Housewife* — prayers and silent conversations with her have the effect of bringing one into harmony with the larger context, the sacred whole, the Great Holy.

Mary the Advocate, or Intercessor, is unique among cosmological religious figures in that she has experienced a full range of human suffering. We can barely imagine the horror of persecution and crucifixion that Jesus endured, but Mary's ordeals are more familiar. She was pregnant and unwed in a village culture. Her new husband at first considered leaving her when he learned she was pregnant. The physical conditions of her pregnancy were far from ideal, as she had to travel a long distance by uncomfortable conveyance very late in the third trimester. Turned away by those who might have helped her, she had to give birth in a stable dug in a shallow cave where domestic animals were kept and then lay her newborn in the feeding trough, or manger. She soon had to flee into exile with her husband and infant, taking no possessions since they had to leave from Bethlehem rather than their home in Galilee. She had to live for several years in foreign exile, presumably poor, until King Herod died and it was safe to return. She had to endure a curt public rebuke from her preteen son when she and Joseph went back for him in the temple. She no doubt worried a great deal during the "lost years" when Jesus' whereabouts were unknown (in the gospels). Once the public record picks up again, when he was thirty, Mary is known to have dedicated herself to her son's unusual work. When she asked him to help the hosts of the wedding at Cana, he again was brusque in his response to her . . . though he did acquiesce and began his ministry then, at her prompting. Finally, she had to endure the betrayal, persecution, and death by public torture of her beloved son. To bury one's child is in itself excruciating, but to see the divine project to which she had assented at age thirteen be met with such extensive and murderous cruelty must have been the most intense of torments. Yet she kept her vigil at the foot of the cross — the *Mater Dolorosa,* the Sorrowful Mother — and then proceeded with quiet dignity throughout the burial and the bringing of the spices to anoint the body.

Just before he died, Jesus said to John, as a representative of all the apostles, that Mary would henceforth be their mother and that they were to regard her as such: "Behold thy Mother." As the mother of

Christians, and later the mother of the Christian Church, Mary was ever forbearing and compassionate, a fount of both divine grace and intercessory powers. In the course of 2,000 years, she has no doubt been called upon and consulted in every possible trying situation, from the intimate to the societal. She is the Advocate of the Poor, in particular, not only because she supported Jesus in his work but also because she expressed strong feelings against the structural violence of oppressive conditions when she declared in the exultant Magnificat that God scatters those who exhibit overweening pride, topples rulers from their thrones, fills the hungry with good things, and sends away the rich empty-handed.

Mary has often been invoked in times of struggle against great odds. In fact, her intercession, obtained through countless rosaries, was credited with Christendom's victory over the Ottoman Empire in the naval battle of Lepanto in 1571, after which Pope Pius V instituted the feast day of Our Lady of Victory. Still, the modern world was shocked in 1986 to see news photographs of throngs of Filipinos "armed" only with statues of the Blessed Virgin Mary as they courageously faced down Marcos's tanks and armed troops during the nonviolent revolution in the Philippines.

At times Mary has been carried into battle by both sides, as in the Mexican revolution. The royalist forces fought under the standard of La Virgen de los Remedios, as had Cortes and his invading conquistadors hundreds of years earlier, while the forces for independence marched under the banner of La Virgen de Guadalupe. Soldiers on both sides wore their particular Marian image sewn on their upper sleeves. It is quite a stretch, though, to imagine that the Blessed Mother endorses battlefield carnage or any other violence as a wise counterforce against oppression.

Mary's Magnificat and the teachings of Christ about one's spiritual responsibility to improve the lot of the oppressed and disadvantaged have come to be known as the "social gospel." Its simple admonition is encapsulated in the gospel of Matthew, chapter 25: The way we treat the least among us is the way we are treating the myriad expressions of the Divine. The social gospel, then, inextricably blends spiritual practice, charitable works, and social justice. The inner work without the outer work is merely a narcissistic extraction from the gospels, while economic activism alone cannot create the quality of social structures that nourish both the inner and outer realms of life and bring them into harmony.

The social gospel lives today not only in the teachings of Christ and in Mary's Magnificat but in the myriad projects and campaigns for ecosocial justice and for peace. One of the Blessed Mother's contemporary titles in Brazil, for instance, is Mother of the Excluded. In El Salvador during the reign of the right-wing paramilitary death squads in the 1980s, Mary was called upon as Mother of the Disappeared.

Every day millions of prayers are offered, including all the rosaries communicated to Mary, Queen of Peace. Like so much else in Marian spirituality, the rosary was one of the targets of the post-Vatican II "deemphasizing," considered a medieval device designed for illiterate folk and certainly not in keeping with the Thoroughly Modern Mary of the Church's new dogmatic constitution. During the early 1970s, ecumenical enthusiasts within the Vatican urged Pope Paul VI to promote two new forms of the rosary. One version lopped off the second half of the classic "Hail Mary" prayer on the grounds that it has a nonbiblical source. The other version reduced the number of recitations of the "Hail Mary" prayer to one-fifteenth of their traditional number, while adding hymns, Bible readings, and a sermon. Fortunately, the pope ruled in 1974 that these new versions should be called something other than the rosary, perhaps "Marian devotion" or "Marian hour." Before he did so, however, these and similar new versions were endorsed in a letter on Marian devotion issued by the bishops of the United States in 1973, Behold Your Mother. With all due respect to the "separated brethren" — because I do not believe that most grassroots Protestants harbor a desire to see other people's beloved spiritual practices dismantled — I am pleased to report that these "progressive" efforts to replace the rosary were thoroughly ignored by the Catholic laity.

The revival of the rosary is one of the triumphs of the current Marian renewal, for its disappearance would be an inestimable loss for Western spirituality. It is a brilliantly multivalent contemplative device. At the most obvious level, the rosary leads one through the major events of the Incarnation, clustered in three groups: the Joyful Mysteries (the Annunciation, the Visitation, the Nativity, the Presentation, and the Finding of Jesus in the Temple); the Sorrowful Mysteries (the Agony in the Garden, the Scourging at the Pillar, the Crowning with Thorns, the Carrying of the Cross, and the Crucifixion); and the Glorious Mysteries (the Resurrection, the Ascension, the Descent of the Holy Spirit, the Assumption of Mary, and the Coronation of Mary). Each mystery, with the exception of the last two, is associated with a passage from the gospels. This succinct compendium is not a complete list of the events in Jesus' ministry but, rather, the main events in his formative years with Mary, his Passion (before and during the Crucifixion), and the divine aftermath of his sacrifice on the cross. The fifteen mysteries were standardized by Pope Pius V in 1569.

On October 16, 2002, Pope John Paul II surprised nearly everyone by expanding the rosary — the first such change in more than 400 years. He added five new "Mysteries of Light," which focus on events in the public life of "the Light of the world," as Christ is called in John 8:12. The additional events — called the Luminous Mysteries, or the Fruitful Mysteries — are the Baptism of Jesus in the Jordan River, his Self-Revelation at the Wedding at Cana, his Proclaiming that the Kingdom of Heaven Is at Hand (and inviting conversion), his Transfiguration while Praying (witnessed by on the mountain by Peter, John, and James), and the Institution of the Eucharist at the Last Supper. Pope John Paul II declared the new Mysteries of Light in an apostolic letter titled *Rosarium Virginis Mariae (The Rosary of the Virgin Mary)*, which he released on the twenty-fourth anniversary of his election to the papacy. It is likely that the pope was motivated by a desire to remind the post-Vatican II Church that Mary is central to remembering and contemplating the story of Christ. In response to the pope's apostolic letter, a Lutheran theologian in Germany wrote that he was pleased and surprised by the "evangelical dimension": "In this letter, the pope emphasizes that the rosary, more than a prayer of words, is a contemplation of the mystery. Certainly today's sensibility and quest is primarily to rediscover a place where the heart rests, where the soul contemplates the mysteries of God and also the ways in which this is possible. We, in our traditions, must rediscover the equivalent ways."[14]

Pope John Paul II simultaneously declared a Year of the Rosary to commence (which was largely ignored by most "progressive" parish priests in the most modern societies). Urging Catholics not to be influenced by theologians who claim that the rosary is out-dated, a superstition, and anti-ecumenical, the pope asserted that the rosary is "a powerful prayer for peace."[15] In his last instruction for the Year of the Rosary, "Mary and the Mission of the Church in the Year of the Rosary," written for World Mission Sunday, October 19, 2003, the pope explained that the Year is intended to encourage the Church to be "more contemplative": Mary, "the contemplative memory of the Church" helps us to acquire that "serene boldness" that enables believers to pass on to others their experience of Jesus. At the "school of Mary," we learn to recognize, in the apparent silence of God, the Word. The Year of the Rosary was timed to occur on the 120th anniversary of the first of Pope Leo XIII's twelve encyclicals on the rosary (1883), the 40th anniversary of the opening of Vatican II, and, at its conclusion, with the twenty-fifth anniversary of Pope John Paul II's pontificate.

A person praying the rosary contemplates several of the events through the experience or the memory of Mary, almost *as Mary,* or at least with deep compassion. Even the Joyful Mysteries contain elements of hardship, such as Mary's uncomfortable journey late in her pregnancy and her giving birth in a stable. The "decade" of ten beads representing the Nativity connotes far more than hardship, though, being the most powerfully multivalent segment in the rosary, along with the later decade representing the Resurrection. The mystery of the Nativity, the emergence of the Savior formed from the body and blood of Mary and delivered into this world through her courage and care, always explodes orderly thought when I reach it. My mind floods first with all I know experientially about the extraordinary female power-mystery of giving birth and then with the miraculous cosmological character of this particular birth. Mary's womb is at once the universe and her body.

Almost all the Joyful Mysteries foreshadow the suffering Mary will experience in later years. Just before the Presentation of the infant Jesus in the temple, for instance, Simeon prophesizes that Mary's soul will be pierced by a sword of great sorrow. In short, a person praying the rosary with a request for compassionate intercession in, say, the illness of a loved one is led to generate compassion *with* and *for* the spiritual figure — and for her Son — to whom one is appealing. Surely this situation is singular in the annals of comparative religion: The Queen of Heaven, or Maternal Matrix, who has experienced extreme levels of human suffering, evokes empathy and compassion as she bestows it. Without any preaching, then, one experiences the link between receiving compassion and the practice of generating it for others.

Each mystery in the rosary yields a "fruit" for contemplation, such as humility, patience, or joy. (Some guides suggest contemplating "obedience" as one reflects on the Annunciation; cosmologically, I suggest that Mary's "obedience" in deciding to participate in the Incarnation, as well as her subsequent growth into cosmological proportions to the Mother of God-the-Son, can be viewed as acts of opening her own existence to the *logos,* or divine order of the cosmos.) Among the more beautiful guides for a contemplative practice of the rosary is a booklet by Domenico Marcucci, *Through the Rosary with Fra Angelico,*[16] which matches fifteenth-century paintings by Fra Angelico with adaptations of the prayer intentions proposed in the late seventeenth century by the Marian theologian St. Louis-Marie Grignion de Montfort. These "fruits for contemplation" are designed to cultivate the spiritual art of compassion. For example, the prayer intention when one contemplates the birth in the stable is "For all those who are in need"; for the finding of Jesus in the temple, it is "For understanding between parents and their children"; for the agony in the garden, it is "For those who are unable to comprehend or accept their suffering"; for the scourging at the pillar, it is "For greater respect for human life"; and for the moment when Jesus, dying on the cross, forgives his murderers, it is "For those who find themselves unable to forgive."

In addition, contemplating the story of Mary and Jesus leads one through a primary cycle of creativity, courage, and new possibilities (the Joyful Mysteries); followed by dedication, emergence, and fruition (the Luminous Mysteries); followed by tribulation, waning, and loss (the Sorrowful Mysteries); followed by regeneration, hope, and potent renewal (the Glorious Mysteries). No matter where a person may be mentally fixated in the cycle because of a particular situation in his or her personal life, the exercise of moving through the progression aids one in achieving psychological and spiritual balance. Perhaps this is so because the Joyful Mysteries are paradoxically seeded with hardship or foreboding such that we celebrate them yet feel ourselves pulled into the process of transformation that follows in the Luminous Mysteries and beyond. The Sorrowful Mysteries are so poignantly saturated with intense suffering, perseverance, and moral courage that the rosary seems to absorb and dilute any woes brought to it. The intensity of suffering then energizes the renewal that follows in the Glorious Mysteries, the abode of grace and abundance. Suffering is experienced through Mary's rosary as a transformative power.

The entire cycle delivers one to a level deeper than the intellectual or the emotional: to the matrix of the *cosmologic,* where everything is held and nothing is lost. From that deep center arise compassion, forgiveness of others, and the acceptance of one's own foibles. In the cosmologic, nothing makes sense except that which is infused with the generous and expansive peace that permeates that level of our being. Praying for peace, then, is less a matter of requisitioning outside intervention than articulating the hope that antagonistic parties, at the level of persons or nations, might experience in their heart-minds the deep, unitive dimension of being.

I discovered that deep stratum when I took up the rosary in mid-life. I had abandoned it after childhood, enticed in college by more intellectual approaches to religious matters. Even though I felt myself being drawn back to Marian spirituality in the 1990s, I was doubtful that a circle of beads could amount to much. Yet, encouraged by a friend whose spiritual trajectory has been similar to mine, I gave it a try, a serious one involving praying the rosary every evening for ten weeks. As it happened, the period during which she urged me to rediscover the rosary was one in which I was trying to resolve and free myself from the mental grip of an unpleasant experience some time earlier. Perhaps because I have practiced mindfulness meditation over the years, I was able to focus my concentration without much difficulty on the multi-layered contemplation involved with the rosary.

At some point I realized in a whole-body, more-than-intellectual way that the suffering of Mary and Jesus is the suffering of the world, that every individual's suffering, including my own, is *the* suffering of the world, not something apart or unconnected. Once this connection was felt — and experienced as profoundly organic — the rosary delivered me to the deep stratum. The sense of oneness there was so powerful that, to my amazement, thoughts that began to take shape, up on the surface level, about who did what to whom were not even interesting enough to finish. Any thoughts that started out in that direction, as they had hundreds of times in my mind for far too long, made no sense in that deep place. They literally felt so illogical as to lack all substance and hold no interest whatsoever. Instead, what did make sense and ruled all thought on that deep level — what I call the "cosmologic" — was the intense awareness that profound connection and love are the truth of existence, enormously more potent and vast than any surface perturbations arising in our lives, no matter how gripping. While on that deep level, every subject that arose in my mind was infused with the powerful truth of love and its joy. No exception was possible, I discovered, as I thought about various prickly persons or situations. Wonder, awe, and gratitude then filled all the space in my mind. The peace I arrived at was dynamic and vital.

Equally surprising was the fact that, later on, I could call up the potent memory of what it felt like to be on that deep level whenever cosmological grounding was needed in the face of difficult matters. The deep truth is always right there, just a thought away — although far more easily accessible if one maintains a daily practice of saying the rosary. This ready recall is, in my experience, a bodily as well as mental process. Perhaps all joy, wisdom, and spiritual experience are a matter of connecting with this deep substratum. There are many paths to it, many names for it, and many ways to nurture the connection.

I do believe, however, that our poor discursive minds are inadequate to effect a profound change of heart, or *metanoia*, in the face of seemingly intractable conflicts that arise in this life. Our surface mind simply digs us deeper and deeper into what seems to us "the natural and obvious response" to whatever has happened. Certainly various particulars causing strife can be negotiated, but the only true freedom from a consuming conflict lies in opening oneself to the larger context and preparing the ground for the possibility of a psychological and spiritual shift. The nature of that shift and the person or persons in whom it might take place cannot be dictated; one can only cultivate in one's situation the preconditions. Doggedly willing a particular change (in oneself or another) or an escape from mental suffering seems to be less effective than keeping one's heart supple, green and juicy (as St. Hildegard of Bingen put it), and emanating loving kindness for all beings. Cosmological grace is apparently attracted to such a field, in which miracles large and small are then sown.

It is easy to understand why the rosary's deliverance of one's heart-mind to the divine "cosmologic" has long been recognized as a spiritual "path of the heart." As such, the rosary is associated not only with personal healing but with efforts for world peace, thanksgiving, or simply felt communion with the Divine. As a weekly cycle of daily prayer, the Joyful Mysteries are traditionally said on Monday and Thursday, the Sorrowful Mysteries on Tuesday and Friday, and the Glorious Mysteries on Wednesday and Saturday (Mary's day). Emphases are added according to the annual cycle of the liturgical calendar, such as praying the Joyful Mysteries every Sunday during Advent and the Sorrowful Mysteries every Sunday during Lent. To accommodate the new Luminous Mysteries, the Joyful Mysteries are now prayed on Monday and Saturday, and optionally on Sundays during Advent and the Christmas Season; the Luminous Mysteries are prayed on Thursday; the Sorrowful Mysteries are prayed on Tuesday and Friday, and optionally on Sundays during Lent; and the Glorious Mysteries are prayed on Wednesday and Sunday.

The subtle layering within the practice of the rosary is contained in a vessel of sounds, repeated in a gentle rhythm to form words that vibrate with connotations of communion: full, grace, with, blessed, womb, holy, Mother of God. The "Hail Mary" prayer, recited thoughtfully ten times for every one "Our Father" prayer, is the mystical rose of the rosary. It begins with Mary's cousin's salutation to her (Luke 1:28) and ends with the hope that "sinners" (literally, in Hebrew and Greek, those who have "missed the mark") will be brought back into balance, into a state of divine grace:

Hail, Mary, full of grace, the lord is with thee.
Blessed are thou among women and blessed is the fruit of thy
    womb, Jesus.

Holy Mary, Mother of God, pray for us sinners
now and at the hour of our death. Amen

Each "Hail Mary," observed the head of the Dominican order in an
address delivered during a rosary retreat at Lourdes in 1989, "suggests
the individual journey that each of us must take, from birth to death. It
is marked by the biological rhythm of every life."[17]

The rosary holds an unbounded space for not only the personal but
also the collective, for the welfare of all beings. The exhortation to pray
the rosary for peace is the common ground linking nearly all visitations
of Mary during the modern era, many of which have been reported
during the current Marian renewal. Another common feature of visitations is the description of the Virgin as radiantly luminous "pure love."
It is difficult, if not impossible, however, for anyone to know and
understand exactly what takes place in these sightings of and conversations with the Blessed Virgin because so many layers of interpretation and presentation grow up around the initial account, which itself
attempts the impossible task of translating a revelatory experience into
words. Sometimes the layers constructed around the initial experiences result in political directives and fire-and-brimstone exhortations
that seem far removed from the quiet dignity of both the biblical Mary
and the compassionate Advocate.[18]

It is possible, though, to consider these events in terms of three
areas: the initial experience reported by one or more people of seeing
and hearing Mary; the accounts and interpretations, plus the debates
over official recognition; and the spiritual outcome of the visitation,
including pilgrims' experiences in the ambiance of the location where
the visitation took place and a widespread spiritual renewal extending
far beyond the site.

The Virgin Mary is reported to have appeared 21,000 times in the
past thousand years. In nearly all cases the Church refrains from either
endorsement or condemnation. It largely ignores the sightings, though
it does not forbid people to visit the sites and pray there. The task of
determining authenticity falls to the local bishop. Only a tiny fraction
of reported visitations win official acceptance, after a lengthy process
during which an appointed commission studies all the documentation,

including not only the testimonies of the people who received the visitation but also medical records related to any miraculous healings and evidence of other extraordinary events.

During the past twenty years, many hundreds of sightings and even sequential visitations have been reported, although none has been officially recognized by the Church. In response to the unexpected boom in reported visitations, officials within the Vatican's Sacred Congregation for the Doctrine of the Faith announced in January 2003 that they are preparing new guidelines that will bring greater doctrinal clarity to the process of determining whether such experiences should be judged authentic. With or without official recognition, however, these contemporary visitations simultaneously reflect and engender the rising surge of Marian spirituality.[19] It should also be noted that apparitions of either Mary or Jesus — who is called Isa bin Maryam (Son of Mary) in the Quran — have reportedly occurred seventy times in Islamic countries since 1985.[20]

The major visitation in recent times — that is, the one that has attracted millions of pilgrims (including my mother and sister in 1991) and inspired prayer groups around the world — began in 1981 in Medjugorje, a rural town in the Croatian area of the Republic of Bosnia-Herzegovina, formerly part of Yugoslavia. Although the authenticity of this visitation is denied by many Church officials (but not by the local Franciscan priests), the event itself has several elements in common with the other major visitations in the modern era. First, Mary appeared to working-class country people. (Catherine Labouré might seem to be an exception as a young postulant in a convent in Paris in 1830, but she was the barely literate daughter of a French peasant.) Second, as in the other modern visitations, Mary appeared to a girl or to a small group that was predominantly female (except at La Salette, France, in 1848, when the pair who saw her was a girl and a boy). Finally, the message relayed from Mary (via 2,000 visitations reported over several years by the six young people who saw her at Medjugorje) was "a call to holiness," a commitment to prayer, fasting, and the self-examination of conscience (formerly called confession, now reconciliation). As contemporary pilgrims to the Bosnia-Herzegovinian site, not all of whom are Catholic, returned home and often related a sense of spiritual renewal to their friends, the Marian "spirit of Medjugorje" spread throughout the world and continues to transform lives.

It is usually the case that the rippling effects following reported visitations soon acquire a vitality of their own, quite apart from the wrangling of the adults who soon become involved and even apart from the spiritual experiences of the young seers themselves. No doubt the sites of the visitations become charged by the concentration of so much prayer offered continually by a steady stream of visitors. The profound transformations, both physical and spiritual, often experienced by pilgrims at the sites are probably brought about by a combination of personal faith, the spiritual nature of the site (which many people perceive as a subtle vibration), the collective ambiance during and after prayer, and the inspiration of Mary herself. A certain energy seems to manifest at sites of the visitations.

The political spin that was attached to some of the early twentieth-century Marian visitations led to several right-wing organizations' claiming the Blessed Virgin Mary as their champion. Organizations such as the Blue Army of Mary and the Legion of Mary, both dating from the 1920s, employ military metaphors connoting aggressive concepts that seem quite far removed from the spirit of the gospel of love. Even the secretive and reactionary organization Opus Dei (The Work of God), founded in 1928 in Spain and now an international network favored by the current pope, emphasizes devotion to Mary as part of its program. Clearly, many groups who favor an intensely patriarchal social system and laissez-faire capitalism (which amounts to "corporate capitalism") view Mary as emblematic of that type of social order. Oddly, they ignore not only the social gospel and the central role of women in the initial ministry and Passion of Christ but also Catholic social teaching. For over a century, the Roman Catholic Church has released papal encyclicals and other high-level documents on a just social order, the conditions of labor, the role of Christianity in social progress, economic development, and the destructive effects of both communism and unchecked capitalism.[21]

Throughout the "Third World" (actually the More-Than-Three-Quarters World), Mary has sustained people in their struggles for social justice. In the Philippines a large statue of Mary, Queen of Peace was installed in a shrine in Quezon City, just northeast of Manila, to commemorate her inspiration in the massive and courageous vigils during the "people power" uprisings against President Marcos in 1986. At that Marian shrine, rather than in a government building, President Gloria Macapagal Arroyo took her oath of office on January 20, 2001, following the widely demanded resignation of President Estrada.

The cries for social justice are increasingly informed, moreover, by an *eco*social political analysis and vision. This broader perspective is replacing the blind insistence found in both humanist Christianity and the ideology of modernity that we live on top of nature and need focus our attention solely on the human project. On the island of Mindanao in the Philippines, the ecosocial orientation has produced an inspiring model of spiritually based activism. A traditional form of prayer to Mary has been expanded to address the destruction of the Creation by "earth-killing enterprises" encouraged by the government in the name of progress. The Earth Rosary, devised by a Columban missionary, Fr. Vincent Busch, interweaves contemplation of the Joyful, Sorrowful, and Glorious Mysteries of Jesus and Mary with the life, death, and restoration of Mindanao's rainforests and mangrove swamps. Strengthened by the rosary's transformative image of resurrection, Catholic communities in the northwest end of the island engage in ecological activism as an extension of their prayer lives. The text for Mary's Assumption, for instance, reminds the faithful that "we can be compassionate because we live on a generous planet. We can feed the hungry because the earth's food cycle faithfully renews the bounty of the land and the seas. . . . Parents, catechists and children care for the earth the way Mary cared for Jesus."[22] Fr. Busch's ecosocial ministry, spanning twenty-five years in the region, is inspired in large part by the ecological theology of Fr. Thomas Berry in the United States.

Along with the slow spread of ecological awareness in recent decades has come the rise of the justice movement for women. As I have noted, "progressive"-feminist Catholic theologians today, who insist quite admirably that the Church should democratize in various ways, often miss the full meaning of Mary in the spiritual lives of grassroots women. Traditionally, most Catholic women have always had a profound understanding of Mary's spiritual presence, especially the combination of her humble empathy, her dignity, and her power. If they encounter a priest who preached the patriarchal version of Mary, railing on about what the Mother of God should mean to women as a model of obedience and what the Blessed Virgin expects of women in the way of submissive behavior, most Catholic women simply put on their best poker faces — I can see endless generations of them sitting in the pews — and think to themselves, "That poor man knows absolutely nothing about the relationship between Mary and women. Yet he stands up there imagining he does, getting red in the face, too. What a curious spectacle."

Those are the kind of women I come from. They never had to say much about their connection with Mary; it was as much a part of them as breathing — and just as nonnegotiable. My maternal grandmother, for instance, made a pilgrimage every year from Cleveland to the national shrine of Our Lady of Consolation in Carey, Ohio, along with a busload of her friends. They were women of substantial form, decked out in their flowered dresses, hats, and white gloves. They were immovable in their love for Mary — and they never missed a trip to her special place no matter what Vatican II said.

Among the Baby Boomer generation, many Catholic women who may or may not have been subjected to patriarchal versions of Mary in their childhood reached their breaking point in the 1970s and early 1980s when they learned about the recurrent suppression of divine and semi-divine female figures in the history of Near Eastern and Western cultures. Often the attributes of these female religious figures survived in greatly reduced form as part of the lore surrounding Mary.[23]

In the white heat of feminism in the 1970s, the Virgin Mary seemed to many of us to be too far gone, too tragically confined by the contours of patriarchal religion. I remember a conversation I had with my mother back then, a time when I was deeply involved in the research that became my first book, *Lost Goddesses of Early Greece*. It went something like this: "Women's status got *worse* — they *lost* rights — when Christianity moved into the Celtic cultures in the Rhineland, northern France, Ireland, and other places in Europe. And Mary! They made her the Mother of God, but she used to *be* God. It was an outrageous demotion. The Church couldn't have gotten even a toehold in Europe or the New World without a Great Goddess on their banners. Mary the Humble Servant of God! *Unbelievable.* Our Lady of Consolation! That's rich. I mean, jeez, exactly what is it we need to be consoled about if not patriarchal religion and society! And I *hate* the way they make the heavy drapery in her statues press her breasts as flat as a boy's! Sometimes it's all I can do not to take a chisel to that marble drapery so her maternal breasts could pop up. The whole thing just drives me crazy!" We were in my mother's kitchen at the time. When I finished my rant, she simply gave me a look that had been perfected by my grandmother in such situations: This girl's had way too much education to understand what's going on here.

A couple of years later, when I was again visiting our family home, after my father's fatal heart attack, I was lying across my parents' bed talking on the phone when my eyes alighted on the small mantle on the facing wall where three statues of the Virgin Mary, some candles, and some silk flowers stood in a row. At that instant I suddenly grasped the entire complex of meaning that had been pushed from my mind: The devotion surrounding Mary is a religion within a religion, a powerful spirituality for women and children and all men who honor the Maternal Matrix. It is thoroughly embedded in the Jesus religion and does not stand apart, yet it also has its own integrity. As obvious as that now seems, I had somehow lost sight of it.

Like other prodigal daughters of Mary, I was able to find my way back to the fullness of her spiritual presence because I had known her so well in my youth. She had been presented to me by my mother and grandmother as Our Blessed Mother who dwells everywhere and is always with us in our hearts.

Mary the Intercessor is called upon to facilitate the healing of both the causes and the effects of cruelty and oppression, but she is also called upon to ease the life passages of all who seek her. In fact, part of the Blessed Mother's message to Catherine Labouré, reported during the visitations in 1830, was that the graces she mediates can flow only to those who ask for them. *Only connect.*

Because of Mary's own experiences, she is never far from life's tribulations and its end. She is called upon to accompany one through a peaceful death, as were so many of her divine female forbears. I do not doubt that communing with male spiritual figures as death approaches brings guidance and relief, but there is an organic logic behind the turning, in so many cultures past and present, to a female form of the Divine or semi-divine: The body of the earth and the body of the mother give us form and sustenance and, finally, receive us back into the vast cosmic field pulsing with the rhythms of arising and passing away, arising and passing away.

Our Lady of Perpetual Help

Queen of Martyrs

Queen of Apostles

Comforter of the Afflicted

Protector of the Oppressed

Mother of the Excluded

Mother of the Disappeared

Mirror of Justice

Chapter Five

Why the Church Deposed the Queen of Heaven

Containing the influence of Mary has been a recurring concern for the Church since the fourth century. As swells of Marian devotion among the laity arose repeatedly over the centuries, causing the Church to enlarge its official recognition of Mary's spiritual presence and significance and to adopt a rich array of devotional practices, certain bishops and theologians in every era have eyed the Virgin warily. Such a huge female presence included with Christ in the central focus of the Catholic faith! Is this really necessary?

The excessive pruning Vatican II performed on Marian spirituality was not an isolated act; it was embedded in a historical stream of sporadic efforts to limit the way in which the Blessed Virgin is perceived. Within that 1,600-year arc, however, the immediate context of Vatican II was the post–World War II era, in which various ideologies of modernity were intensified with a macho show of intellectual and political force. These academic and cultural currents influenced, in particular, many of the young, university-educated European priests in the 1950s who subsequently played the role at Vatican II of assertive "modernizers" of doctrine and devotions. The public rationale the Church gave — and continues to give — for the radical "modernizing" of the Blessed Mother was the sudden need for rapprochement with the other two branches of Christianity, the Protestants and the Orthodox.

In September 2000, however, after nearly forty years of denying the full spiritual presence of Mary, largely phasing out her rosaries and novenas, deleting her hymns and prayers, and getting rid of most of her images or moving them to more discreet locations so that "the separated brethren" would not be visually offended, the Vatican's office of the Sacred Congregation for the Doctrine of the Faith sent the ecumenical movement reeling when it released a thirty-six-page document titled *Dominus Iesus*. The statement addressed the "errors and ambiguities" of certain Catholic theologians who seem to regard non-Catholic religions as being on an equal level with Catholicism. In contrast to such relativism, it asserted, the Roman Catholic Church is the sole path to salvation for all humanity.[1] Imagine the surprise of the theologians who had been participating in ecumenical dialogues with the Church for decades, only to learn that Rome's goal all along was to simply incorporate them! Imagine, as well, the surprise of participants in interfaith dialogues with the Church who had assumed that all religions were equally respected. (Two years later, however, prominent Catholic scholars who are part of the ecumenical Christian Scholars Group on Christian-Jewish Relations issued a statement, with their colleagues, repudiating "supersessionism" and declaring, instead, that "God's covenant with the Jewish people endures forever." That is, it was not replaced, or superceded, by God's covenant with the followers of Christ.[2])

A few months after *Dominus Iesus* was released by Cardinal Ratzinger's office in the Vatican, Avery Dulles, a Jesuit who had recently been appointed by the pope to the College of Cardinals, responded to a reporter's question about the shockwaves caused by that declaration with this tidy clarification: "It is a defect of other forms of Christianity if they do not acknowledge the authority of the bishop of Rome."[3] On February 22, 2001, the pope issued a letter to the German cardinals reminding them that, as *Dominus Iesus* had specified, the primacy of the Catholic Church must be the firm basis for ecumenical work.[4] Surely this position is more offensive to the "separated brethren" than are statues of the Virgin Mary. A few months later, the Orthodox churches were openly hostile to the pope during his visits to Greece and later to Ukraine. Whatever ecumenical progress had been made was severely undercut when the Protestants and the Orthodox were summarily informed that the Vatican views ecumenism as an annexing of their churches.

With regard to the fate of Mary, the declaration *Dominus Iesus* raises a central question: If her full spiritual presence had to be sacrificed for the potential of an ecumenical reunion of the three branches of Christianity (an egalitarian vision that, it turns out, is not of any real interest to the Roman Catholic hierarchy), one must ask whether the rallying cry of *Ecumenism!* all these years has been a front, an excuse for "modernizing" Mary and various "old-fashioned" devotional practices nearly out of existence.

Over and over again, the accounts of ecumenical dialogues follow a familiar pattern. When issues are put on the table that carry differences so strong as to preclude consensus, the matter is resolved by agreeing that the particular difference will be left alone and accepted by all parties involved as "a matter of faith." In this way, the 480-year-old areas of incompatibility are addressed — until the Virgin Mary is brought up for discussion. At that point, teeth grind, eyes narrow, and posture straightens rigidly: time for a showdown amid the détente. The Protestant theologians make clear that it would be thoroughly impossible to expect them to make any movement whatsoever toward the Catholic sense of Mary — even the post–Vatican II minimalist version (in which the Nazarene housewife is still Assumed into heaven and glorified as a queen!). In dialogue after dialogue, the Catholic and Protestant conceptions of the Virgin and their respective relationships with her are usually found to be highly charged issues that cannot seem to be acknowledged, left alone, and respected as differing "matters of faith."

Throughout this book, I consider several factors contributing to such a line-in-the-sand stance regarding Mary. Several modern Catholic theologians, by the way, position themselves almost entirely on the Protestant side of that "line," being more than willing to jettison any remaining vestige of Marian spiritual tradition in the Church, ostensibly for the sake of ecumenism. Such ready appeasement regarding Mary was a concern in Pope John Paul II's letter to the German cardinals, mentioned above, in which he urged them to proclaim the Catholic faith "in all its fullness and all its beauty."[5]

I deeply appreciate the ecumenical and interfaith impulse toward rapprochement — which has evoked, at long last, the pope's apologies to the native peoples of the New World for centuries of barbaric treatment; to the Jews for the Vatican's shameful passivity during the Holocaust, and for teaching Catholic children for centuries to regard Jews as "Christ killers"; and to the Orthodox Church in Greece for harmful actions in the past. Yet the meaning of "ecumenism" is to go to the deepest roots of one's spiritual tradition and then celebrate the common ground with other traditions. The operative common ground with Protestants and the Orthodox that guided the ecumenical decisions of Vatican II was not the deepest Christian roots but, rather, the dominating context in which all religions and other institutions find themselves today: modernity. In a "rationalized," text-based, "tough-minded" version of religion for the modern age, what could be more incongruous than a place of honor for the Maternal Matrix, a female spiritual figure writ large who links human and divine, Earth and heavenly cosmos?

Rather than positioning Mary as the deal-breaker of the ecumenical project, it would be far wiser to reframe the issue with a both/and response: Ecumenical gatherings of the three branches of Christianity in various locations around the world could honor Mary's biblical presence — while still allowing the Catholics and the Orthodox on their own respective turf to honor Mary's mystical, cosmological dimensions as well. After all, many Protestant churches in Europe and the United States have introduced new honor and even formal devotions to their traditional (strictly biblical) version of Mary since Vatican II (while *not* expanding their Mariology). In Sweden, for instance, medieval hymns to Mary, unsung since the Reformation, have been restored in recent years to the hymnals. This increased honoring of the strictly proscribed biblical sense of Mary — which has always been present, if sometimes buried, in the spiritual orientation of several Protestant denominations — could become a point of reunion among the branches of Christianity *without* the biblical*only* perception of the Virgin having to become the sole understanding of her. That is, full honor to the biblical sense of Mary would be given, even in quarters where she has been stiff-armed, but it would also be deemed acceptable that Catholics and the Orthodox additionally perceive a biblical*plus* sense of Mary.

Perhaps most importantly, a reframing of ecumenical and interfaith dialogues should include — and make central — the severely degraded state of the Creation. Modernity's disconnecting us from the unfolding story of the Earth community and the universe has resulted not only in the ecological crises but also in our collective refusal to take seriously any part of the Creation other than modern, industrialized humans. We seem unable to turn our religious attention from narratives of vertical transcendence to the literal common ground beneath our feet. What do Protestant, Catholic, and Orthodox Christians say and do about the overarching spiritual *and material* crises of the Creation? Nearly nothing? Instead, they dig into their trenches and do battle over whether Mary is too large or too small. How severe do the crises have to become before *ecological ecumenism* appears obvious?[6]

It seems that the wisest course for ecumenism would be for the Western branches of Christianity — that is, Protestantism and Roman Catholicism — to lean in the direction of the Eastern Orthodox, who have cultivated both a rich sense of Mary's mystical, cosmological presence *and* a well-developed tradition of regarding the Creation as sacred. The formative theologians of the Orthodox tradition perceived divine grace diffused throughout nature. Moreover, they have declined to make many doctrinal definitions of the Blessed Mother, preferring to let her extensive spiritual presence manifest itself in art, liturgy, and daily practices. She is known as the Virgin of Tenderness and Our Lady of Perpetual Help. She is called the Foundation of Earth, More Sublime than Paradise, Life-Giving Fountain, Joy of All Afflicted, Joy of Joys.

Russian Orthodox theologians generally interpret Mary as continuing the spiritual presence of Sophia, the figure in Hebrew Scripture who is a manifestation of divine wisdom. According to the Book of Proverbs, Sophia was the partner with God from the beginning of time. Mary, sometimes depicted as Maria Sophia, is regarded as the matrix of profound silence and grounding from which manifested the Word of God in Jesus Christ. The Orthodox theologian Vladimir Zelinsky explains that Mary was the all-important "site" of the encounter between God and humankind. Consequently, her mystical presence is petitioned not as a mere "instrument" by which one connects with the Divine but as an expression of "Heaven" itself because it is Mary who "has made the Sun of Justice rise."[7]

The linkage between Mary and Sophia is only one of numerous references in Hebrew Scripture that can be read as predicting or foreshadowing the coming of Christ. Isaiah 7:14, for instance, declares, "Behold, a virgin will be with child and bear a son, and she will call his name Immanuel." The linkage of such foreshadowing was essential to demonstrate authenticity because "the Jesus cult," as it was known for the first fifty years, was considered a sect within Judaism. Yet Judaism was dwarfed by another, much larger context in which Christianity grew: the pagan world of the Mediterranean basin. At the time of Christ, some 90 percent of the people in that area were pagan. Their spiritual practice was centered on ancient expressions of the Divine embedded in mythic stories that informed their cultural history.

The Early Church Fathers were demonstrably anxious about their pagan competition, especially Goddess religion, and are generally credited with fighting off any such "corruption" of the Christian faith. Although this view has dominated Church history, the early laity have not received credit for safeguarding the course of Christianity from veering too far in an all-male direction. The early Christians were well aware of another new religion in their midst, Mithraism, which was extremely popular among soldiers in the Roman legions and had spread throughout the entire Roman Empire. It featured a young male god who neither owed his existence to a woman (he was born of a stone) nor had any relationship to women at all. Mithraism, though a strong presence, was hardly an appealing model for women, who constituted a large portion of the converts to early Christianity. On the cultural level, the notion of a lone male denied the balance common in most families in Mediterranean cultures, in which the male/father has authority but the female/mother has power. On the spiritual level, the model of the lone male denied the deeply seated resonance associated with the ancient perception of a Great Mother who symbolically embodies cosmological forces. Hence, the early laity, and some clergy, gradually sought to bring fundamental balance to the story of the Incarnation by venerating a Mary who not only assented to the will of God but grew through her piety, her ordeals, and her unique ontological relationship to God-the-Son to possess bountiful powers of compassion and intercession. She would have quasi-divine powers, while not being fully divine. Yes, the Man from Galilee would be accepted as the Messiah, but the presence of the sacred female would live on in more-than-human Mary.

In embracing a full and rich theology of the Incarnation, the laity honored Mary as a profound matrix from which Christ's life took form and in which it unfolded. While this perception of a Christian Great Mother naturally found common ground with many familiar aspects of Goddess religion, it is not the case that the early Christians "took a tumble" into believing that Mary was endowed with beneficent powers merely because they happened to live among various "corrupting" forms of Goddess spirituality that had shaped religious life for thousands of years. Rather, they saw correctly what the new Christian story needed. Had they not insisted on increasingly seeing in Mary the Goddess-like powers of efficacious compassion that complement, yet do not overshadow, the spiritual authority of the male Savior, it is likely that "the Jesus cult" would not have survived much longer than Mithraism.

In the early centuries of Christianity, Mary was hailed by theologians as the New Eve, opposite in every way to the Eve of Genesis, whose supposedly faulty character was embellished with misogynist enthusiasm by the Early Church Fathers. The second-century theologian Justin Martyr seems to have been the first to make this connection, accompanied by the corollary that women are fallen Eves.

Mary's great role of mediator, however, was also formalized in the early centuries of the Church. This Marian dimension emerged initially in the Eastern Church but developed in the Roman areas as well. Irenaeus (a second-century bishop of Lyon) and Origen (an early-third-century theologian in Alexandria and, later, Caesarea), for instance, each taught that Mary was an intercessor and mediator for the faithful. Cyril, a fifth-century patriarch of Alexandria, wrote a hymn to Mary as "Mediatrix of the World." Irenaeus and Origen additionally perceived Mary cosmologically. They each emphasized that the Incarnation was a cosmic event, linking heaven and Earth — as opposed to Paul, for instance, who taught that Christians need to transcend cosmic forces to connect with the greater God of grace and freedom. In another sharp contrast to both Irenaeus and Origen, Tertullian (an early-third-century theologian in Carthage) sought to deny any extraordinary, or cosmological, powers to Mary on the grounds that they were too similar to those of Isis. Like thousands of clergymen after him, he praised Mary primarily for her obedience. Clearly, his fear of too great a Mary within Christianity was also linked with his contempt for women, each of whom, he taught, is an Eve: the devil's gateway, the first deserter of divine law, and the reason Christ had to die.

During the early centuries of the Church, many of its officials sought to subsume the growing adaptation of Great Mother imagery, channeling it from the Nazarene mother of Jesus to the institution itself. They decreed, without great effect, that the Church itself was the Second Eve (redeemer of the fallen First Eve), the Virgin Mother, and the Bride of Christ (a term that refers to Mary's spiritual Coronation). Although these appropriations failed to stem the tide, the phrase "Holy Mother Church" survives today from that era.

By the end of the fourth century, Mary was widely honored as a regal figure of great spiritual power. Controversies still arose, however, over the dual nature of Christ's parentage and hence his substance. Arius, a charismatic presbyter in Alexandria, declared that Jesus was not fully divine. That is, Arius asserted that Jesus' essence was similar to, but not the same as, that of God. Although this position was condemned by the bishops' Council of Nicaea in 325, the Arian heresy lived on for another century, causing the Church Fathers to emphasize the supernatural and fully divine nature of Mary's pregnancy.

A related controversy developed in 428 when Nestorius became patriarch of Constantinople and railed against those referring to Mary as Theotokos (God-Bearer, or She Who Gave Birth to God), which he found too similar to the pagan beliefs of Goddess religion. Indeed, both Isis and Cybele were called "Mother of the Gods," so calling Mary the "Mother of God" was blatently syncretic in the eyes of the patriarch. He allowed that Mary should be considered the mother of the humanness of Jesus but not the mother of his divine nature. In response, Cyril, the bishop of Alexandria, attacked Nestorius for dividing Christ into two separate natures. To settle the issue, a council of the bishops of the Church met in 431 in Ephesus, where many Christians believed Mary had spent her last years in the care of the apostle John. They met, in fact, in the Marian church that had been built adjacent to the ancient temple of Diana (called Artemis by the Greeks), whose religion had been suppressed by Emperor Theodosius fifty years earlier, depriving the populace of their goddess. A surviving column with Diana's image was incorporated into the church, symbolizing — at least in the minds of the laity — the common ground shared by the two Great Mothers and the passing of the torch in the new era. Because Cyril was able to call the vote at the Council of Ephesus before the arrival of the Syrian bishops, who supported Nestorius's position, the "Nestorian heresy" was condemned, and Mary was declared Theotokos.

This elevation of Mary's official status to "God-Bearer," popularly understood as Mother of God, brought the Church hierarchy up to speed with the laity, who cheered the decision in the streets surrounding the bishops' council. The declaration of Theotokos, issued from the city widely associated with Diana of Ephesus, was responsible more than any other clerical intervention in the history of the Church for officially enlarging the role and perception of Mary of Nazareth. All subsequent elevations of the Virgin follow from this decision. Moreover, all such elevations, even into the mid-twentieth century, followed the same order: The laity precede the hierarchy in perceiving an expanded sense of Mary's spiritual presence and the increased honor it evokes.

Almost immediately after the bishops' decision at Ephesus, speculation arose in theological circles concerning the death, or dormition (falling asleep), of the Theotokos. The belief common among the laity was that she had been assumed into heaven in body and soul because Christ would not allow his mother's body to remain on Earth decomposing in a grave and would want her — body and soul intact — with him in heaven. The celebration of Mary's Assumption spread from Eastern Orthodox churches and was eventually set, in 600, on August 15, where it has remained ever since.

Soon new iconography developed to depict the birth of the Theotokos. She was moved, moreover, from the sidelines to the center in paintings and mosaics of the nativity. New icons also changed her depiction when holding Jesus from profile to full frontal position, an aesthetic presentation that was otherwise reserved for royalty and divinities. On either side of the Theotokos, archangels alighted to flank the noble defender of the faith, the spiritual queen of Christianity.

In short, poor Nestorius, deposed and excommunicated after Cyril's ambitious campaign against him, had inadvertently brought about that which he feared most: the enthusiastic acceptance by the official Church of goddess-like attributes for Mary, which had long been recognized by the laity. Yet Nestorius had merely presented the Church with an excuse to open a channel for a tide they could not turn back. Following his expulsion, his Nestorian sect attracted many adherents at first but eventually died out.

Several centuries later, in the Middle Ages, Marian spirituality reached its apogee, inspiring more devotions than ever, new music to accompany them, and some of the finest art and architecture in the history of the West. Elegant Gothic cathedrals arose in Chartres, Paris, Reims, Amiens, Rouen, Bayeux, and elsewhere as palaces for the Queen of Heaven. Between 1150 and 1250 over 80 cathedrals and 500 churches were under construction in her honor.

While various interpretations of Marian doctrine were debated by the medieval Scholastic theologians, grassroots Christians invented exaggerated legends about the Virgin that took on a life of their own. Stories circulated about her successfully intervening on behalf of even the most scurrilous of villains about to be sent to hell because God so loved Mary that he could not deny her. In some legends the Virgin thwarted the power structure in heaven and on Earth merely because she could, which delighted the peasantry. A few voices within the Church — including even "Mary's troubadour," St. Bernard of Clairvaux — urged moderation on the grounds that Mary, the perfect intercessor, needed no attributes attached to her. Still, the homespun stories of the Virgin and various saints continued to proliferate.

Once the medieval worldview was eclipsed by Renaissance human-ism, depictions of Mary changed dramatically. In fact, humanist changes in Marian art had already been apparent in the late medieval era when Mary enthroned, who previously had been approached only by angels, was now crowded by saints or wealthy patrons, sometimes looking over her shoulder. By the second half of the fifteenth century, paintings of the Annunciation in several countries presented a large and rather fierce Gabriel, who now occupies the symbolically dominant side of the composition (the right), and a smaller Mary who is now docile or even cowering, rather than deliberating. Matthias Grünewald's famous paint-ing of the Annunciation in the Isenheim Altarpiece (c. 1510-15) occupies the extreme end of this trend — his Gabriel a huge, overpow-ering bully, his Mary a helpless heap.

In Italy the humanist artists did not wish to run afoul of the Church, so they often painted traditional religious subjects, but they boldly declared the assertions of the new thinking through their work: *Man is the measure of all things! Humans are the crown of creation!* Painting Mary as a housewife (a somewhat glamorous version when a patron's wife was the model, a somewhat frumpy version when the artist's servant was the model) was claimed, theologically, to emphasize the fully human nature of the Incarnation. Visually desanctifying Mary, however, also served the political agenda of Renaissance humanism.

The artists of the High Renaissance no longer depicted Mary in celestial glory or mystical allure. Instead, she is situated in domestic scenes or else framed by a neoclassical arch. Her prominent halo is now merely hinted at with a thin golden line or is gone entirely. Her face often lacks intelligence, and her expression is likely to be vacant or even coquettish. Raphael, Correggio, Caravaggio, Titian, Da Vinci, Del Sarto, and others signaled this turn. Mary sits far less often on a throne than a garden bench with imposing neoclassical architecture behind her, denoting the new and looming influence of Greek (that is, secular) thought. In short, several decades before Luther and Calvin declared the Virgin to be *just a housewife,* the painters of the intensely masculine Italian Renaissance paved the way for a more "rational" view of Mary. (In Spain, however, painters continued to glorify Mary in her cosmological fullness throughout the seventeenth century.)

By the time Martin Luther published his 95 Theses on Indulgences in 1517, there were many patterns of excess within the Church. He was understandably disgusted with the Vatican's scheme for raising money: the corrupt practice of selling indulgences, which involved the transfer of merit accumulated by saints to shorten a sinner's time in purgatory in exchange for not merely prayers, as was traditional, but also an obligatory donation to the Church of Rome. (This shameful fundraising scheme was devised largely to pay for the Vatican's ambitious architectural projects by prominent Renaissance artists and designers.) Although the impulse behind the Reformation was entwined with new feelings of nationalism in emergent modern states, its theological arguments were wide-ranging and, for most of northern Europe, ultimately convincing. The fundamental goal of the Reformers was to assert the direct, unmediated relationship between the individual and God. In doing so, they shifted the emphasis in their new version of Christian spirituality from the sacramental experience to a text-based faith. Luther insisted that Scripture-based faith is the sole means by which an individual might experience God's grace. Nothing else — not good works; not the ritual experience of the seven sacraments; not the community of nuns, priests, and saints; and certainly not the intercession of the Virgin Mary or any particular saint — was necessary or proper. Luther disavowed all the sacraments but two, the eucharist and baptism. Instead, he lay great emphasis on hearing the Word of the Lord read, preached, or sung, going so far as to assert that the ears are the only organs of a Christian. (He disapproved, however, of the brutal destruction of all imagery that took place in some churches early in the Reformation when they were appropriated from the Roman Catholic Church.)

The Reformation's attitudes toward Mary were framed initially by the pronouncements of the founding fathers — Luther, Zwingli, and Calvin — who began from quite different perspectives. Luther was an Augustinian friar and a professor of biblical studies who had been trained in medieval Scholasticism. Early on, just after he had been excommunicated in 1521, Luther wrote a fifty-seven-page commentary on the Magnificat (Luke 1:46-55), Mary's famous prayer proclaimed early in her pregnancy. In this essay Luther interprets Mary's exultant declaration through the lens of his core theological message, the "radical sovereignty" of God. He emphasizes that Mary was a "poor, despised, and lowly maiden, who served God in her low estate."[8] Explicating a zero-sum Mariology, Luther asserts that "the vain chatterers who preach and write about her merits" (that is, the Catholics) diminish the role of God's grace: "For, in proportion as we ascribe merit and worthiness to her, we lower the grace of God." Therefore, he reasons, those who would show Mary proper honor "must strip her of all honor, and regard her low estate."[9] This position is consistent with Luther's view that *all* possible honor must be given solely to God: "For we desecrate God's name when we let ourselves be praised or honored."[10] With this conviction in mind, Luther deflected upward any praise for having initiated and led the Reformation, famously observing that it was God Himself who had reformed the Christian church, while he had merely drunk Wittenberg beer. Luther further taught that those who find in Mary "great and lofty things" are contrasting us with her instead of her with God.[11] Just to be on the safe side, Luther advised, "For it is better to take away too much from her than from the grace of God. Indeed, we cannot take away too much from her, since she was created out of nothing, like all other creatures."[12] He allows that Queen of Heaven is "a true enough name and yet does not make her a goddess who could grant gifts or render aid, as some suppose when they pray and flee to her rather than to God."[13] In his "Sermon on the Afternoon of Christmas Day" in 1530, Luther exhorted the faithful to "accept the child and his birth and forget the mother, as far as this is possible, although her part cannot be forgotten, for where there is a birth there must also be a mother."[14] After all, Luther pointed out, the angel who appeared to the shepherds at the time of the Nativity announced that the Savior had been born not to Mary but to all people: "I bring unto you glad tidings of great joy: for unto you is born this day the Savior."[15]

In the German-speaking regions of Switzerland, the Reformation was furthered by Ulrich Zwingli, a Renaissance humanist who had learned Greek and Hebrew and was much impressed by Erasmus's edition of the Greek New Testament. It is likely that he also knew of Erasmus's scathing condemnation of the devotions practiced at Walsingham, the renowned Marian shrine in England. Zwingli himself was chaplain from 1516 to 1518 of the major Marian shrine in Switzerland, Einsiedeln, which houses a black madonna. Although he preached often to the pilgrims there, he always limited his mention of Mary to biblical events. In 1519 he read some of Luther's early works and, five years later, published *Commentary on True and False Religion* when he was head of the Gross Münster church in Zürich. Throughout his life, Zwingli's teachings on Mary were primarily pastoral, asserting to the faithful that no petition should ever be addressed to her or any saint. Rather, he taught, Christians should admire the gifts Mary received from God, emulate through contemplation the way she held these things in her heart, and imitate her example of piety, obedience, and humility.

The second wave of the Reformation was spearheaded by Jean Calvin, who was born in 1509 and hence felt even greater distance from the medieval devotion to the Virgin Mary. His father lay under excommunication by the bishop of Geneva for several years, and Calvin did not hesitate to declare that the pope was "the Antichrist who usurped Christ's place as Head of the church," adding that "what are called temples among the Papists are only filthy brothels of Satan."[16] Calvin felt that Catholics had made an idol of Mary by fraudulently ascribing to her that which is God's alone; in doing so, Catholics had "stripped Christ of his spoils."[17] The point of the Virgin Mary, he taught, is that she exemplifies the way in which we should receive the Word of God in our hearts. God placed her in the miracle of the Incarnation as a picture, or cipher, to remind us how totally one should respect the Word of God.

I must pause a moment at the conclusion this summary of the Reformers' Marian views to observe that although the argument of the "progressives" at Vatican II for minimalizing the meaning and status of Mary in Roman Catholicism was said to be based on the latest developments in post-World War II, "scientific" methods of biblical exegesis, it certainly sounded — and still does — remarkably like the very arguments made by Luther, Zwingli, and Calvin. Because the post-World War II movement within Catholicism to adopt the "modern" and literary way of reading Scripture, such that the significance of Mary was radically diminished and she was understood to be merely a cipher in Scripture, arose among a few theologians in Germany, it seems that they, more than Catholic theologians in other countries, absorbed the influence of their Lutheran peers. Within only a few years, many of the young German and other European Catholic theologians were fully convinced that Mary's role in the Incarnation and the Redemption was essentially passive and that she had no spiritual presence of the sort that had been increasingly discerned by the faithful as the Christian religion grew and developed. In short, the mystical nature of her becoming the Mother of God-the-Son was simply denied.

To return to the historical survey, it can be said that most of the subsequent leaders of the Protestant denominations — including the Calvinist Presbyterians, who eventually held sway in Scotland — soon ignored even *Mary, Just a Housewife*. That extreme diminution is justified by some Protestant theologians today who argue that the founding Reformers would not have bothered to include any Mariology whatsoever had they had the benefit of modern advances in "scientific exegesis" of Scripture. In any event, the Reformers' streamlined, text-bound version of Christianity contributed cultural patterns that moved the West a giant step closer to the modern mentality: the focus on the individual over (religious) community; the introduction of reductionist, rationalist practice to the exclusion of ritual experience; and the semiotic interpretation of symbols as mere referents (signs that *refer* to something else, or remind us of something), rather than multivalent expressions of participatory consciousness. Then, too, the fact that some of the Reformers called the pope "the Scarlet Woman of the Apocalypse" and did away with the role of nun for women in the Protestant churches — not to mention dethroning and closeting the Great Mother — reflects a more hard-edged masculine cast to both doctrine and practice, which influenced the course of modern thought.

In England and France secular replacements for the Virgin Mary were developed in the hope of inspiring loyalty for political causes. Queen Elizabeth I became known as the Virgin Queen (for whom the state of Virginia was named) not because she was physically virginal when she ascended to the throne but because she sought to mirror the attributes of the Queen of Heaven, who had recently been deposed in newly Protestant England. Elizabeth, although solidly Protestant, was anointed during her coronation with oil said to have been given to Thomas à Becket by the Virgin Mary. (This ritual was begun with Henry IV but was discontinued by Elizabeth's successor, James I, as a popish superstition.) She also continued the healing ritual called the Royal Touch, in which monarchs since Henry II touched the afflicted during a full religious ceremony. After Elizabeth's ascension to the throne, references to the Virgin Mary and the saints were deleted from that healing ritual so that the only remaining beneficent mother was the queen, as civic intercessor and Defender of the True Faith.[18] In 1570 Queen Elizabeth was excommunicated by the pope.

Still, the cultural memory of England's earlier devotion to Mary, so fervent and widespread that the country was once known as "Mary's Dowry," must have survived on some level through many generations.

When American Protestant ministers and laywomen who were pre-dominantly of English descent mounted a movement in the nineteenth century to establish Mother's Day in the United States, they chose a Sabbath day in May, the month of Mary. According to a historian of the nineteenth-century "cult of motherhood," this new day of reverence was a partial recovery of the connection Protestants had lost with Mary after the Reformation.[19]

In Italy, as we have seen, Mary was stripped of her halo and cosmological associations by Renaissance humanist artists, who intro-duced symbolism from classical Greek mythology, such as the pome-granate, and who favored neoclassical architecture or domestic scenes as the background. Most often they painted *Madonna e Bambino*. In the Protestant countries, Mary nearly disappeared as a subject in paintings, especially during the eighteenth century, when the intensified secular humanism of the Enlightenment targeted Marian images and devo-tions as problems far worse than various corrupt religious practices such as selling indulgences. Marian spirituality epitomized for the Enlightenment zealots the preposterously wrong turn taken by the medieval era in the West's grand march from classical Greek rational-ism to the "tough-minded" neoclassical thought of their time, which was infused with the mechanistic worldview of the Scientific Revolution.

In Mary the French *philosophes* and their violent foot soldiers saw a debilitating superstition that was blocking the triumph of the Age of Reason. Her centuries-old statues were targeted for destruction during the French Revolution, which raged on as a protracted civil war in several regions after the initial events in Paris. Yet the symbol for the new civic culture being born was a secular version of female deliver-ance based on the Virgin's name: Marianne, a working-class heroine courageously leading the people to democracy and secular enlighten-ment. In an even bolder appropriation, the Revolutionaries invaded the Cathedral of Notre Dame in Paris and erected a large female statue called the Goddess of Reason.

Beginning in the 1830s, a grassroots renewal of Marian spirituality manifested itself in Catholic cultures of Europe, especially in France and environs. From that decade until the end of World War I, a series of visitations were reported, spawning several new pilgrimage sites. The Church encouraged this show of fervor (although it continued to withhold any official recognition of the vast majority of visitations of the Virgin Mary that were reported) because it felt itself to be aggressively threatened throughout the nineteenth century by the new secular culture of modernity. No doubt that is why the rather desperate measure of "papal infallibility" was introduced then and was used, for the first time, to further glorify modernity's prime target within Catholicism: the Blessed Mother. Still, Pope Pius IX's definition in 1854 of the Immaculate Conception of the Virgin Mary *as revealed dogma necessary to salvation,* rather than a doctrinal teaching, shocked some Catholics and nearly all Protestants. Most of the Catholic grassroots, however, rejoiced that their beloved Holy Mother was now situated at the very core of official Catholicism, even in the modern era. By the beginning of the twentieth century, several Catholic leaders predicted that we were entering a Marian Age.

Between 1849 and 1940 the Vatican received a stream of eight million petitions requesting a second infallible papal declaration, this time defining the Assumption of the Blessed Virgin into heaven. They came not only from the laity but also from 3,387 cardinals, archbishops, and bishops. When Pope Pius XII finally defined the Assumption in 1950 as an infallible revelation of church dogma, the same pattern of responses erupted as had one hundred years earlier. Protestant theologians and leading clerics wrote strongly disapproving articles to the effect that the pope's action was "religiously dangerous," having widened the division of Christendom. A few disgruntled voices within the Catholic Church complained that the declaration should have simply amplified the doctrine, rather than raising the Assumption to the level of dogma (that is, an article of faith). The vast majority of the Catholic laity and clergy, however, were delighted that the Church was again honoring Mary.

Buoyed by the papal definition of the Assumption, a movement intensified among some of the laity and clergy for yet a third infallible papal definition of the Blessed Mother, although this one attracted less support than the previous two efforts. The group sought papal recognition, as an article of faith, that Mary was Co-Redeemer with Christ, meaning that she was *with* him in the salvific task in a unique way. At that point the brakes were slammed on, mostly surreptitiously. On public, if unofficial, levels the Vatican let it be known throughout the

1950s that no such definition would be forthcoming so soon on the heels of the last one. In private circles, a few theologians and members of the Church hierarchy initiated discussions about the need to become more acceptable to Protestants and the rest of the modern world by "rationalizing" Catholicism and vastly reducing Marian spirituality.

Various concerns converged in the planning of Vatican II in the late 1950s. (Vatican I had been convened in 1869 to define and clarify the newly introduced concept of papal infallibility.) As I have noted, the vast majority of subjects proposed for reform at Vatican II had to do with the great liberalization of attitudes toward the world at large, the lay apostolate, the self-organization of nun's communities, and the countless internal matters of organization and operation. All of those impressive accomplishments could surely have been achieved, however, without gutting the full spiritual presence of Mary.

The rallying cry of the "modernizers" of Mary at the Council was informed by several currents in intellectual life in the post-World War II period. First, many of the young intellectual priests and theologians had come in contact with the modern trends in biblical exegesis and other areas of theology; they wanted to be able to participate in the new "scientific" and "tough-minded" semiotic analyses. In addition, there was a current of fear that the new methods of biblical exegesis and archaeology might prove the Church wrong on some matters. Lopping off Catholicism's least "rational" and most nonbiblical element — that is, the Queen of Heaven — seemed to many of the intellectual priests to be a prudent move for the Church. Second, the grip of Freudian theory in postwar intellectual circles was making it embarrassing to have a "mother fixation" on such a huge scale. The Freudian view is a cozy fit, of course, with male anxiety in patriarchal cultures concerning the elemental power of the female because the Freudian spin both legitimates and assuages the fear implanted by patriarchal socialization in male minds. Third, something needed to be done to improve relations with both the Protestant and the Orthodox branches of Christianity in the wake of the papal definition of the Assumption. Several of the critical articles by Protestant theologians had been extremely condemnatory — and, apparently, for many of the intellectual priests, largely convincing. The solution that neatly addressed all three of these problems was to move the Church closer to the modern, sophisticated (and Protestant) interpretation of Mary so as to achieve an ecumenical rapprochement. This new direction was launched by declaring that ecumenism was suddenly absolutely essential, a top priority of great immediacy for the Roman Catholic Church.

But why then, after more than 440 years? The three branches of Christianity had been humming along on parallel tracks, with very little concern among their respective laity in recent centuries about the internal beliefs of the other branches. Why did ecumenism suddenly become a burning necessity for many in the Roman Catholic hierarchy in the late 1950s, making it the impetus that shaped most of the doctrinal and liturgical changes decreed by Vatican II? Perhaps there was a fourth influence in the mix: During the 1950s the Islamic world began to identify itself as a unified, politicized bloc. Children in the Near and Middle East were instructed in schools to think of themselves as "Arab" rather than Egyptian, Syrian, Jordanian, and so forth. Did the emergence of this united force — which was unfavorably disposed toward Christianity after suffering through the exploitative colonial era (and, before that, the Crusades and the expulsion of the Moors from Spain) — convince the Church that it was time to circle the wagons? If so, that self-protective action could be accomplished only if Catholicism became far more palatable to the Orthodox and to Protestants — and did so very soon, very sweepingly, and very quickly. To please the Orthodox, it would have to open dialogue about the old rifts. To please the Protestants, it would have to become more strictly text-based and less mystical and sacramental. The idea of a second Vatican Council met all these criteria.

For reasons both psychological and political, then, the full spiritual presence of Mary was targeted by the "progressives" at Vatican II as being particularly unmodern. After they (narrowly) won the vote about including a "modernizing" chapter on Mary in *The Dogmatic Constitution on the Church (Lumen Gentium),* it is clear that the "progressives" maintained the upper hand in drafting the content. The wording, however, is quite vague and circumspect in many places, reflecting the almost 50/50 split in the vote count and the struggles over various drafts. In the chapter, the full title of which is "The Role of the Blessed Virgin Mary, Mother of God in the Mystery of Christ and the Church," the meaning of Mary is reconfigured according to the "ecclesio-typical" interpretation: The Blessed Virgin is to be understood as a model, or sign, or "type" of the Church. Much of the text consists of a summary of her biblical life along with citations from the Early Church Fathers praising — *guess what* — Mary's obedience. All the Marian titles, including Mother of the Church, are dropped from usage here, with the exception of Mother of God. "Mother of the Church" and all of Mary's even longer standing titles, it was explained, do not fit the modern way of reading the gospels since Mary is now understood to be merely a cipher representing the Church in the text!

Particular emphasis is placed on clarifying that the "salvific influences of the Blessed Virgin on men" (that is, her powers as Intercessor) flow solely from "the superabundance of the merits of Christ" rather than any qualities of her own. After intense debates over whether to omit or include Mary's titles that express her dimension as advocate and mediator, a compromise was struck such that those titles appear only once and in an ambiguous manner. That is, the Council notes in section III of the Marian chapter that historically "the Blessed Virgin is invoked by the Church under the titles of Advocate, Auxiliatrix, Adjutrix, and Mediatrix," but the Council itself refrains from using any of those titles. In fact, the Council trumps all of those Marian titles by stating directly, at the beginning of that section, "We have but one Mediator": Christ.[20]

Moreover, the constitution produced at Vatican II pointedly omits mention not only of the commonly invoked but controversial title "Co-Redeemer," the unique co-participant who was profoundly *with* but not equal to Christ, but also the entire Mariological cluster of concepts derived from the fact that Mary's participation in the Redemption was unique because of her ontological relationship with God-the-Son. Some "progressives" have subsequently asserted that the title "Co-Redeemer" was used only by a few "rabid Marianists" and never officially. Consequently, they insist, it should indeed be omitted from even a historical list of past Marian titles. This claim is not true, however. The title was used frequently by many respected writers and by popes from Leo XIII (1878-1903) through Pius XI (1922-1939). As for grassroots evidence, I shall weigh in here with a bit of documentation to add to the proof that Mary was indeed widely considered "Co-

Redeemer" prior to Vatican II: an excerpt from my childhood coloring book, *Mary, Full of Grace,* which I came across recently while rooting around in my mother's basement in Columbus, Ohio. Published in 1954 with the imprimatur of the bishop of Milwaukee, a paragraph near the end of the book states,

> Jesus chose the day of His supreme sacrifice to announce the highest dignity of His holy mother. As she had a special role in the conflict with the serpent she would have a special share in the victory — the defeat of Satan and sin, the restoration of grace. Mary was, in a sense, co-redeemer with her Son. He made her the distributor of all graces, our spiritual Mother. This was his last gift to saints and sinners before dying.

In the closing sections of the chapter on Mary in *Lumen Gentium,* the Council Fathers note that the "special cult" of the Blessed Virgin is fundamentally different from the "cult of adoration which is offered to the Incarnate Word, as well as to the Father and the Holy Spirit." That is, the Church has always taught that Mary may be accorded special veneration *(hyperdulia),* which is greater than the veneration accorded the saints *(dulia),* but she may not be accorded adoration *(latria),* which is reserved for God. Marian piety, the chapter states, is acceptable as long as it remains "within the limits of sound and orthodox doctrine." In expressing pious appreciation of "the duties and privileges of the Blessed Virgin," Catholics are to "abstain zealously from both all gross exaggerations as well as petty narrow-mindedness in considering the singular dignity of the Mother of God." The Council was particularly concerned that Catholics not indulge in any expression of Marian spirituality that could mislead "separated brethren" (that is, the Orthodox and especially the Protestants) about "the true doctrine of the Church." True devotion proceeds from true faith, rather than "transitory affection" or "a certain vain credulity."

Whew. Even the pope was shocked. He tried to intervene twice during the Council, hoping to prevail upon the modernizers to at least preserve the Marian title of "Mother of the Church." During a ceremony on October 11, 1963, the first anniversary of the opening of the Council, Pope Paul VI prayed, "O Mary, make this Church, which is His and yours, as it defines itself, recognize you as its Mother and

Daughter and elect Sister, as its incomparable model, its glory, its joy, and its hope."[21] During in an address the next month, at the closing of the third session, he again championed part of the position of the dejected Marianists, who were only slightly in the minority: "To the glory of the Blessed Virgin and for our consolation we declare that the Most Holy Mary is Mother of the Church. . . . "[22] Two years later, at the closing ceremony of the entire Second Vatican Council — set, ironically, on a Marian feast day, December 8, 1965 — the pope no longer referred to Mary with the now disallowed title "Mother of the Church," but only as "the Mother of Christ, . . . the Mother of God, and our spiritual mother."[23]

Several of the bishops and cardinals watched the closing ceremony through their tears. Amid its many triumphs in the areas of the laity, religious orders and communities, and attitudes toward other religions, drastic doctrinal changes had been made to deep regions of Catholic spirituality. Some of the changes in liturgical practices seemed ham-fisted, and, most tragically, the recognition of the mystical character of the Maternal Matrix in the Incarnation and the Redemption — indeed, in the life of the Church — was denied entirely and was thoroughly eradicated from the modernized version of Catholicism.

In hindsight, it seems curious that there was no strong middle position on Mary at Vatican II. I suppose the severe polarization developed because the core issue underlying the biblical*plus* versus the biblical*only* debate was an either/or proposition: Either Mary has more-than-human spiritual capabilities (in which case the traditional perception of her makes sense) or Mary does not have more-than-human spiritual capabilities (in which case the strictly biblical perception of her makes sense). What the Council Fathers should have been debating is the question of whether or not a village girl's central participation in a mystical birth of cosmological import, her experience of growing God-the-Son from her very flesh, *changed her ontologically*. To millions of Catholics through the ages, it had always made sense that Mary, by virtue of becoming the human Mother of God, moves into a space that did not exist before: For eternity she is more than human but less than divine, a unique mediator intimately linked with both humans and the Divine. This extrapolation seemed obvious within the sacred narrative because all those millions of Catholics in all those centuries noticed that a woman is subtly but irrevocably changed after growing a person inside herself. Mary, it follows, must have experienced far more of a transformation than usual since the being in her womb was God.

On the other hand, the men who wrote the gospels were strongly influenced by local cultural assumptions of their time: Jewish tradition held that a woman is rendered unclean for several weeks by the act of giving birth, and Aristotelian science had widely established the notion that woman is simply an incubator that receives the tiny person contained in the male "seed." Understandably, the scribes of the gospels, with the exception of Luke,[24] give Mary scant attention, viewing her essentially as a rent-a-womb. This assumption that Mary's role and experience in the gestation of God-the-Son was passive and static was emphasized by Luther, who taught that Mary was "no more than a cheerful guest chamber and willing hostess."[25]

Fortunately for Christianity, the sacramental imagination of the faithful did not freeze with that local, first-century rendition of the Incarnation. For centuries the laity grasped that the story of the mystical birth and sacrifice of God-the-Son is bigger, much bigger, than words. They sang it. They prayed it. They celebrated it. They contemplated it. They carved it. They painted it. They built their roadside shrines. They shaped their communal lives around it. They cherished the sacraments that hold it. They absorbed the Mystery of Jesus and, in, of Mary — and only occasionally had need of the received words. They joined their inner lives with the immensity of the Incarnation and the Redemption, the Ascension and the Assumption. Layer by layer, the people, rich and poor, high and low, responded with aesthetic, nonlinguistic depth to the Great Mystery. All that is now cancelled by a reification of the text? Does it not seem odd that the orientation that is thoroughly glued to the first-century text and fourth-century theology is called "progressive," while the orientation that has always creatively engaged the sacramental imagination with the cosmological, expansive, unlimited heart of the Mystery is called "regressive"?

Vatican II was dissolved and dismissed upon completion of its monumental task. Four years later, in 1969, the Church published the post-Vatican II liturgical calendar, which had been "modernized" and "uncluttered" by dropping several popular feast days of Mary's (and those of several saints, as well) and by reducing others to optional commemorations. Five years after that, Pope Paul VI tried to put the best possible spin on the situation by issuing the apostolic exhortation *Marialis cultus* (The Cult of Mary) to reflect on the "evolution" of Marian prayer since the Council. He sought to correct the well-founded impression that the rosary had been deemphasized, but he suggested that henceforth it should be appreciated as "excellent preparation" for and a "continuing echo" of the mass.

Certainly the laity were shocked by some of the decisions of Vatican II. In truth, even the clergy and theologians who were called to Rome for the Council were initially surprised by the grand project. One of the relatively few surviving Council Fathers from Vatican II, now a retired bishop in Canada, told me recently that the announcement of and invitations to the Second Vatican Council "came out of the blue." Reflecting on its work and effects, he gently but firmly asserted that the Council had properly disallowed "the traditional, overly emotional" Marian devotion — which, he noted, "makes her into a goddess." He insisted, however, that the widespread removal of her statues and phasing out of the rosary in the wake of the Council were caused merely by misunderstandings and overreacting, simply a "pedagogical problem."

I had heard this explanation before, but if the radical demoting of Mary was merely a mistaken interpretation of Vatican II's diminished delineation of her spiritual presence, why was no correction attempted? If the "disappearing" of so much Marian practice was not the result desired by the Council Fathers, why did they not issue an outpouring of articles and sermons in the years following Vatican II urging a cessation of "overly anti-Mary" developments? Instead, a great silence descended concerning Mary, who was suddenly regarded by the modernized Church as uncomfortably anachronistic.

That period of heavy silence about Mary was confusing to most priests as well as the laity. Rather than a worldwide conspiracy among Catholic priests to demote the Blessed Mother, there was an unmistakable perception that the theological leaders of the Church, that is, the Council Fathers, had shifted the ground under Mary and that one had best try to figure out how to get into sync with the new mood of the Church. Fairly quickly, Mariology — especially any teachings about

Mary as Mediatrix of divine grace — was played down and soon phased out entirely at most seminaries. In truth, however, the majority of priests and nuns as well as lay people initially had no idea how deep and far the implications of the somewhat oblique Council pronouncements on Mary were about to reach.

Surely the "progressive" Council Fathers themselves must bear responsibility for the repression of Mary in the decades following Vatican II. Their dominant stance in the chapter on Mary in the new dogmatic constitution does not merely warn against excess in honoring Mary in her traditional role as intercessor and conduit of Christ's grace. Rather, it shrinks her role to "maternal duty" toward the faithful. The Council Fathers' Marian chapter certainly gives the impression that the modernizers would have liked to eliminate altogether Mary's role as even a "care-giving" intercessor among the faithful. As that undoubtedly would have caused riots, they at least cut her down to a size more comfortable for themselves and more acceptable to the Protestant "separated brethren."

What was crucial at Vatican II, the elderly Council Father explained to me in our conversation, was that Mary henceforth be seen as a *member* of the Church, not a force above it. Marian devotion had grown to unacceptable proportions, many felt, because a theology of the Holy Spirit had atrophied in the Roman Church, unlike in the Orthodox churches. Hence the Holy Spirit needed to be elevated and Mary demoted. Once again, a crisply rational reason for repressing the female was confidently crafted. The nonexistent competition between Jesus and Mary was transformed into a new theological competition between the Holy Spirit and Mary.

In the wake of Vatican II, the prayer known as the Apostles' Creed was replaced in the mass (except on certain occasions) with the Nicene Creed, in which a passive Mary is "overpowered" by the Holy Spirit to initiate her pregnancy: "He [Jesus] was conceived by *the power of* the Holy Spirit and born of the Virgin Mary." More recently, during the Year of the Holy Spirit (1998), a rosary based on "the mysteries of the Holy Spirit" was promoted.[26] It emphasizes the Holy Spirit's powerful presence at the Annunciation, the Visitation, the Crucifixion, and Pentecost. While this customized rosary includes the "Hail, Mary" prayer, the second half of that beloved prayer has been lopped off on the grounds that it is not from a biblical source and, hence, not "in line with Vatican II." Other post-Vatican II efforts to help the rosary "evolve" include interpretations that shift the focus from the Virgin Mary to God the Father, insisting absurdly that the "Our Father" prayer recited once in between each set of ten repetitions of the "Hail Mary" prayer is really the more important prayer since the abundance of Mary's prayer indicates that it is merely background material!

In March 1987 Pope John Paul II composed a more strongly Marian interpretation of Vatican II's decisions than was his predecessor's *Marialis cultus*. In order to launch the Marian Year, he issued *Redemptorius Mater (The Mother of the Redeemer)*. It is a lengthy explication (seventy-nine pages in booklet form) divided into three sections: Mary in the Mystery of Christ, The Mother of God at the Center of the Pilgrim Church, and Maternal Mediation. The entire text is larded with biblical citations and sprinkled with reminders that it is in line with Vatican II, but beyond that, it is infused with a warm and tender devotion to Mary. The third section, in particular, reflects a lifetime of communion with Our Lady of Czestochowa and other forms of the Blessed Mother. In this text, the pope honors — not merely tolerates — the rich source of Marian spirituality that lies within "the historical experience of individuals and the various Christian communities present among the different peoples and nations of the world." Not surprisingly, he includes an admiring reference to St. Louis-Marie Grignion de Montfort, an early eighteenth-century missionary in western France who created an exuberant explication of the rosary and Marian devotion, *The Secret of the Rosary,* based on his observation about the biblical account of the Incarnation: Jesus had to entrust himself to Mary, and we are to imitate Jesus. Therefore, concluded St. Louis de Montfort, the Blessed Virgin is a strategic and central element in the divine plan for our salvation.

Throughout his tenure, Pope John Paul II has held the line against any further "modernizing" away of Marian spirituality — while, unfortunately, making disappointing decisions in numerous other areas, such as failing to support noncommunist social-change advocates in Latin America (refusing, for instance, to even receive Archbishop Romero, prior to his assassination by right-wing hit men in El Salvador); furthering the ruination of the Creation through overpopulation and imposing great hardship on women (by forbidding contraception); aiding reactionary organizations, such as Opus Dei; and banning even *discussion* of the ordination of women. On the other hand, he has drawn on a beyond-left-and-right activist philosophy known as "personalism" (prominent in the social theory of French and Polish Catholic intellectuals since the 1930s) to issue strong condemnations of both state socialism and corporate capitalism, has exhibited a bit of ecological concern, and has repeatedly sought the forgiveness of peoples hurt by the Church in the past. Adding to the admirable column of his actions, the pope surprised both feminists and conservatives when he told a crowd of pilgrims in St. Peter's Square, in September 1999, that God has both a male and female nature and can be referred to as "God the Mother"![27] A similar declaration had been made by his predecessor, Pope John Paul I, shortly before his death: "God is both mother and father and is more mother than father." Perhaps elderly men feel free at the end of life to kick over the patriarchal barricades in their spiritual lives.

The current pope has been on the Marian path since his adolescence, when he served as president of the large Marian society in his hometown. As a young Polish priest, Karol Wojtyla consecrated himself to the Blessed Mother, considering her the spiritual guest in his soul, as the apostle John had done. When he was made an archbishop, Fr. Wojtyla inserted into his coat-of-arms an unmistakable Marian symbol, a large "M," which he carried into his papal seal years later. Similarly, his papal motto continues his earlier declaration of his spiritual consecration to Mary: *Totus tuus* (My Entire Self Is Yours). This pope routinely ends his letters to lay groups by commending them "to the loving protection of Mary, Mother of the Church." He has even used the term "co-redemptrix" six times in his papacy to describe Mary as being uniquely and inherently involved with Jesus in the Redemption. In March 2001 he celebrated the 750th anniversary of the brown scapular of Our Lady of Mount Carmel by asserting that wearing the scapular "nourishes the devotion of believers and makes them sensitive to the Virgin Mary's loving presence in their lives."[28]

Later that year, in his address at the Vatican the day after the terrorist attacks on the World Trade Center and the Pentagon, the pope expressed "profound sorrow at the terrorist attacks that yesterday brought death and destruction to America" and ended with this appeal:

"May the Blessed Virgin, Mother of Mercy, fill the hearts of all with wise thoughts and peaceful intentions." A few days later, speaking in Frosinone, Italy, he said, "Mary welcomes the dead, consoles the survivors, supports those families who are particularly tried, and helps all to resist the temptation of hate and violence and to commit themselves to the service of justice and peace." In April 2003, the pope told a gathering of young Catholics in St. Peter's Square, "In this troubled moment of history, when terrorism and wars threaten agreement among people and among religions, I want to entrust you to Mary so that you become promoters of the culture of peace that is more necessary than ever." He prayed that young people would find refuge under the mantle of Mary and that she would make "the beauty of Christ shine in them."[29]

He may well be the last pope to encourage engagement with the fullness of Marian spirituality. It would not be a bit surprising — in light of the current unexpected and largely uncontrollable Marian resurgence, including the aggressively rebuffed *Vox Populi* petitions — if a litmus test were applied to candidates during the election of John Paul II's successors: Are they on the side of the "minimalist Marian" modernizers . . . or are they "soft on Mary"? Surely the recent ecumenical "breakthrough" that moved the Roman Catholic and Lutheran churches a large step closer to "full communion, or merger" — that is, the joint decree signed in Augsberg in October 1999 resolving their 482-year-old core theological argument about the role of faith and good works — does not bode well for Marian spirituality. Would not such a merger, or even a partial joining, require a staunchly post-Marian pope?

Even before Vatican II, many parish-level Catholic priests, especially in certain countries, routinely pounded home the interpretation of Mary as a domestic model of female obedience, embodying a perfect level of submissiveness and docility against which every woman is supposed to measure herself. Hearing only that version of the meaning of the Blessed Mother, countless young women born after World War II turned away from Mary and often from the Church entirely. Vatican II then raised the emphasis on Mary the Obedient Housewife to the level of the new dogmatic constitution of the Church, causing a few sectors of the emergent feminist movement to take note in the aftermath and object to the bias. In 1974 Pope Pius VI tried to soothe the situation via his apostolic letter titled *Marialis cultus,* in which he asked the offended parties to understand that certain "sentiments about the Mother of Jesus" had merely reflected the social realities of past centuries and were not true to the biblical portrait of Mary. He urged Catholics to think of Mary as far more than a woman focused solely on her Son: She was a woman of action who "helped to strengthen the apostolic community's faith in Christ." Pope Pius VI also noted that Mary should be appreciated as the first and most perfect of Jesus' disciples: She heard the word of God and acted on it.

It has long been apparent that the Catholic right and the Catholic left interpret the "woman of action" in different ways. The current regime in the Vatican, especially Joseph Cardinal Ratzinger's administration in the office of the Sacred Congregation for the Doctrine of the Faith (SCDF), has demonstrated repeatedly that appropriations of the Blessed Virgin Mary by right-wing organizations are more acceptable to them than those adopted by left-wing or even nonideological, community-based organizations that reject the socialist model of a state-owned economy but seek to spread wealth and ownership as broadly as possible. In the 1980s the SCDF meted out one-year silencings and applied other pressure tactics to such distinguished liberal theologians as Hans Küng, Leonardo Boff, and Matthew Fox.

Even seasoned observers, however, were stunned by the action taken by Cardinal Ratzinger on January 2, 1997: He actually excommunicated a seventy-five-year-old priest in Sri Lanka for having published a long article, "Mary and Human Liberation," in a 1990 double issue of a journal with a circulation of 600 readers.[30] What was Fr. Tissa Balasuriya's radical position on Mary's significance? In truth, he seems to interpret the gospels and the very meaning of Christ as being solely political. Seen through that lens, Mary's cosmological dimension, her bountiful body of grace, and her intercessory role are viewed as archaic European cultural constructions that are not only nonbiblical but are worse than irrelevant because they "domesticate" people by luring them into a private spirituality instead of an activist Catholicism. Balasuriya asserts that traditional Mariology is based on imagined religious myths about which we can have no verification: the Immaculate Conception, the virginal conception of Jesus, the perpetual virginity of Mary, Mary as "Mother of God," her bodily assumption into heaven, and her role as mediator of grace and Co-Redeemer. (Balasuriya takes a literal, materialist — hence dismissive — view of these attributes, and he seems to exhibit no awareness of Mary's cosmological dimension as Maternal Matrix, with its ancient roots in the pre-Christian lineage of the symbolism of the sacred female.)

Balasuriya maintains that it would be far better to consider Mary the "tough, ordinary woman of the people" that she actually was. He lays great emphasis on Mary's Magnificat and concludes from it that Jesus' strong social conscience must have been formed under his mother's influence during his boyhood. Balasuriya is not convinced that Mary thought of her son as the Son of God; rather, she knew him as a courageous crusader for social justice and salvation on all levels who paid the price for challenging a repressive regime. Balasuriya has proposed "Marian Stations of the Cross," which incorporate the social (that is, political) pathos of the Passion of Christ.

The entire point of Christianity, according to this interpretation, is the social gospel and the rescue of the poor today. For good reason, Balasuriya locates the cause of much of the suffering in Third World communities in the policies and practices of the globalized economy and the *carte blanche* given to transnational corporations in the new world order under the General Agreement on Tariffs and Trade (GATT) and its enforcement agency, the World Trade Organization (WTO). He also notes that the status of women within the Church is sadly lacking in justice since they are barred from the priesthood.

The SCDF's initial critique of the article, released on July 27, 1994, ironically complained that Balasuriya fails to appreciate the fact that the chapter on Mary in Vatican II's dogmatic constitution, *Lumen Gentium,* disavows nearly all the "anachronistic" aspects of Marian spirituality that Balasuriya himself considers ridiculous. What the SCDF found scandalous was Balasuriya's seeming denial of several core beliefs of Catholicism concerning both Christ and Mary, as a result of his predominantly political interpretation of the Incarnation. What I find puzzling is Balasuriya's two-track, either/or sense of Catholicism (*either* private *or* activist). Activist Catholics all over the world have been combining the spiritual strength of Mary's full (traditional) presence in their lives *along with* social-change work and community development for several decades. She is certainly far more than a grassroots activist from Galilee.

As for the other protracted Marian struggle with Vatican officials (other than the pope), does it matter whether the six million Marian rebels in the Vox Populi movement prevail over their formidable opponents in Rome, especially Cardinal Ratzinger's SCDF? Given the institutional politics, such an outcome would require a miracle. In light of Mary's resilience over two thousand years, however, the question of elevating three of her pre-Vatican II titles to the level of infallible dogma is merely another play of the warp and woof in her luminous gown.

Perhaps it is sufficient that Professor Miravalle sounded the charge with the Vox Populi petition . . . and millions rallied on behalf of the Blessed Virgin. It is surely inspiring that one person at a small Franciscan College in the Appalachian foothills of Ohio plus a handful of colleagues and supporters — including those who, following an inspiring trip to Medjugorje, founded the Queenship Publishing Company in Santa Barbara — could build a worldwide movement in a few years. Win or lose, their materials have educated millions about the theological case for honoring Mary in her grand proportions (while not requiring adherence to the founding Vox Populi members' own social and political conservatism). By inference, they have shone a critical light on the matricidal moderns at Vatican II. Most importantly, though, Vox Populi has provided a vehicle through which grassroots devotion to the spiritual Great Mother of the West has once again found public expression, even in our hypermodern age.

Still, so much has been lost. In Mary the extremely ancient female expression of the sacred has been kept alive in the West — even through its repression by antifemale, antinature Greek rationalism and the renewal of that repression by Renaissance humanism — until it was decisively *cut* for the women and men of Protestant northern Europe in the sixteenth century. It lived on in the spiritual lives of Catholic women and many men — until that last thread, too, was *cut* in the 1960s by the effects of Vatican II. The modernizing "renewal," as Vatican II called its work, essentially reinforces the age-old insistence that power flows *solely* from and through the male to the female; any variation, however partial, will not be tolerated. The time is long past due for the aggressive patriarchal forces hiding behind that particular "renewal" to engage in an examination of conscience.

Stop teaching young people that Mary is a problem, a danger zone within Catholicism. I heard that warning from a young man in his late twenties, a college graduate, when I rode in his taxi to the airport in Columbus a few years ago. As soon as I got into his cab, I could see it was unusual — a very large sign hung over the back of the front seat advertising an upcoming Knights of Columbus raffle, a hapless saint dangled from the rearview mirror, and various magnetic religious medals were affixed to the dashboard. We chatted about our common background in the Church and, though he seemed a bit rigid, I eventually brought up Mary. "Oh, Mary," he said gravely, "You gotta be careful about Mary." He went on with what I knew would be the Knights of Columbus rap on her, as I had clipped a K-of-C coupon from the Sunday newspaper ("What do Catholics believe about the Virgin Mary?") and had sent away for their booklet, *Mary, the Mother of Jesus*. Its message, unsurprisingly, is that Mary is a model of cooperation through obedience. So when the young cabbie launched into his lecture, I wasn't listening. I drifted off immediately, thinking, "No, *I* don't have to 'be careful about Mary.' *I* know her intimately. *You* have to be careful about her, lest her heart melt your own and hold you in a cosmological embrace so profound that all your patriarchal structures would seem bizarre." When we reached the airport, I gave him a good tip. You gotta feel sorry for the Motherless sons of this world.

Catholic men who are at least my age have experienced both the fullness of Mary in the first part of their lives and her near absence since Vatican II. As I was discussing the topics in this book with a friend of mine, his conversation turned to a recent tragedy, the suicide of his elder son's friend, a sophomore at a respected university. No one close to the boy could think of any reason why he did it. My friend was silent a while, then brought up our earlier subject and explained something to me about the male psyche: "There's so much pressure on young men to see whether they've got what it takes, whether they're good enough to make it. They desperately need an underlying matrix that lets them feel everything is all right. Mary provided that for my boyhood and my entry into the world of men. Her loss in these young lives today is immeasurable . . . and they don't even know it." I thought of Andrew

Greeley's poem about the fate of Marian spirituality after Vatican II, "Our Lady's Day in Harvest Time": "The blue mantle hangs useless from the peg.... Summertime — and yet we are cold.... we orphans, chilled and alone, among the rotting roses."[31] In a similar vein, the distinguished Swiss theologian Hans Urs von Balthasar has observed,

> Without Mariology, Christianity is in danger of becoming inhuman. Without Mariology the Church becomes functionalistic, without soul, a hectic enterprise without a resting place, alienated by over-planning. Because in this male-masculine world one new ideology replaces another; everything becomes polemical, critical, bitter, humorless, and ultimately boring. People desert such a Church in droves.[32]

Quite right. Yet one hopes that the presence of Marian spirituality is embraced in men's lives not merely to rescue them from the "boredom" of patriarchal institutions but to *change* those institutions and social systems, to bring them closer to the Marian ideals of empathy and compassion. It is unlikely that the Blessed Virgin sees herself as a support for practices that are grossly unjust and harmful to women. Nonetheless, one can easily find examples of men who compartmentalize the comfort of Mary's female presence apart from their own patriarchal behavior. They honor the sacred dimension of the feminine writ large but cannot manage to acknowledge it in actual women.

Millions of Catholic women and men all over the world honor the full spiritual presence of the Blessed Virgin Mary. I believe that a great number of them join me in expressing the following sentiments to all those in the Church hierarchy who are bent on repressing her:

> Here's the deal: You men cannot have it both ways. Christianity and then Catholicism could not have spread as far and been taken into the hearts and minds of so many for so long without the enormously appealing presence of Mary in her cosmological fullness. She has drawn to her countless converts and lapsed Catholics. You both want and need all she brings to the Church, yet you now insist on jamming her into a little box so that her reduced form could be more easily managed for your current purposes. It is ever thus with patriarchal institutions: You could not survive without the presence and succor of the female, yet you cannot let her *be herself*. Mary has a history, a

lineage, and a powerful complex of characteristics — all of which have enriched Christianity. Why not honor that richness? Can you not at least learn from the past that if you forbid her full presence it simply grows back even stronger in the hearts of the faithful? If you remain bent on repressing her, you will fail . . . and you will damage your own spiritual life in the process. You simply have no idea what you are tampering with and violating. While you fixate on what one biblical passage or another says about Mary, you miss entirely — as Christ did not — deep engagement with the Maternal Matrix.

Mother of the Dispossessed

Chapter Six

Mary's Biblical and Syncretic Roots

Across borders of language and culture, a special kinship has linked millions of women for the past thousand years. They are related not through a surname but through the resonant variations of the name of the Blessed Virgin: Mary, Maria, Marie, Marija, Marianne, Marijanka, Marilyn, Marie Thérèse, Maria Elena, Mary Beth, Marian, and many more. In Central Europe, Catholic families sometimes gave their sons the middle name of Maria, as well, especially in Austria, Germany, and the Netherlands. Examples are the poet Rainer Maria Rilke, the novelist Erich Maria Remarque, and the actor Klaus Maria Brandauer. An Austrian friend of mine told me that his grandmother walked into town from their farm every week for some forty years to have coffee with her three best friends—who, like her, were all named Maria. I, too, was enrolled in that spiritual sorority, for my middle name is Marie, in honor of her.

The international kinship of Marian naming is embedded in the far larger spiritual kinship with all whose formative years were shaped—a little or a lot—by the presence of Mary in their lives. Our First Holy Communion procession outside the church to the statue of Mary, the pearly rosary I received on that day, the crowning of the May Queen in Mary's month, the little statue of Mary I was given to keep on my dresser, the countless recitations of "Hail Mary, Full of Grace," and my mother's and grandmother's low-key but unmistakably essential Marian spirituality—all these were common to a life shared with Mary. Even today I can hear in my memory the robust voice of our short, barrel-chested, and much beloved Irish American parish priest in the 1950s, closing his sermons and announcements with a vigorous coda that filled the church: "And remember the sick and the needy in your prayers to Our Blessed Mother."

Our Blessed Mother. We were all *held.* More than that, we were all held *together.* But how? Mary means so much to so many because the deepest spiritual and cultural streams converge in her presence. She is at once the Mother of each nation and the Mother of All Nations. In every Catholic country, a national Marian presence has evolved that includes attributes long associated with ancient religious expressions of the divine and semi-divine female in that culture. It was through Christianity's merger with these deeply embedded symbols of spiritual cultural that the new religion was able to take root so firmly. A large measure of Mary's appeal, then, is her inclusive and syncretic nature, which the Church, oddly enough, is loathe to admit, preferring to ignore the obvious.

Once Christianity became firmly established in various countries, the clergy downplayed and then denied its syncretic religious lineage. Their intensive dismissal, alas, fits a familiar pattern: Patriarchal institutions and movements have often achieved success only with desperately needed female presence and potency, which is subsequently shoved aside as being merely instrumental, something once useful but now superceded and properly forgotten. In most quarters of the Catholic Church, the very mention of the abundant evidence of continuity from the pre-Christian female divinities to the Blessed Virgin Mary is considered if not heretical at least in poor taste.

Instead of a supersessionist position — that is, the insistence on a radical break between the cosmological, goddess-like attributes in the spiritual story of the Virgin Mary and those of her female religious predecessors — the Church could more logically conclude, from their perspective, that *of course* all the powerful streams of ancient religions flowed into and found a Christianized place in the "greater glory" of the new religious era. All (neolithic Goddess) roads lead to Mary! The Church might well, in fact, be expected to reason that Christianity is so spiritually compelling (setting aside for a moment the many forced conversions and other horrors) that it is not surprising that it attracted earlier religious forms into its fold. Syncretic forms, then, would be acknowledged approvingly as testament to the spiritual allure of Christianity.

That response was, in fact, the one expressed by a group of Italian bishops after a slide presentation several years ago by the late archaeologist Marija Gimbutas in which she explicated numerous instances of continuity between an attribute or form of an indigenous goddess in neolithic Europe and those later attributed to the various national versions of the Blessed Mother.[1] The good fathers did not become apoplectic, as do many spokesmen for the Church, at the evidence of this continuity. Rather, Professor Gimbutas related to me, those bishops apparently felt that nothing is taken from Catholicism by acknowledging this irrefutable syncretism and that, indeed, it is deeply satisfying to realize that some aspects of Catholic practice have such deep cultural roots.

In fact, Mary's biblical story echoes those of her historical predecessors in several respects. Consider three key elements in Scripture: Mary produces a child parthenogenetically (that is, without benefit of sexual intercourse); it is a male child who is born at the Coming of the Light (winter solstice) and who becomes an important leader; and her divine son-god dies and arises at the vernal equinox. (Easter is set by the Church on the first Sunday after the first full moon following the vernal equinox.) Although the Church ignores such correspondences, these events in Mary's biblical life link her clearly with the pre-Christian neolithic traditions. Common to most of them was a goddess who produced a divine child through her own powers — or a mortal woman who was impregnated by divine intervention (such as the Holy Spirit), producing a demigod or hero. The goddesses Isis, Hathor, Inanna, Ishtar, Demeter, and Cybele were all, like Mary, both virgin and mother. Many of them produced a son-of-a-virgin who was half human and half divine, who was brought forth from a hidden place in the earth (for example, the cave-like stable in which Jesus was born), and who died and was reborn. In short, the biblical story of Mary and Jesus carries into a new era religious elements that are extremely ancient.

The roots of Goddess spirituality in Europe extend at least to 25,000 B.C., as indicated by artifacts from the upper paleolithic era. The archaeologist Marija Gimbutas concluded, after an extensive study of the pre-Indo-European symbol system (prior to 4400 B.C.), that ritual-ized depictions of various goddess forms were expressions of cosmo-logical processes, such as coming into being, maturing, passing away, and regenerating into new life.[2] By the time of the neolithic era, well established by 6000 B.C., one or more versions of the Goddess's mythic presence had been elaborated in nearly every region of south and southeastern Europe, as well as elsewhere in the Near East. The Goddess was considered symbolically a virgin, a *parthenos,* meaning not necessarily unacquainted with sex but a female figure who was one-in-herself, independent, not owned by anyone, and was possessor of vast powers of generation and regeneration. Some goddesses were said to partake of a ritual bath of renewal at a sacred site every year. Aphrodite, for instance, renewed her virginity annually by walking into the sea from the shores of Paphos.

Still, modern readers may wonder, "Why a goddess, "virgin" or otherwise? What's the point? Weren't they just primitive fertility-cult fetishes?" The dogged intoning of that sweeping dismissal in modern schooling is remarkably uninformed. Actually, the pre-Christian god-desses of Europe and elsewhere reflect complex dynamics and local particularities within the sacred whole. They were revered as the embodiment not only of elemental processes such as birth, death, and regeneration but also abundance, wisdom, justice, the arts, the home, and numerous other areas of life. In fact, *Goddesses in World Mythology,* a biographical dictionary published by Oxford University Press in 1993, cross-references 11,000 goddesses in *fifty-eight* categories of their attributes and powers. Fertility is merely one among the many.

But still, *why a Goddess?* The answer is the same as to the question *Why a God?* — only more so. Consider the basics: At every fraction of a second, the universe lays out trillions of possibilities for itself. Some paths are taken, others not. We humans call the profound creativity of the cosmos Ultimate Mystery, the Divine, Cosmic Consciousness, Goddess, God, the Tao, the Great Spirit, the Great Holy, or other names. We use the poetic devices of symbol and metaphor because only symbolizing can express in a multivalent, evocative way our necessarily partial and incomplete apprehension of the Divine. Our experiences with the ineffable resist capture by language or even highly charged symbols.

To cultivate communion with ultimate mystery, human societies have identified it in the presence of certain animals, impressive natural forces, or the ephemeral Taoist sense of "the Way." In cultures that consider themselves more "advanced," however, collective narcissism won out: Their sense of the Divine usually looks remarkably like themselves, either female or male. Historically, "Goddess" long predates "God" for a few very logical reasons. First, a sensible representation of the Divine should partake of the cosmological dynamics that shape our physical reality: Early cultures everywhere could not help but notice that the tides of the female body (menstrual cycles) flow in rhythm with the twenty-eight-day cycles of the moon and the tides of the sea; that is, the female body functions on cosmological time. Second, both Earth and female were bountiful, producing plants, animals, *and people* through their cyclical changes. Then, after the female had waxed as round as the full moon and issued an infant, her breasts created milk to keep the newborn alive. Third, everyone could see that without maternal care and caring there would be no human life. So the living symbol of the Divine was most often cosmological, bountiful, and caring: It was female. Moreover, everyone who came from the body of a mother and The Mother was kin.

From the Stone Age to the present age, these spiritual touchstones of divine creativity in human experience have been revered. Mary Ever Virgin — cosmological, bountiful, and caring — lives in the hearts of millions today as she and her predecessors always have. Is not this remarkable 25,000-year spiritual stream cause for celebration rather than denial? Can any other cultural continuity compare? Her numinous resilience stands alone.

Numerous symbolic associations were transferred from goddesses to Mary. Birds, which appear frequently near her in the Early Christian frescos in the catacombs of Rome, had long been considered emblems of the soul in several Goddess religions. The dove, associated with goddesses of wisdom such as Inanna and Aphrodite, are sometimes seen in medieval art hovering over Mary's head, where they indicate the seven gifts of the Holy Spirit: wisdom, understanding, counsel, fortitude, knowledge, piety, and the fear of the Lord.

Like countless goddesses before her, Mary has a strong association with the moon. In addition to Mary's role as mediator between humans and the Incarnation, the logic of this symbolism resides in the periodicity of women's blood tides and the lunar cycles, from which the association with constancy is derived. The waxing, full, and waning phases of the moon were associated in Greece and elsewhere with the Triple Goddess. In Egypt and then the entire Roman Empire, Isis was associated with the moon and its gentle light, thought to bring life-giving moisture to plants and animals. Goddesses linked with the moon were also felt to control the tides and so were protectors of those at sea.

Several Near Eastern forms of the Goddess converge directly in Mary's story as it was shaped in the early stages of Christianity: Mariamne, the Semitic mother-god and Queen of Heaven; Aphrodite-Mari, the Syrian version of Ishtar; Isis as Stella Maris, star of the sea (the pole star of the Earth's axis); Maryam, the Ethiopian goddess; and others. Some legends held that Mary was the Fate-virgin, the first of the three temple Moera, or triple "Marys," who spun the thread of destiny. A Coptic text identified Mary as that same triple goddess of fate, incarnate as the three Marys who kept their vigil at the foot of the cross when Jesus was crucified. In the Orthodox tradition and in Gnostic texts, Mary is strongly associated with Sophia — who is Divine Wisdom and the World Soul — in Hebrew Scripture. Sophia herself was often associated with the goddess Isis or Hathor and was sometimes known as the Goddess of Wisdom. An embodied bridge between Goddess religion and the forbears of Mary may have been Sarah, the woman who married Abraham and gave birth to the lineage of the Jewish people. Some scholars assert that Sarah was significantly involved with the Old Religion, that of the Goddess.[3] When Sarah died, she was interred in the womb-necropolis of the Goddess of the Anakim.

In the earliest phase of Christianity, as the "Jesus sect" within Judaism began to spread throughout various cities of the Roman Empire around the Mediterranean basin, where some 90 percent of the population was pagan, the sacred story about a virgin mother, who had been impregnated by (a) God, and her sacrificial son, who arose from the dead, was received as a conceivable variation on a very old theme. Later, the emergent Christian teachings about a triune concept of the Divine (that is, the Trinity) were reminiscent of the older triune form of the Divine in Goddess religion. The Triple Goddess was known in several forms in various areas, such as the pre-Greek triad of Artemis (tender maiden / waxing moon), Selene (bountiful mother / full moon), and Hecate (wise crone / waning moon). (The official Trinitarian formulation was finally declared by the bishops' Council of Constantinople in 381.) In addition, Mary's sacred maternal role was familiar to many of the converts. The goddess Isis, popular in Roman culture, was often depicted seated on a throne and holding her small son, Horus. Once Christianity became established, and the Christianized Roman Emperors began to suppress paganism, these statues were gradually renamed "the Virgin Mary" or became models for new Marian statues. Since Isis was dark-skinned, having come from Egypt, such statues and scores of similar dark goddesses became known as "black virgins" or "black madonnas." Many shrines to Mary as the black madonna in Sicily and other parts of southern Italy, for instance, are located on or near sites of neolithic Goddess religion.[4]

In the fourth century, a group of Christian women in Thrace and Upper Scythia (lands west and north of the Black Sea) created their own rituals to the Blessed Virgin Mary in which they offered sacred loaves to her in a ceremony that lasted several days. This practice, having ancient roots in Goddess religion, was found alarming by the local bishop. The women were derided as "Collyridians" (meaning followers of a small loaf of bread) and were soon declared heretics.

As Christianity spread across Europe, its gradual acceptance was greatly facilitated by the convergence of local goddesses with the Great Mother of the new faith. In Wales, Mary and the White Goddess were conflated to yield the White Mary. In Ukraine and Russia, the iconography of Mary-Rusalka, a tree goddess associated with birds and animals, became intertwined with the symbolism of the Virgin Mary, particularly the tree of life symbol, as well as the birch tree and water. In the Baltic cultures, several characteristics of Zemyna, the goddess of fertility, renewal, and justice, were blended into the symbolic presence of the new arrival, Mary. In Russia and Siberia, the birth goddess and earth goddess Kildisin was merged with Mary, as was the virgin goddess Boldogasszony in Hungary. In the Basque country, the Virgin Mary was merged with the indigenous goddess Mari. In Greece, Mary sometimes became the new occupant of goddess temples, such as Athena's Parthenon, but more often churches were built in her honor over or near the ancient sites. In Italy, churches named for Mary were constructed over the cave of the Magna Mater in Rome and elsewhere over shrines to the goddesses Juno, Isis, Minerva, and Diana. These are but a few examples of a list that extends to every Christian country in Europe. In fact, several cultural historians have concluded that the early Church would have been a failure but for the broad appeal of the Blessed Virgin Mary.

In North America, Mary met her match, so to speak, in an indige-nous goddess who lived on a hilltop that is now part of Mexico City. Together they became the Virgin of Guadalupe, patron saint of Mexico and protector of the poor. Her image spread throughout Central America and parts of South America and was eventually carried lovingly across the border to the United States, where it is a common sight in Catholic churches today. By all indications, she seems to be impervious to the Marian diminution declared by Vatican II. As the version of the Blessed Virgin that is indigenous to the Americas, the spiritual allure of Our Lady of Guadalupe has spread far beyond communities of Mexicans and Mexican Americans, her nearest rela-tions. Lately I have noticed her image in the homes of many American women whose backgrounds are not Latino or even Catholic.

As elsewhere, the broad appeal of Mary in any particular version is so spiritually organic that words cannot capture its fullness. Still, a few reasons for the Virgin of Guadalupe's widening circles come readily to mind. First, she is one of the most cosmological depictions of Mary: Wrapped in a cloak of starry heaven, with the rays of the sun emanating behind her, she stands poised on a crescent moon. One or two of these elemental associations were often conveyed in medieval European iconography of the Virgin, but not usually all three. Another of Our Lady of Guadalupe's cosmological dimensions is her state of preg-nancy with the Divine: she is cosmologically *bountiful*. Second, her complexion is light brown, so she is clearly emblematic of native cultures and the new nationality born from the union, usually not voluntary, of indigenous women with the Spanish conquistadors. That is, she is a maternal figure of the dispossessed and dominated who, without military might, caused the brutal invaders to kneel in worship before her. Such a satisfying reversal — one that has remained in place for 470 years. Third, Our Lady of Guadalupe is spreading across North America because she is the face of the Blessed Virgin that emerged from this continent.

The story of the Virgin of Guadalupe takes place only ten years after the conquest of Mexico by Cortes and his legions. Before dawn on December 9 in 1531, an Indian man, a widower who had been christened Juan Diego by the invaders, was crossing the foot of a hill that had long been associated with Tonantzin, a Totanec goddess of earth and crops who eschewed the Aztec preference for human sacrifice. Oddly for that time of year, he heard birdsong, a multitude of birds singing back and forth in soft and sweet harmonies. He looked toward the top of the hill where the music seemed to be coming from and saw a shining white cloud that was brightest at the center and was surrounded by a rainbow. As he stood wondering if he had been transported to an ancestral paradise, the birds fell silent, and Juan Diego heard his name called with the affectionate diminutive *my little son* in his native language, Nahuatl. Following the sound to the top of the hill, he saw a beautiful lady standing amid the rocks, mesquite, and cacti, all made luminous by the radiance of her garments. She asked where he was going. When he replied that he was on his way to mass in Tlatelolco, the lady told him, "I am the Ever-Virgin Holy Mary, Mother of the God of Great Truth." ("The God of Great Truth" was a term used by the Spaniards to distinguish their god from that of the Indians.) She would like a church, she explained, to be built on that very hilltop, Tepeyac, from which she would dispense her loving compassion to all who seek her help in their work and in their sorrows: "I am your merciful mother and the mother of all the nations that live on this earth who would love me, who would speak with me, who would search for me, and who would place their confidence in me." She then instructed Juan Diego to tell the bishop in Mexico City what he had seen and heard and to relay her request for a church.

In the corridors of power, Juan Diego was made to wait a very long while before finally being received by the bishop, who did not find the Indian a trustworthy source of information. He dismissed Juan Diego, telling him to return some other time so that he could be questioned more thoroughly. Juan Diego returned to Tepeyac the same day and reported the bishop's response to Mary, suggesting that his lowly status made him ineffective as a messenger and that she should select someone more highly valued in the new society, perhaps a Spanish nobleman. Addressing him as her abandoned son, the luminous vision told him to return to the bishop the next day and repeat his story, making clear that he is sent by "the Ever-Virgin Mary, the Mother of the God Teotl."

Again, Juan Diego's earnest account was translated to the bishop, including Juan Diego's recognition that the lovable Mother of Teotl was the same Mother of the Spaniards' *Dios* in the form of Jesus Christ. The bishop this time told the Indian to bring him some proof of the alleged visitation, a sign that he was indeed sent by the Lady from Heaven. Although the bishop sent some retainers to follow Juan Diego, he disappeared in the mist in the vicinity of the hilltop Tepeyac, where he related the bishop's demand to the luminous Lady. Juan Diego was told to return the following morning, Monday, for a sign to take to the bishop, but he did not do so because one of his uncles, Juan Bernardino, had become seriously ill with a fever, probably smallpox or typhoid. Early on Tuesday morning Juan Diego was dispatched by the family to bring a priest so that his uncle could receive Last Rites.

On this errand he avoided crossing the top of Tepeyac and took a lower route, as he feared that the Lady would reproach him for failing to come the previous morning. The Virgin, however, appeared in his path. She assured Juan Diego that there was nothing to fear, neither for himself nor his uncle, who was already made well, adding, "Am I not here, your mother? Are you not under my shadow and protection? Am I not your foundation of life? Are you not in the folds of my mantle, in the crossing of my arms? Who else do you need?" She asked him to climb the hill, gather the flowers growing there, and bring them to her. Although puzzled, since not even cacti bloom in December, Juan Diego climbed the hill. There he saw many varieties of fragrant roses, free of frost and shining with dew that looked like pearls. He tied two corners of his *tilma* (a blanket-cloak woven from the fiber of the maguey cactus) together behind his neck, forming a pouch with the free-hanging half, and gathered the roses, which were varieties that grow in the region of Castile in Spain. When he rushed them down the hill to the Lady, she arranged the roses in the pouch and instructed him not to open his *tilma* to anyone until he was in the presence of the bishop himself.

Juan Diego then hurried to the bishop's office, where he was made to wait even longer than before. When the retainers rudely demanded to see what he was carrying, Juan Diego realized that his only hope of being admitted to the bishop's chamber was to show them a bit of the fresh roses. On being informed of this, the bishop ordered him to be shown in immediately. Juan Diego then told his story to the bishop and several other officials who were present. When he untied the bottom of his *tilma,* causing the roses to cascade to the floor, the Spaniards' eyes grew wide. They sank slowly to their knees. It was not the out-of-season Castilian roses that struck them with such awe but an image on the *tilma* of the Blessed Virgin Mary exactly as Juan Diego had described her.

Bishop Zumarraga prayed with tears and sadness that Our Lady might forgive him for failing to believe in her presence. He then reverently carried the *tilma* to his chapel and later to a public display in the cathedral, where crowds soon gathered to pray. He asked Juan Diego to stay with him for the rest of the day and to show him the next morning the place where the Blessed Virgin had appeared. Construction of the church and hermitage she had requested began immediately; once completed, Mary's home on Tepeyac would house the *tilma* for all to see. Finally Juan Diego was able to return home, where he found his uncle, Juan Bernardino, fully recovered. His uncle, too, had been visited by Mary, who told him the name by which she wished to be known in Mexico: The Eternal Virgin Mary of Guadalupe.

The name *Guadalupe* was the Castilian appropriation of the Nahuatl name related to the Spanish officials by Juan Bernardino. The Nahuatl name for the luminous lady was probably Tlecuauhtlacupeuh (She Who Comes Flying from the Light like an Eagle), or Tequantlaxopeuh (She Who Banishes Those Who Ate Us), or Coatlaxopeuh (She Who Crushed the Serpent's Head). The correspondence to the sound of the Nahuatl name that made eminent sense to the Spaniards was *Guadalupe,* a town in the province of Estremadura in Spain, home of Cortes and many of the conquistadors. It is also the site of a famous medieval Marian shrine in Spain, Our Lady of Guadalupe. While it is true that the Spaniards' acceptance of the brown-skinned Virgin of Guadalupe at

Tepeyac accelerated conversions to the Catholic Church in Mexico, it was henceforth a national church with La Morenita (the small dark woman) at the fore.

The theologian Virgil Elizondo has suggested in *Guadalupe: Mother of the New Creation* that the title by which the dark-skinned Blessed Mother introduced herself to Juan Diego — "the Ever-Virgin Holy Mary, Mother of the God of Great Truth" — had deep significance for a conquered and degraded people. In view of the widespread rape of Indian women by the conquistadors, the abandonment of the *mestizo* children, and the shame felt by the Indian men because they could not stop these violations, the eternal virginity of the pregnant La Morenita was a sign of the resilient integrity of those who have been sexually violated and humiliated. On Tepeyac, Mary took on the flesh of the Indian women of the Americas. Untouched by abusive hands, she is "husbandless" but bears new life within her. As one of the conquered peoples, she understands brokenness, yet her presence reminds them that a divine virginal purity lives within, even when assaulted by sinful men.[5]

The story of the Marian visitation in Mexico was recorded in 1648 by Fr. Miguel Sanchez, a creole Franciscan, who drew on the traditional oral account of the events. A long poem in Nahuatl, the *Nican Mopohua,* also relates the story. This native narrative, originally thought to date from the mid-1500s, was "found" (or composed) the year after Sanchez's recording of the oral sources. The most dramatic evidence of the visitation, however, is the mysterious *tilma* bearing the image of Our Lady of Guadalupe. In 1981 two astrophysicists from the National University of Mexico were invited to study the pattern of the stars in the Virgin's cloak. They found that it replicates the sky of December 12, 1531, as seen from the Valley of Mexico at 10:40 A.M., the time the image on the *tilma* was first unfurled. In the cloak, the constellation of Virgo (the Virgin) can be seen over Guadalupe's heart, the aurora borealis crowns her head, and Leo (the Lion of Judah) appears over her womb.

The fabric and coloring of the *tilma* have been officially investigated in 1556, 1666, 1756, and 1977. The most recent of those studies employed infrared photography and computer enhancement. What puzzles both artists and scientists who have examined the *tilma* is the startling clarity of the image superimposed on material woven from crude cactus fibers. Such material would be expected to disintegrate within twenty years, especially since it was damaged in a flood in 1629 and was touched and kissed countless times before it was put under glass in 1647. The image has neither cracked nor faded even though the figure has never been sized nor the paint varnished. In 1791 during a cleaning of the metal frame, nitric acid was accidentally spilled on the image but somehow caused no damage. In 1921 anticlerical leftist operatives placed a bomb in the flowers under the *tilma,* which hangs under glass in the Marian basilica on top of Teyepac, now surrounded by Mexico City. No serious injury occurred during the blast, and the glass over the *tilma* was not even broken in spite of forces so strong that a heavy iron cross nearby was twisted out of shape and the immediate area was pelted with shattered masonry, marble, and stained glass.

I have related the story of Our Lady of Guadalupe in full not because it is more important than the Marian visitations in other cultures but because all North Americans should be familiar with it as one of our informing spiritual expressions. In fact, Elizando, who has written insightfully on the cosmological dimensions of the Guadalupe visitations, has concluded after decades of reflection on her impact that no other event since Pentecost has had such a "revolutionary, profound, lasting, far-reaching, healing, and liberating impact on Christianity."[6] Guadalupe brought about the conversion of the Church in the New World, thereby bringing new cosmic life to the new humanity.

Undeniably, Nuestra Señora de Guadalupe is the soul of Mexico. When Pope John Paul II visited Mexico City in 1998, twenty years after his first trip there, huge crowds waved souvenir fans imprinted with two images: a large picture of the Virgin of Guadalupe looming over a smaller one of the pope. Knowing he is a pope who loves Mary, the multitudes cheered him in the midday heat all along his route and at a mass celebrated in a soccer stadium, as they held high their pictures of Guadalupe. During that visit, the pope declared that Our Lady of Guadalupe is now Patroness of the Americas and that December 12 is henceforth an official feast day of the Catholic Church in North and South America.

Guadalupe is at once protective, compassionate . . . and subversive. As Margaret Randall writes in the engaging collection *Goddess of the*

Americas / La Diosa de las Americas: Writings on the Virgin of Guadalupe (1996), when the Virgin was initially rebuffed by the bishop, "she had a strategy that would work. . . . Our Lady of Guadalupe is a warrior."[7] That rich anthology of Mexican and Mexican American poets and writers is dedicated by the editor, Ana Castillo, as follows: "In Her name — Whose Love is Endless, Who has never abandoned us. On the contrary, we have left Her too long."

This sense of the Virgin of Guadalupe as a powerful presence has also been explicated by Clarissa Pinkola Estés. In an essay titled "I Am Your Mother," she begins by declaring, "The Mother I know is not clean and demure. She is called La Conquista, meaning The One Who Conquers All and also Mother of the Conquered. She is a high-spirited Jewess and a *force majeure Azteca*." Noting that there is speculation today about whether Juan Diego really existed, Pinkola Estés comments, "Meanwhile, Our Lady, Seat of Wisdom, pays no attention. She keeps appearing to those in need without anyone's permission, without any institution's sanction." In reflecting on the words spoken by Our Lady of Guadalupe to Juan Diego on the morning he avoids the top of the hill — that she is his Mother, that he need not be afraid of anything, that he is under her protection — Pinkola Estés illuminates the deep connection between "La Nuestra Señora, this Mir-yam, Maria, Madre Guadalupe" and the history of the Mexican people:

> The meaning in these words cannot be interpreted by the cosseted or by those who are secure. They must be interpreted by one who has been conquered. To such, they command: "Get up off your knees. . . . You were not born to beg for your life, to be happy with crumbs. Proclaim that I am with you, that you move under my aegis, that you are mine and I am yours." She makes clear, "You belong to no ruler other than the greatest Source imaginable. You are not abandoned, for I am here, and I leave no one stranded."[8]

Catholic spirituality as it is actually *lived* in every Catholic culture is shaped by syncretic mergers with the Blessed Virgin Mary. Yet it should not be concluded from all this convergence in the presence of Mary that she is the "tainted," pagan part of Christianity, while Christ is the pure part. His story was also mythologized in similar ways in the decades following the death of the historical Jesus, a Jewish "agitator" executed by the Roman occupation forces. The heroic end of Christ's life mirrored familiar stories of the dying and returning gods such as Osirus, Adonis, Attis, and Dumuzi. Each was accompanied in his life by the Goddess in some form: Isis with Osirus, Venus with Adonis, Cybele with Attis, and Inanna with Dumuzi. Some scholars also see traces of Zoroaster and even Dionysos in the story of Jesus. Certainly the influence of the cult of the Roman god Mithras is evident.

Remarkably, the Victorian mythologist, James George Frazer, author of *The Golden Bough,* managed to retain his professorship at a Christian university in England while proving that nearly all the elements in Christianity had been adopted from pagan sources. We should hardly be surprised, for that is how human nature, and indeed all of nature, functions: Life evolves via an interplay of novelty and continuity. The latter is very difficult to kill off, even though the ideologues in every triumphalist movement always try. In religion, Judaism declared a radical break from paganism in Canaan, and Christianity subsequently declared a radical break from both Judaism and paganism. In politics, the Enlightenment declared a radical break from all such religious foolishness; the Nazis declared that the beginning of their Thousand-Year Reich was a radical break from all that came before; and various communist governments declared Year Zero or Year One when they took power. Yet the past always lives on in the present. Denying that dynamic is a futile strike against our evolutionary nature and hence is unhealthy.

While it is true that Mary's role of mediator was foreshadowed by various passages in Hebrew Scripture, her role of compassionate Great Mother to whom mortals turn in times of need was also foreshadowed by the ancient goddesses, such as Tonantzin on the Mexican hilltop Tepayac. Mary's predecessors were often seen as protectors of a region or a sector of life, such as protector of the arts or the home. In many cultures their help was invoked for the fertility of fields, for safety on a journey, or for just deliberations in civic institutions. Even the rationalist civil society of classical Greece swore their oaths of honor by invoking the name of Gaia, Mother of All, or other goddesses.

The characteristics of Mary and her predecessors are viewed in "sophisticated" quarters of academic religious studies today as more or less meaningless in terms of conveying any spiritual reality ("reality" being seen as an entirely relative concept) but valuable as clues to the "identity formation" of the groups who expressed them. That is, the deconstructionist perspective sees religion as nothing but a social construction, a cultural structure that reflects and addresses the concerns of a particular people, usually in ways that legitimate the power of some people over others. Contrary to this assumption of extreme relativism, which holds that actual truth or inherent value is impossible since all concepts are simply made up, one can see that to be culturally connected to the cosmological realities is to participate consciously in the truth of our larger context, rather than falsely deny it. What can be said of peoples who elaborated an intimate, poetic symbol of the Maternal Matrix, the life-giving "plenum" from which all forms manifest and pass away in this universe, is not that they were childlike and ignorant but that they were perceptively aligning their deepest spiritual identity with the larger, profoundly relational reality, rather than holding it at arm's length, as does the ideology of both modernity and deconstructionism.

Indeed, it seems that the modern impulse to shrink and devalue the influence of the Maternal Matrix can have repercussions in a people's collective psychology. Is it a coincidence that the northern European cultures that dumped "*big* Mary" in the sixteenth century are commonly perceived as being colder and fostering an insular sense of self in their people? Or was it the other way around: Did those cultures go along with the Reformation's radical diminution of the Blessed Mother because she stood for a profound interrelatedness in life that they simply did not feel?

Speaking from the perspective of depth psychology, C. G. Jung declared in *Answer to Job,* 1958, that the papal definition of the Assumption of the Blessed Virgin into Heaven as dogma of the Church in 1950 was the most important religious event since the Reformation. When a longing for the exaltation of the Mother of God passes through the people, Jung felt, they are signaling their desire for the birth of a savior and peacemaker whose "birth in time" can be accomplished only when it is "perceived, recognized, and declared by man." Jung seemed to anticipate the great debate that was to split Vatican II a few years later over the modern "ecclesio-typical" view of Mary as a mere cipher, or sign, in the gospels that represents the Church: He warned that, just as the person of Christ cannot be replaced by an organization, so Mary cannot be replaced by the Church. "The feminine, like the masculine," Jung wrote, "demands an equally personal representation."[9]

So I am grateful for the male poets, painters, and composers and the choirs of male voices singing Mary's praise. They give me hope. I am grateful, too, to the often exasperating Roman Catholic Church for creating and protecting (until Vatican II) a prominent space for the Great Mother of the West. To imagine the cultural history of the West without her is a bleak exercise indeed. Nobel Laureate Seamus Heaney feels that the Irish Catholic poet's imagination, for instance, has been blessed because he partakes of the "ancient feminine religion of Northern Europe, which offers him a lens through which he looks at a landscape which has become a memory, a piety, a loved mother."[10] Hence the Muse lives on. Heaney has often suggested that Marian folk-religion both molds and expresses the deepest core of a people, incorporating the tender, primal, and maternal power of nature as part of the complex forms of Marian Christianity. Many of his poems express the difference he noticed during his youth in Northern Ireland between Protestantism and Protestant ways of working, thinking, and praying, which were "masculine, active, hard, phallic," and Catholicism, which was "yielding, maternal." The historian of Christianity Eamon Duffy has noted, "For Heaney, Christianity without its Marian dimension is an arid, abstract thing, like the mind of the Presbyterian neighbor, 'a whitewashed kitchen, hung with texts, swept tidy as the body o' the kirk.'"[11]

One may even deduce that the convergence of the ancient Motherline, via Mary, with Christianity not only contributed spiritual continuity to balance the new venture but also explains a theological puzzle as well. Christ's gospel of love is profoundly relational and compassionate, but where did that emphasis come from if he was solely an offspring of the legalistic and sometimes punitive Yahweh? Where else could Jesus' emphasis on loving compassion and forgiveness have come from but the other half of his cultural and spiritual "DNA": Mary and the long lineage of mother goddesses she continued. Not all goddesses are peaceful, but Mary's primary identity as Great Mother brought the relational logic of compassion, or maternal ethics, into her son's

Incarnation, which yielded a truly new story. The wrathful sky-god — who long pre-dates his Hebraic form as Yahweh — is tempered at last.

In reflecting on this theological insight in the fall of 1999, as the new millennium approached, the memory of my childhood catechism came to mind. The *Baltimore Catechism,* with its light blue and white cover, was the booklet of religious instruction used in parishes and schools across the United States during the post-World War II period. It was straightforward and supremely confident: *You have questions? We have answers!* We children read the questions (*Who made us? Why did God make us?* and so on) and memorized the answers given under each one, reciting them back to the nuns. It has occurred to me, however, that a more historically informed theological reflection about the syncretic nature of Christianity and its early blending with aspects of the extent Goddess religion might result in some different answers — as well as different questions. Here follows, then, an imaginative catechism in the form of a prose poem. The final question is a pop quiz, which the seekers themselves — that is, the catechists — must answer.

A Catechism on Mary at the New Millennium

Why do we mark the millennium?
Because two thousand years ago Mary gave birth to a miracle.

What sort of miracle?
She gave birth parthenogenetically
to a son born at the coming of the light of Winter Solstice
who died and was reborn at the Vernal Equinox.

Why those three particulars?
It was the Ancient Way,
the neolithic tradition of the Great Mother goddesses.
Mary followed it perfectly.

But why?
Greece had fallen.
Hera was reduced to an impotent shrew,
Athena made a Zeus-born martinet,
and Gaia — even Gaia, Earth Mother of All —
was paired off with Ouranos to breed . . . what?
The new thug-gods and titans and strife.
Babylonia, too, was long lost to the coup,
with Tiamat murdered by Marduk,

who then slashed her primordial corpse.
Nor had Canaan escaped the new order:
   Even Ashtoreh was now called a whore!
   They smashed her images,
   felled her sacred groves,
   slew her faithful.
On Sinai, Olympus, and Abu
   the new sky gods entrenched for their reign,
      with Earth no Great Mother but mud at their feet.
They shut down forever (how smug they all felt)
   the Way of the Mothers,
   which knows
      All beings born of the Earth are kin,
   and which insists
      Deep relationships have deep responsibilities.

What happened then?
There was one last chance for the Motherline —
   with its blood-tides and life-milk and care,
      with its full-moon bellies, its nectar and bliss —
   to assert the primacy of compassion over legalistic whim:
   a merging of the lines. In Israel!

Much earlier, Sarah the Priestess had tried
   — with the patriarch Abraham —
   to link the two Ways,
      but her guidance was soon overrun.
This time a *divine* convergence
   would join the new Era of the Sky God
      with the ancient wisdom of EarthMotherLove.

Mary, a simple Jewish peasant girl (with Sarah in her veins!),
   would give birth to a miracle.
   In her paleowomb she would grow a Redeemer,
      formed of the Motherline and the Sky God,
   a holy child whose passion would be the Gospel of Love.

Had Mary no visitation, then, from the archangel Gabriel?
She did.
It was a beautiful annunciation of feminine finesse:
   Hearing the angel's message
   of God's desire for a son,
      she demurely replied, "So be it."
Mary even added joyfully, "My soul exalts the Lord!"

And so it did, for she was deeply pleased
   with the joint parentage of her child,
who would merge the heart and mind of both traditions.
She quickly took a kindly old man, a carpenter,
   for a husband and earthly father
      for the Christ child.

Did Jesus honor the Motherline within him?
   Like Olympian Athena before him,
   he thought himself born of pure fatherwill.
      Still, he drank in Mary's sustenance —
         all three Marys', Martha's, too,
      wondering why, it often seemed to him,
      they nearly knew his words before he spoke.
   So he might well have said,
      as the end drew near and his followers felt such fear,
      might well have approached the Blessed Virgin and,
         placing his hand so tenderly on his source,
         declared to all:
         "Upon this womb I build my church."
   Instead he called on Peter.

Of course, of course — Mary remained devoted.
She was there at the foot of the cross, kneeling for hours,
   silently emanating waves of love and deliverance
      as her son gasped his long, slow death.

Where were the male disciples?
   Well, those Roman soldiers were so intimidating.

Oh.

And then?
   Then the "Jesus movement" spread,
      first as a Jewish sect, later as a new religion
         cutting a Faustian deal
         for the remnants of the Roman Empire.
   Once again, the persecuted became the persecutors,
      succumbing to history's brutal lack
      of imagination.

But the Gospel of Love remained core!
   For most of the faithful, yes.
      The bishops, however, were captured
         by temptations of power

and expansionist dreams.
They directed a second great merger,
this time forced and complete,
deploying the image of Mary
as its front.
They built churches and cathedrals
over sacred springs, groves, and wells
of the old religion
all over Europe,
turning the local goddess
into a Christian saint
or even a version of Mary herself.

Didn't that strengthen the Motherline within the merger?
Look around. Need you ask?
The Law of the Mothers was rescinded —
and banished again and again.
So Mary asserted her presence . . . twice.
In the High Middle Ages,
all the great cathedrals of gothic elegance
arose in her honor:
The Queen of Heaven.
For more than three centuries
her *caritas* and compassion
shaped the Western world.

That didn't save the "Infidels" slaughtered in the Crusades.
Nor the women later burned as witches.
Nor the Jews forced into ghettoes.
Nor the native peoples of the New World,
martyred by Christian greed.
Nor the Africans taken as slaves.
Mary was violated by those failures,
then batted aside by the modern era
as irrational pap.
Luther forbade her "idolatry";
Vatican II followed suit.
Odd how nervous she makes some men feel.

And the second return of her presence, after the modern chill?
Now. Right now. Don't you see it?
Remember the Filipinos
bearing her statue

as they faced down Marcos's tanks?
Remember when *Solidarnosc,*
sustained by Our Lady of Czestochowa,
took on an empire?
Then there are the millions who will never
make the news.
Have you seen the faces of the poor,
   lit from within as they honor Our Lady of Guadalupe,
     cloaked with starry heaven,
     framed by the rays of the sun,
     and balanced on a crescent moon?
Have you heard their sweet songs
   to the Great Cosmic Mother?

At the dawn of the new millennium,
   six million strong petitioned Rome
   to restore Mary's former title: Co-Redeemer of the World.
     A merging of the lines —
     with both still present!
   The people see it clearly; the theologians fail.

Mary is the grand convergence —
   of space, belief, and time.
All three Abrahamic religions meet in her presence,
   the cosmic dynamic that cares.

She absorbs the world's suffering,
   gives peace in return.
     Hail Mary, full of grace!
   Hail Holy Queen, Mother of Mercy,
     our life, our sweetness, and our hope!

For two thousand years she has held us,
   the Great Mother of the West.
So — *why* do we mark the millennium?

Because Mary has made us twice blessed.

On several occasions I have presented this catechism at conferences as a dramatic reading with a small chorus reading the questions. The piece seems to be a rather invigorating experience for the performers and inspiring for the audience as well. No doubt, many Catholics and most other Christians will pronounce it a deplorable instance of *Going Too Far.* Yet the modernizers have been insisting since Vatican II that

Marian spirituality must "progress." Very well. The debate, then, should simply be over the direction of that progression. I find their direction to be regressive, constrictive, and antifemale, while I find my prose poem to be a measure of "progress" indeed, albeit playfully hyperbolic in spots.

The theological insight that Mary not only raised Jesus with the relational logic of maternal ethics — later called his Gospel of Love — but also contributed that psychological propensity to the formation of his body-mind in the womb is not, of course, the reason that Mary has traditionally been considered Co-Redeemer with Jesus by many in the Catholic clergy. There is a biblical and doctrinal case for this Marian title. The Vox Populi movement cites the foreshadowing of such a role in Hebrew Scripture (especially Genesis 3:15 and Isaiah 7:14), several passages in the New Testament (especially Luke 1:28 and 2:35 and John 19:26), and traditional Church teachings. Defenders of Vatican II's diminution of Mary assert, however, that she was never widely or officially regarded in the Church as Co-Redeemer. To counter, Vox Populi likes to cite a statement from the current pope: "Mary's role as Coredemptrix did not cease with the glorification of her Son." The full argument put forward by Vox Populi makes a convincing case that Mary participated in a special way *with* Jesus in what came to be known as the Christian path of redemption from sin and salvation in God's grace.

Admittedly, the two halves of the Virgin Mary's significance — the human and the more-than-human — seem barely congruent. Catholics seem invariably drawn strongly to one half or the other. "Progressives" find Mary's "glorified," cosmological version to be insupportable and distasteful, while others like myself have never once thought, from childhood on, of the powerfully compassionate Our Lady of Everything as merely a domestic role model, activist or otherwise. The key to understanding the continuity between the strictly biblical Mary and the biblical*plus*, cosmological, mystical Mary is the temporal expansion of the Redemption: The spiritual presence of the Blessed Mother grew and expanded along with the Redemption project from the final moment of Christ's sacrifice on the cross. Moreover, the cosmological context itself provides the continuity between human Mary (a particular expression of universe life) and grand-scale, cosmological Mary (a symbolic presence of the Maternal

Matrix, or the life-giving and supporting dimensions of the universe). Together, she is the cosmological, writ small and large.

Following the Crucifixion, the tiny "Jesus sect," bearing the redemptive story of Mary and Jesus, spread gradually through the eastern Mediterranean lands and eventually over all of Europe, its spiritual presence expanding syncretically, culturally, and cosmologically. Had it not grown in these ways, Christianity would have died out early on. In this chapter I have sought to demonstrate that not only did Mary play a unique and central role in the Incarnation and the Redemption but she is also inherent to other essential kinds of redemption and salvation in a cultural context of great complexity that extends beyond the focus of Christian religion:

- Mary saves us from loss and discontinuity by connecting us with 25,000 years of our spiritual and cultural history of the sacred female.
- Mary saves us from fragmentation of two sorts: she tenderly illuminates a people's collective and particular identity, while uniting ethnic and cultural diversity as the Mother of All Who Seek Her.
- Mary saves us from denying the kinship among Judaism, Christianity, and Islam: All three live in her spiritual presence.
- Mary saves the Christian faith from what C. G. Jung called "the odium of being nothing but a *man's religion* which allows no metaphysical representation of woman."[12]
- Mary saves us from the profound alienation of the modern mind, connecting us with the creative source of spiritual fecundity and the maternal ethics of compassion.

All five of these Marian blessings are related, of course, and they are not cause for gratitude among those Christian clergy who fear that glorifying the female somehow unleashes dangerous forces. That attitude, expressed in an Anglican book of essays, *The Blessed Virgin Mary* (1963), is still in play in certain Protestant circles: John de Satgé, an evangelical canon, warned in his essay, "The evangelical has a strong suspicion that the deepest roots of the Marian cultus are not to be found in the Christian tradition at all. The religious history of mankind shows a recurring tendency to worship a mother-goddess." *Well, of course!* Moreover, he continues, "the cult of Mary may be an intrusion into Christianity from the dark realms of natural religion. . . . an older religion, a paganism."[13] Dark realms? Christianity from the very outset was a convergence of the earth-honoring Motherline with the cult of the sky-god Father. The new Father-Son religion was immeasurably enriched by the compassionate and cosmological attributes of the Blessed Virgin Mary.

Mary's partial "goddess nature" — her larger, cosmological dimension — cannot be severed from the whole of her, from who she is and what she does in the fullness of her own integrity.

Mother of God

Queen of Heaven

Mother of Our Creator

Queen of Angels

Virgin Most Powerful

Chapter Seven

Her Mystical Body of Grace

In Mary the cosmological body of grace is merged with the bountiful female body. Grace — in a cosmological rather than a denominational sense — is our conscious experience of the unity in which we are embedded. It is our perception of the larger reality, the sacred whole, infused with the divine creativity called God, Goddess, or the Great Holy. We can speak of the cosmological *body* of grace because the cosmos constitutes a unity, unfurling the curve of space/time within the gravitational embrace. As for the bountiful female body, it too has always been a source of elemental mystery. Its blood tides flow in rhythm with the moon, then pause when it swells as round as a full moon and grows people from its flesh, keeping the newborns alive with food it has transformed into milk. Even in the age of science, mysterious paradox survives within this body. How could the tenderness of belly and breast accomplish such tough feats? The female body, both vulnerable and hugely resilient, has always attracted a charged reaction from culture, especially from the deepest pool of cultural response: religion. Honored or feared, the female is the matrix, the life force, the incomparable sanctuary.

The image of grace emanating from the *embodied* spiritual presence of the compassionate Blessed Mother presents a desperately needed corrective balance to Christianity's skewed conceptualization of spiritual life: its fixation with vertical transcendence *above* body and nature. Mary radiantly embodies transcendent grace, often in close association with the natural world, its hills, springs, and grottos.

Spiritual engagement with Mary — whether prayer, contemplative exercise, or conversation so intimate it needs no words — involves the entire bodymind. All energy, all cells and pulsing rhythms seem to enter into communion with her. Perhaps women and men experience this attunement somewhat differently. No matter what the details of Mary's statues, women know what it feels like under her robes, breasts rising as we breathe, sensations flickering here and there, the comfortable repose of our flesh. She knows all this about us, too. Knows how trauma lodges for decades in the organs and cells of our deeply relational selves. Knows what a broken heart feels like, the numbness of great loss of any sort. Knows the wrenching place where tears come from. We never have to explain (as if anyone could). She knows.

Is it otherwise for men who love Mary? In defense of the papal declaration that Mary's Assumption into heaven was henceforth an article of faith, the novelist Graham Greene, a convert, wrote in an essay in *Life* magazine in October 1950: "The Supreme Being, the Trinity, the Creator of all things, such phrases may once have excited thought, but they do so no longer. . . . But the statement that Mary is the Mother of God remains something shocking, paradoxical, physical."[1] The combination of near divinity with the procreative powers of the female body may indeed seem shocking in the modern era when the masculine is the norm and the feminine far less. Yet it was not always so.

Before and after the intensely masculine worlds of classical Greece and Rome, which viewed the female as an anomaly, she was culturally honored. The divine creativity of the cosmos and the Earth itself were often associated with a version of the Goddess in pre-Indo-European neolithic Europe, an era in which widespread burial patterns indicate roughly equal status between the sexes or somewhat greater honor for women. Later, in the city-states of Greece and the empire that was Rome, a few forms of the Goddess lingered on, but women were declared not rational, not citizens, and not primary (they were merely "misbegotten males" in Aristotle's influential view).

In the hands of the Early Church Fathers, Mary's "immaculate" status came to connote far more than her freedom from Original Sin (a concept invented by Augustine, not Jesus). She was deemed "immaculate" primarily because she was said to have been granted a divine exemption at the moment of her conception such that her soul was spared the stain of the Adamite sin. Further elaboration of the Virgin's "immaculate" state followed, however, and reflected the "internal logic" of certain patriarchal concerns (such as the desire for sex but the disgust at one's own lust and craving, and the "womb envy" that causes patriarchal cultures to devalue or denigrate menses, pregnancy, and childbirth): Mary's parents' coital union when she was conceived was said to be free of the concupiscence usually involved with coitus. Moreover, the Virgin herself was declared to be free of the monthly cycles of women, according to fourth-century theologians.

Regarding the delivery of the Christ child, Augustine, Ambrose, and Jerome all insisted that Mary was "ever virgin," or a perpetually "closed gate" before, during, and after childbirth. Ambrose explained that since Mary's hymen was not ruptured during Christ's miraculous delivery, Jesus was spared the usual "contagion of earthly corruption" involved with normal conception and birth: "For only the Lord Jesus was holy among all those born of a woman."[2] While it is perhaps clinically interesting, in terms of the misogynist psyche, that the holiness of Jesus is linked so closely with his deliverance from the normal maternal processes of birth, a far-reaching effect of these elaborations in the Western branch of Christianity was the denigration of sex, the female body, and birth-giving.

The Eastern Church Fathers avoided such bizarre extrapolations by holding that Mary's perpetual virginity was spiritual in nature. By adopting this definition, they carried on the ancient, symbolic meaning of virginity as it had long been held in many pre-Christian traditions: the perpetual renewal of the natural world in the earth-body of the sacred female. In addition, understanding Mary's perpetual virginity to be spiritually symbolic accommodates the references in the gospels to Jesus' brothers (including James, who was the head of "the Jesus cult" in Jerusalem for thirty years after the Crucifixion) and perhaps sisters (although some scholars believe that these relatives were either cousins or half-brothers and -sisters from an earlier marriage Joseph could have had).

Western Christianity maintained that the Blessed Mother's body was decidedly unlike other female bodies except in one respect: The first-century writers of the gospels and the fourth-century Early Church Fathers applied to Mary the contemporary physiological assumption, from Aristotle's science, that females are simply passive incubators for the tiny child who is carried in the male "seed." Following from this assumption of passive child-bearing in the gospels, Luther argued, as we have seen, that Mary should be regarded as "no more than a cheerful guest chamber and willing hostess."[3] This view seems to be prevalent as well among many "progressives" since Vatican II, who see no reason to think Mary was ontologically changed by bearing God-the-Son and, therefore, no reason to think she grew to have more-than-human capabilities. If we wish to reflect on the Nativity, however, why limit ourselves to such erroneous first-century assumptions about female physiology?

Theological reflection in every age ideally energizes the contemporary engagement with the Mystery of the Incarnation by bringing to bear the fullest, most current knowledge about the Creation. Twenty-first-century physiology reveals that a mother's body receives some of her fetus's cells and DNA, which can remain in her indefinitely.[4] Therefore, Mary's body contained cells of God-the-Son for the remainder of her days, which she spent as the First Disciple of the "Jesus sect." That is, divine presence entered Mary from the moment she assented at the Annunciation, and it never left. Moreover, contemporary science tells us that pregnancy and child-birth alter the mother's brain by creating new neural pathways.[5] Imagine the neural pathways that would develop in a woman's brain while God-the-Son was gestating within her and growing from her very flesh! Of course, Jesus was physiologically fully human, but he was also fully divine — and they both knew that, which surely must have lent a profound dimension to their intimate connection. That elemental connection became part of Mary forever. The Catholic tradition of *mystical* engagement with the *mystical* birth of Christ has long intuited this aspect of Mary's spiritual being: Mary after Christ was more than human, the luminous Blessed Mother. During the first several centuries of Christianity, this was particularly apparent to the laity. Many grassroots Christians considered Mary to be the Theotokos long before the Early Church Fathers decreed the title official.

With the great florescence of religious culture that infused Europe during the Middle Ages, female embodiment was honored once again in the West, as it had been in pre-Christian and pre-Greek times. The returning Crusaders brought back to Europe, beginning in the early twelfth century, numerous Near Eastern goddess statues, prayer beads, and the rose, all of which influenced the creative burst of new religious imagery and practices. Yet the impulse for the great medieval honoring of Mary — at once intensely spiritual and physical — was indigenous. It burgeoned forth as a profound correction, in all quarters of medieval society, of that which had been denied for several hundred years by the grimly misogynist Early Church Fathers in the era that used to be called the "Dark Ages." This pall was replaced finally by an extraordinary flowering of creativity. The breadth and depth of aesthetic brilliance evoked by communion with the Maternal Matrix during the Middle Ages in art, architecture, and religion has never again been experienced in the West.

Before considering medieval religious symbology, I must forewarn modern readers that the focus of so much spiritual energy on the female body in the twelfth through the mid-fifteenth century will probably seem as foreign as stepping into the neolithic heyday of the Goddess, say, 3000–1500 B.C. Even after immersing myself in this research, I find I can barely imagine the gestalt that must have resulted from the rich cultural and spiritual weave of medieval images of female embodiment. I experience that aesthetic and spiritual orientation more as an ache and an absence than as a collection of historical facts. For modern women, surely, there is pathos in the allure we feel for a Marian spiritual culture across vast stretches of barren time.

In truth, modernity's war against Mary is yet another strike against beauty itself. In a reactive swing against beauty as being too "femmie" and too dangerously moving (*horrors, to be entangled with feelings and possibly not in control!*), the foundational modern movements sought to situate all truth and value in media that are well suited for control: the text, empirical measurement, and instrumental logic. Even modern philosophy, via Kant, dismissed beauty as a simplistic, even if universal, human perception compared to what the modern philosophical male mind can grasp as "the sublime." In the modern world, beauty is considered merely epiphenomenal, quite beside the point. The fact that *nature* and *the female body* are the two associations most closely linked with *beauty* is more than coincidental to their being devalued in the ideology of modernity. In fact, one finds at the deepest layers of the "disciplined" modern thought a programmatic focus: The practices and assumptions of modernity evolved to soothe the fears and insecurities of males who have been raised with patriarchal socialization. Because nature and the female body have long been perceived as dangers by the patriarchal mind, they are, therefore, thought best conceptualized in patriarchal culture as *nothing very important.* Their beauty has no real hold on the truly "tough-minded." It follows that the deeply resonant spiritual beauty in the pre-Vatican II rituals honoring Mary were thrown out the window like so much old trash by the modernizers. The more thoroughly schooled in the ideology of modernity were the anti-Mary, antimystical young theologians and Council Fathers, the more their capacity for beauty had been killed off. They were Motherless sons marching in the new army, laying down the new law of a more virile, modern religion.

Yet we are now delivered to a different time, a historical moment supple with a rising vitality. I find that I have been changed by my immersion in the nonmodern outpouring of aesthetic and spiritual homage to Mary's mystical female body. I have sensed the possible: a world infused with her grace once again, not only as an aggregate of individuals' spiritual practices but as a collective engagement with female spiritual presence and embodiment writ large. I believe that a multivalent balance between male and female spiritual presence and imagery, far more complex than a simple polarity, might be restored once again.

Let us turn, then, to the sources and expressions of the Marian era that immediately preceded modernity, less with an emphasis on particulars than on the resultant ambiance of honor to the cosmological female.

In the Middle Ages, the procreative aspects of Mary's body were celebrated in spiritual language that partook of romantic imagery. The inspiration for such metaphors was the erotic Song of Songs (Canticle of Canticles), a love dialogue between a bride and groom in Hebrew Scripture that grew out of the oral tradition prior to 200 B.C. and may have originated, in part, in an earlier spiritual-erotic orientation, perhaps devotions to the goddess Ashtoreh (Astarte) or Inanna. (Judaism has a far more positive attitude toward sex than does Christianity but is less body-honoring than its predecessor in the Holy Land, Canaanite Goddess religion.) The Song of Songs was the most frequently commented upon book of the Bible during the twelfth and thirteenth centuries; by the following century, it was the most frequently quoted text from any source. The groom became Christ, while Mary represented the Church as the Bride of Christ. In twelfth-century Provence, in the south of France, metaphors for the Virgin Mary sometimes merged with the troubadours' songs of courtly love, in which passion and reason are reconciled for the elevation of humankind.

In both the Song of Songs and medieval writings about the Blessed Virgin Mary, the virginal female body — in particular, the womb and its approach — is called an enclosed garden. In visual depictions, Mary as Garden is seated within a walled garden (*hortus conclusus*), the heavenly paradise where she is now enthroned. In this association, Mary was again contrasted with Eve: Mary, the New Eve, brought redemption in the heavenly garden of paradise, while Eve had brought the fall in the Garden of Eden. (Note, however, that the meaning of every element in the Judeo-Christian story of Adam and Eve was turned inside out from its significance in the earlier, Goddess religions of the region. The snake was previously a symbol of regeneration and renewal, shedding and growing its skin repeatedly. The tree was previously the sacred bough, the tree of life. The female was previously honored, not vilified.)

One medieval legend that certainly pushed the limits was the mystical unicorn hunt, which was set in the heavenly garden with Mary at its center. Christ is the unicorn, an animal so swift and powerful that no man can catch it, but a pure virgin can lure it to her lap (or womb, as the Incarnation). The unicorn is eventually struck by arrows, as Christ was pierced by the Roman spear. This fanciful theological extrapolation was condemned by the Council of Trent in 1563, after which time it faded from use.

Like the garden, the rose was charged with bodily and spiritual significance in the medieval mind. The connotation of the red rose as a symbol of Venus (one of the goddesses called "Queen of Heaven," along with Isis, Hera, and Astarte) was brought back to medieval Europe by the Crusaders. Eventually, roses that were red, the color associated with love and suffering, were associated with Christ's bleeding wounds, while roses that were white, the color associated with purity, connoted the Blessed Virgin. The roses known to medieval Europe were not the tulip-shaped, modern hybrid tea roses common today; rather, they were usually single roses with five petals that arch open almost flat or else semi-double roses with a loosely open, cupped shape. Although the "rose" had long been a colloquial term in Europe for the female anatomy ("the little rose beneath the rosebush"), it was Christianized in the medieval world: Mary indeed had and was a rose, now celebrated as the Gate of Heaven, the mystical gateway of the Incarnation. The beauty and purity of Mary's intimate passageway was also symbolized by the white lily.

The rosary was developed at various sites in Europe between the eleventh and thirteenth centuries but was preceded in the East by knotted prayer cords used in Byzantine Christian practice, the Islamic chaplet of 99 beads, and the Hindu mala of 108 beads. Some of these Eastern "rosaries" were no doubt brought back to Europe by the Crusaders. The Western rosary had its origin in repetitions of the *Ave Maria* ("Hail Mary") prayer, which begins with two verses from Scripture. It opens with the archangel Gabriel's greeting to Mary at the Annunciation, "Hail, Mary, full of grace" (Luke 1:28, though a more accurate translation is "Hail, Mary, greatly favored one" or "long favored one"), and then melds with the greeting spoken by Mary's cousin Elizabeth at the Visitation, "Blessed art thou among women, and blessed is the fruit of thy womb" (Luke 1:42). By the eleventh century, it was widely believed that offering these words to the Blessed Virgin — 50, 100, or 150 times, counted on knotted cords or strands of beads — brought her joy by recalling the miracle to which she had assented. By the latter half of the thirteenth century, a manuscript titled *Aves as Roses* appeared in Latin, Catalan, and German. Eventually the *Aves* — called a collection of roses, a *rosarium* — were accompanied by a set of meditations based on reciting the 150 Psalms of Hebrew Scripture, interpreted as references to Christ or Mary.

In the late Middle Ages an emphasis on reenacting the life of Christ, especially the Passion, combined with the well-established metaphors of garden and rose. This narrative structure transformed the string of 150 beads into symbolic chaplets, or crowns, of rosebuds, while the meditations were divided into contemplation of the Joyful, Sorrowful, and Glorious Mysteries of Jesus and Mary. (The insertion of the Mysteries was initiated in Carthusian monasteries in fourteenth-century France.) In Germany a popular text on the rosary that was published around 1430, *Our Lady Mary's Rose Garden*, explained, "The [red] rose is the Word that the First Gardener, Who planted paradise in the beginning, planted in Mary's earthly womb."[6] She is the fertile earth that gives sustenance and life itself to the Savior. Guides to the rosary titled *The Garden of the Soul* became widely available during the 1500s.

With so much bodily specificity in the medieval honoring of Mary, it is not surprisingly that her breast milk was revered as the elixir of life that had brought the Incarnation to fruition. The earliest image in Christianity of the nursing Virgin (*Maria lactans*) is a late-second-century wall painting in the Roman catacombs of St. Priscilla. The painting reflects the influence of well-known images of the goddess Isis enthroned and offering her breast to the son-god Horus; the two were central figures in a religion that had spread from Egypt through much of the Roman Empire around the Mediterranean. Centuries later, during the medieval intensification of Marian spirituality, her breasts were understood to yield the miraculous milk of paradise. A popular legend held that Bernard of Clairvaux, the twelfth-century Cistercian monk who composed intensely beautiful Marian prayers, was reciting the *Ave Maris Stella* as a sickly child before a statue of the Virgin in the church of St. Vorles in Chatillon-sur-Seine when he came to the words "Show thyself a mother" and was amazed to see that the Virgin had appeared to him, pressing her breast and letting three drops of heavenly milk fall onto his lips. The legend — painted by Perugino, Filippino Lippi, and Murillo with Bernard depicted as an adult — assured all that the Blessed Virgin Mary may bestow material signs upon the faithful, granting even the very milk that had nourished the Savior. In some medieval depictions, streams of Mary's breast milk, the spiritual nectar of wisdom and mercy, flow like astral light into the mouths of people suffering in purgatory.

Medieval Christians were fascinated, if not obsessed, with the idea of holy relics — a splinter from the "True Cross" on which Jesus died, a finger bone of a saint, or, better still, some physical manifestation of the Blessed Virgin. Since Mary's milk was associated in medieval piety with her powers of healing and intercession with Christ, vials of what was believed to be the preserved substance itself eventually appeared at most of the major Marian shrines. Sometimes the dried miraculous milk was said to liquefy on certain holy days (feast days in the Church calendar). This excessive literalism was, of course, one of the targets of the Reformation. Calvin scathingly observed in his *Treatise on Relics* that although even the smallest town and convent display some of the Virgin's milk, she could hardly have produced so much even if she had been a wet nurse or a cow! His real target, however, was not the devotional excess but the spiritual exaltation of the Virgin.

The simple dress, or shift, said to have clothed Mary's body when she gave birth to the Savior was another relic that surfaced during the Middle Ages (and is still displayed in a glass case in Chartres Cathedral). Her body itself, it had long been held, had been "assumed" into heaven by Christ once her life on Earth had ended. Her role as the Queen of Heaven, in particular, sparked the imagination of medieval artists and composers. Later she was also called Queen of the Universe.

Mary as the Seat of Wisdom, or Throne of Wisdom — also known as the Virgin in Majesty — was a common image in the medieval world. Several notable examples were carved of fruit wood or set in stained glass during the twelfth and thirteenth centuries in France. In none of the Gothic cathedrals was the Seat of Wisdom depicted with more arresting grandeur than at Chartres, where the palace to the Queen of Heaven rises from the plain of Beauce, an hour southwest of Paris by train. As tourists and pilgrims approach the entrance, they are funneled single file into a simple wooden passageway that eases them from the sunlit jumble of the cathedral square into the gripping calm that lies beyond the inner door. Once they step inside, a vast enclosure of space soars before them with an almost unbearable grace. The tall rows of fluted pillars lining the nave, the exquisite contours of the vaulted ceiling, and the sensuous curve of the ambulatory wall all serve to deliver one's gaze to the central focal point: the great stained-glass window of the enthroned Virgin in Majesty looming high in the distant wall. Framed by a large mandorla, the Queen of Heaven reigns with a luminous dignity at the exact center as the Seat of Wisdom. Her small son is held securely on her lap as a profusion of jewel colors glow around her, forming reverent angels.

Most visitors are momentarily stunned the first time they enter the cathedral of Notre Dame de Chartres, then amble off quietly to explore, but I found I could not move at that point for what seemed like a lifetime compressed into something more intense. Standing just inside the door, 136 meters from the great window at the opposite end of the church, I slowly realized that although my eyes were held magnetically by the iridescent image of Mary enthroned, my bodily awareness was feeling, as much as seeing, everything at once. The entire enclosure felt like an enormous womb-body with the Holy Mother at the head — although that simile did not occur to me until much later when the experience was reduced to memory and would allow the approach of words.

My own body began to move toward the Virgin, sliding first one foot and then the other across the large smooth stones set into the floor of the narthex. It, too, delivered me toward the luminous Seat of Wisdom, for I found that the expansive entryway was slanted slightly upward, toward her. I slid slowly up the incline, my gaze still held by the looming figure of Mary but also aware of the slightly convex stones beneath my feet. Polished by 800 years of pilgrims' tread, the grid they formed had long since been softened into rounded corners and meandering sides, framing rich hues of gold, tan, and blushed beige as they caught the filtered light.

Once across the narthex, I found myself drawn slowly down the center aisle of the nave. As I approached the wide transept, my head now tilted back so that my eyes would not be torn from the great window, a sound reached my ears. In this silent space? With some effort, I grasped that the sound, which seemed to go straight from my ears into every cell in my body, was music: a choir, a group — not a large one — of sweet voices, a simple but lovely melody. I was literally pulled toward it, turning left, where I found myself facing the enormous north rose window, though I could barely take it in as the singers drew me closer, turning me now to the right, where they stood in a small chapel surrounded by about three dozen listeners. I saw that some fifteen women and three men were singing to the Blessed Virgin Mary in the form of a sixteenth-century black madonna, Our Lady of the Pillar. (The original wooden statue and column of jasper is said to have been presented to St. James by the Virgin Mary during a visitation in Spain in the year 40.) The pillar, I knew, was a stylized "tree of life" symbol long associated with pre-Christian goddesses and with Mary; when shown with the latter, a trunk-like pillar symbolizes the tree of Jesse (Isaiah 11:1). The dark brown wooden statue on top of it — the

Blessed Virgin holding Jesus, both wearing gold crowns — was only about fifteen inches tall and was dressed in a brocade gown. This elevated statue was set inside a fluted alcove of dark polished wood and flanked by dozens of containers of flowers, both cut and potted, plus scores of lit candles. As I drew near the singers, I found that this intimate chapel was extremely peaceful, a pocket of tenderness within the soaring walls and cavernous space.

I wanted to see the faces of the people singing to Mary, so I edged among the many observers and those praying until I was next to them. They were all fair with light brown or gray hair; their ages, I guessed, were between twenty and sixty. As they sang, all kept their gaze fixed on Mary, their faces lit with a purity and devotion that seemed radiant. I could not make out their language, so after they finished I asked the young woman beside me. It was Lithuanian, she smiled. I understood then that they were pilgrims who had journeyed across northern Europe to the palace of the Blessed Mother in order to sing their body-prayers to Marija.

Why does Chartres Cathedral have such an arresting effect that, for many, seizes the bodymind in an intense field of unity? Much has been written on the proportions of sacred geometry that comprise the design: the metaphysics of measure, number, and weight in which the Chartres Platonists excelled. The majestic handling of light and harmony, regarded in medieval thought as the formative and ordering principles of the Creation, has also been analyzed in depth. Less well known, though, is the fact that this masterpiece was built, in part, by local parishoners as a remarkable spiritual practice, a sort of local crusade during three periods corresponding with the Crusades to the Holy Land. Rich and poor alike in the town of Chartres and its environs bent their backs in harnesses to pull oversized wagons from the stone quarries five miles away. The "chariots" were pulled in complete silence, sometimes by as many as one thousand people. During rest periods nothing was heard but prayers, confessions, and the forgiveness of trespasses against one another.

In an eyewitness account, the Archbishop of Rouen wrote, "At the voice of the priests who exhort their hearts to peace, they forget all hatred, discord is thrown aside, debts are remitted, the unity of hearts is established." If anyone was "so far advanced in evil as to be unwilling

Joe Brainard, *Untitled (Madonna)*, 1966, mixed media collage, 21" x 16".

Petah Coyne, *Untitled (Mary/Mary)*, 1999-2000, mixed media, 104" x 77" x 31".

Susan Plum, *Lady-Unique-Inclination-of-the-Night,* 1998,
Recycled ironing board, roses dipped in wax, river rock, dried
rose buds, dragonfly stamp, 9' x 8' x 5'.

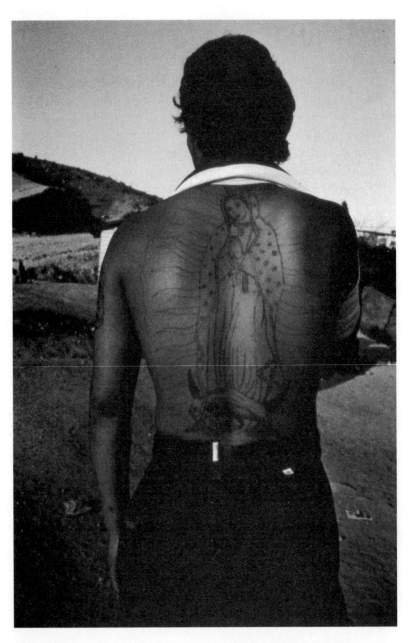

Graciela Iturbide, *La Frontera (The Border)*, Tijuana, 1990.

Raechel Marie Running, *Homage to Our Lady of Guadalupe,*
2002, mixed media and digital illustration from original photo.

Joseph Stella, *The Virgin,* 1926, oil on
  canvas, 39.5" x 39".

Christopher Castle, *Madonna of the
  Vines,* 1998, egg tempera, 9" x 7".

Robert Lentz, *Madre de los Desaparecidos / Mother of the Disappeared,* 1986, acrylic and 23-karat gold leaf on tempered masonite, 15" x 12".

Kayla Komito, *An Irish Mary: Our Lady for Girls in All Seasons*, 1997, watercolor, 15" x 11".

Mario Parial, *Our Lady of Mount Carmel / Nuestra Señ ora del Carmen,* 1992, acrylic on canvas, 48" x 36".

Ioana Datcu, Mother of Sorrows, 1999, mixed media and acrylic on glass, 14" x 11".

Mary Zarbano, *Pietà,* 2000, mixed media, 30" x 43".

Rose Wognum Frances, *Star of the Sea: Star of Evening, Star of Morning, Radiant Queen,* 1993, paint on canvas and wood, tooled gold leaf, incised copper, silk, beads, 30" x 27" x 4" with doors open.

Bernadette Bostwick, *Mary of the Cosmos,* 2002, acrylic on Russian White Birch wood, 11" x 8.5".

Kate McKenzie, *In Her Tender Arms,* 1998, acrylic on paper,
36" x 26".

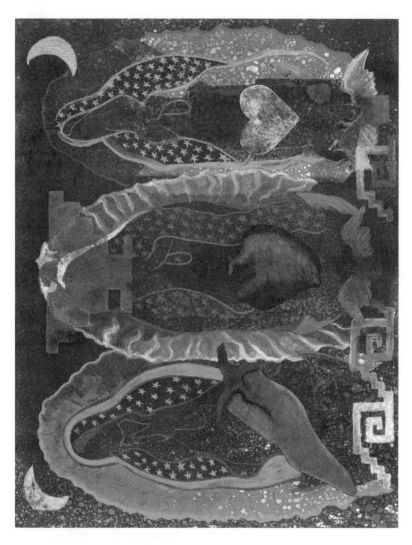

Rosa M. Huerta-Williamson, *Madre de las Americas / Mother of the Americas,* 1995, monoprint and collage, 11.5" x 15".

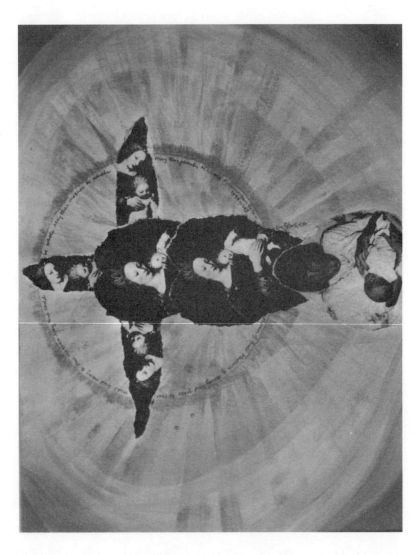

Pamela Eakins, *Mother of Grace,* 1998, mixed media, 11" x 14".

to pardon an offender," he was banished from the work by his peers, and any offering he had placed on the wagon was rejected. The end of the day's toil was also described by the archbishop:

> When they have reached the church they arrange their wagons about it like a spiritual camp, and during the whole night they celebrate the watch by hymns and canticles. On each wagon they light tapers and lamps; they place there the infirm and ill and bring them precious relics of the Saints for their relief. Afterward the priests and clerics close the ceremony by processions which the people follow with devout heart, imploring the clemency of the Lord and of his Blessed Mother for the recovery of the sick.[7]

The extraordinary presence of the cathedral of Notre Dame de Chartres is surely a result of both its inspired design and remarkable construction practices, yet it overwhelms any attempt to violate its mystical presence through analysis. One feels the interior of the cathedral in ways that the internal monologue in one's mind cannot even approach. To visitors whose spiritual lives have been touched or shaped by Mary, the indefinable dynamic of her *maternal body* suggests itself, if not quite consciously, as one faces the Virgin in Majesty in that vast and elegant space with the curving walls of the womb-like cathedral extending from either side of her image. In that palpable context, some feel that the large labyrinth set into the floor in the center aisle of the nave represents not only the contemplative path to Jerusalem and the esoteric structure of the universe (based on a thirteen-point star polygon) but also Mary's labial rose, through which the Incarnation entered the world. (Originally, a centaur or minotaur, symbol of the masculine, emerged at the center, or omphalos, of the labyrinth on a metal disk, which was reputedly seized for cannon fodder during the Napoleonic wars.) In fact, the rose, the intimate symbol of Mary, is found throughout the cathedral. As Henry Adams explained to his modern readers in *Mont-Saint-Michel and Chartres* with feigned pique, "Even twentieth-century eyes can see that the rose redeems everything, dominates everything, and gives character to the whole church."[8]

The year after my pilgrimage to Chartres Cathedral, the small side chapel honoring Our Lady of the Pillar, where I had heard the

Lithuanian pilgrims sing, was destroyed. After one hundred years, it was strategically "remodeled" in the fall of 1998 in ways that made the area as inhospitable as possible: A bright light was directed down onto the dark madonna, so glaring that she appeared almost white; all chairs and kneelers were removed except for three that were elevated in front of the statue, blocking any approach to it and discouraging the act of praying there by turning it into an elevated public display; the flow of tourists was channeled directly through the middle of the formerly peaceful sanctuary; and the abundant display of flowers and candles was removed.

Why this attempt to discourage devotions to the dark madonna? Was it simply "in line with Vatican II" and something the Church had been intending to get around to for thirty years? Was it ordered in the wake of the high-level rebuff in 1997 of the worldwide Marian petition drive by the Vox Populi movement? Or had there been yet another flare-up of that perennial problem for the Church, the association of the dark madonnas with the Goddess? Shortly after the "remodeling," the rector of the cathedral met with a woman who was making plans to bring a group there. On learning she was from California, land of errant thought, he hastened to interject that there are no goddesses in Chartres Cathedral because Mary is always depicted with her son! So were several ancient goddesses, of course, but his anxiety is telling. The following year, for reasons that are unclear, the small chapel to Our Lady of the Pillar was largely "demodernized" and restored to a version that approaches its former ambiance of devotional plenitude and tranquility — a happy, if puzzling, ending to the assault on that sacred space.

While the medieval cathedrals not only soared toward the abode of the Queen of Heaven but also suggested her ineffable spiritual presence, medieval painters were faced with a different sort of convergence: the task of expressing pictorially Mary's spiritual presence and her physicality as both the maternal and the eternal. This challenge proved so intriguing that it shaped the course of Western art. In fact, a young friend of mine told me after touring the great art museums of Italy that she had nearly stopped reading the title plates next to the paintings because they all said the same thing: *Madonna e Bambino*.

The vast outpouring of Christian art during the past two thousand years could not have been predicted by the first several centuries of the new religion, for Christianity inherited from Judaism a central focus on holy Scripture and an initial reluctance to depict the Divine visually. The Jewish prohibition against such depictions rests on theological grounds but was originally a response to strategic considerations as well: When the Levite tribes arrived in Canaan, Goddess spirituality was still alive and thriving in the Near East. The indigenous religious worldview from which the Levites sought to distinguish their sky-god orientation included ritual and pictorial honoring of the female and the sacred bough, plus ecstatic dance and other temple practices. In sharp contrast to their competition's celebratory focus on body and nature, the Levites emphasized the word: commandments, texts, and laws. Moreover, images of the goddesses and their son-gods were smashed, while all visual expressions of the Divine were outlawed in Judaism and later in Islam. When the "Jesus cult" gradually separated from Judaism several decades after the Crucifixion, it maintained the Judaic focus on the word. Although Christianity discontinued the ban against images of the Divine, that loophole should hardly have made any difference since everything essential was contained in the gospels and other texts comprising the New Testament. Yet an enormous body of art has accompanied Christianity — most of it about the Blessed Virgin Mary.

It almost seems that the proportion of texts to paintings is roughly symmetrical but obverse with regard to Jesus and Mary: A huge number of books and other texts have been generated about Jesus, while a comparatively small number of paintings of him have been created (usually depicting either his birth or death); regarding Mary, the ratio is roughly the opposite — at least until the past century, when a stream of Marian books appeared. For more than a thousand years, Mary's bountiful body of grace has engaged the imagination of count-less artists and inspired communion with millions of viewers. Perhaps this is so because art can approach the ineffable in ways more powerfully evocative than a text, although that alone would not explain the great number of paintings of Christianity's Great Mother.

From the earliest times, the elemental capabilities of the female body have been regarded as having symbolic correspondence with the tides and moons and with the mysteries of birth and life support, that is, the mythic drama of our existence. Like all religions, Christianity is about the relationship of humans to the larger reality, the Divine, approached poetically through a particular mythic event or story. That relationship is larger than any one religion's approach to it and certainly larger than any text. Art can allude to the numinous in multivalent ways, as does the Blessed Virgin Mary herself. It is not surprising, then, that artists working in such an evocative medium were attracted to a female spiritual symbol that denotes both the human and the transcendent.

The creation and contemplation of such art is a practice of the *via pulchritudinis* (the Way of Beauty), a term used by Pope Paul VI at the conclusion of the Mariological Congress in Rome in 1975. Mary is an iconic expression of the complementarity and harmony of human and divine beauty.[9] As such she is the true Seat of Wisdom, the embodiment of Sophia (Wisdom) in Hebrew Scripture, with whom she is sometimes merged pictorially as Mary Sophia.

Mary was the first Christian figure depicted in iconography. Initially, expressions of her physicality drew from the long tradition of Goddess art. An early fresco in the Roman catacombs portrays Mary as a half-length figure facing the viewer with her arms straight out to the sides but with elbows bent and palms facing outward, the *orante* (praying) pose of the Great Intercessor. This is the dominant image of Mary for the first six centuries, perpetually praying for the children of God, with her arms uplifted, at the foot of the Cross. After the fourth century, altarpiece mosaics were the medium in which Mary the Intercessor was usually created, often in the Greek style showing a static, colossal, and mysterious Great Mother. From the Roman goddess Diana and several Near Eastern goddesses, she inherited her association with the crescent moon, although Mary is often shown standing on it, indicating the new Christian view of nature. In Marian symbolism the moon also connotes her position as mediator between heaven and Earth.

Statues of Mary were initially modeled on those of Isis enthroned with Horus on her lap, which were common throughout the Roman Empire. Often those very same statues were simply renamed "Mary." (Isis also contributed another well-known pose, her pre-Christian *pietà*: She sits erect with her dead son lying stiffly across her lap. The image of a goddess mourning her son was common to several traditions in the region.) In images of an enthroned goddess, her body itself was understood to be the Throne of Wisdom, or Seat of Wisdom, whether or not she is holding a small son-god. The many statues of Mary carved in twelfth- and thirteenth-century France as the Throne of Wisdom, or the Virgin in Majesty, were often painted with blood-red polychrome for her gown and dark blue for her cloak. These Seat of Wisdom statues are called black madonnas, or dark madonnas, because the skin tone is the brown or grey color of the fruit wood from which they were carved. The features are often strong and the posture always regal. They may be the most compelling expressions of Mary's spiritual presence ever created, for they exhibit a gravitas and maternal authority that is never seen again. Subsequent centuries transform her image into a Baroque cloud-dweller and finally, in the nineteenth century, a handmaid of the Lord dressed in baby blue (the color of the heavens) and white (the color of purity) who stands gazing toward heaven with no hint of maternal potency.

So powerfully evocative were the small Throne of Wisdom statues in the great medieval shrines that even enemies of the Church responded to their charged embodiment. To destroy symbols of Catholicism, one would think that they need only be smashed and broken up, yet some of the statues of Mary in Majesty were literally executed in the manner of the day. For example, in England in the mid-sixteenth century, heretics and traitors were commonly burned at the stake before a crowd of witnesses. In that milieu, Thomas Cromwell, Chancellor of the Exchequer, Secretary to King Henry VIII, and "the architect of the English Reformation," zealously impressed upon public consciousness the new role of Protestanism as the sole religion of the state. In one of his demonstrations of the new order, Cromwell ordered that the Marian statue in the famous shrine at Walsingham be brought to his courtyard in London, in July 1538, and there burned before witnessing officials.

Some 250 years later, French Revolutionaries seized the enthroned statue of Mary from the shrine at Le Puy, which is the starting point of the renowned pilgrimage route across the south of France and then across Spain to the shrine of Santiago de Compostella, the burial site of St. James. (This famous pilgrimage, drawing people from the many kingdoms of medieval Europe, yielded the saying "Europe was formed on the road to Compostella!") The statue of the black madonna of Le Puy, then, had great significance. During the French Revolution, it was blindfolded and taken to the public square in front of the city hall where crowds of Revolutionaries chanted "Death! Death! Death!" until the small wooden Mary was guillotined.

These remarkable assaults on statues of the Mother of the Church as if they were actual female bodies illuminate the power of symbol in ways our modern minds can barely grasp. A religious symbol was not perceived as a simple logo or "sign" reminding the viewer of a concept. Rather, the premodern mind was sensitive to multivalent connotations and fields of meaning. The visual metaphors mentioned here and in the previous chapter are only a fraction of the symbol system that developed around the Blessed Virgin and flourished for centuries until Vatican II. From the medieval convergence of Mary's story with the Song of Songs came not only the image of the walled garden and the rose, but also the sealed fountain, the Lily of the Valley, the Cedar of Lebanon, and the Tower of David. Flowers of all sorts near Mary symbolized the blooming of the world in grace and spiritual beauty. White lilies, representing her purity, were nearly always present in paintings of the Annunciation, as was an olive branch in the hand of the archangel, for he brought peace from heaven to Earth through the assent of Mary. Fruits were emblems of the fruits of the spirit, such as joy, love, and peace. The pomegranate had long been a symbol of hope and, when vertically slit to reveal its red interior, of female fruitfulness; in Marian symbolism it denotes both the Mother of Divine Hope and the *Virginitas fecunda* (fertile virgin). An apple near Mary denotes her role as the New Eve.

Her association with fecundity on a grand scale is also expressed in her connection with the verdant month of May. Previously, the Greeks had celebrated the goddess Artemis and the Romans the goddess Flora in May, followed by centuries of medieval honoring of the pagan Queen of May. The earliest recorded connecting of Mary with May appeared in the thirteenth-century *Cantigas de Santa Maria* by King Alfonso X of Spain. Existing practices were eventually described, expanded, and made official through three Jesuit books during the eighteenth century: *The Month of May or the Month of Mary* (1725), *The Month of May* (1758), and *The Month of Mary* (1785), the last of which was reprinted over 150 times in the nineteenth century and several times in the twentieth century. During the Victorian era, the Jesuit poet Gerard Manley Hopkins wrote one of his most famous poems, "May Magnificat," about Mary's month as a time of "growth in everything":

> All things rising, all things sizing,
> Mary sees, sympathising
> With that world of good,
> Nature's motherhood. . . . [10]

On May Day in many traditional Catholic cultures, statues of Mary are still decorated with flowers and carried in processions. In the more "modernized" countries, the Marian procession to crown her statue with a wreath of May flowers — which is remembered by nearly everyone who attended a Catholic elementary school prior to Vatican II — is long gone.

Marian symbolism also associates her with wisdom. When she is depicted holding a book that is closed, it represents the Virgin herself, particularly the closed pathway to her sacred womb. When it is open, it is the Book of Wisdom. Mary in the act of reading denotes her mystical character as Seat of Wisdom, as well as her continuation of the female presence of Wisdom — that is, Sophia — found in Hebrew Scripture. This continuity in the person of Mary was demonstrated aesthetically by picturing her with certain figures from Hebrew Scripture such as Moses, Isaiah, Ezekiel, David (both a prophet and her husband's ancestor), Ruth, Rachel, Judith, and Esther. The wisdom and piety of her motherline were depicted in late-medieval statues of Mary with her mother and grandmother, particularly in fifteenth-century Germany.

Following the Reformation, Mary largely receded from view in northern European painting and received a change of clothes in subsequent Catholic art. Throughout the centuries she had been pictured in a red gown and a dark blue cloak. The gown was often embroidered with gold patterns in medieval paintings, but it was always red or a dark rosy hue. Red has extremely ancient associations with the female — brides in India and China, for instance, traditionally marry in red — because fecundity depends on the presence of the blood tides and their providing sustenance for the baby during nine months of gestation. In fact, the origin of the Sanskrit word *ritu,* or ritual, was the blood mysteries and rituals of the female.[11]

In time, however, red came to be associated in the West with illicit sexual passion. No doubt because some of the more strident voices of the Reformation began referring to Mary (and the pope and the Catholic Church) as "the Whore of Babylon" described in chapter seventeen of the Book of Revelation, the Catholic Counter-Reformation subsequently decided that white would better suit the Virgin in matters of fashion. In 1649 the Sevillian painter Francisco Pacheco wrote a guide for orthodox iconography, *The Art of Painting,* in which he specified that Mary's gown in paintings of her as the Immaculate Conception (a theological concept that infuriated the Reformers) is always to be white, though her cloak would remain blue. That color scheme has become widely identified with her, with a slight alteration: In the nineteenth century her dark blue cloak was made pastel. The only trace of the red dress remains with Mary Magdalene.

The other major change in depicting the Immaculate Conception was the priggish displacement of the rays of grace that streamed from Mary's breasts in several medieval works: Subsequently, grace is shown to stream downward from her extended palms or, in later eras, from luminous rings on her fingers. Moreover, her depictions became far more flat-chested than her earlier forms. It seems hardly coincidental that this more modern and more "rational" version distorts and denies Mary's bodily grounding in the elemental power of the female. Of course, no one was fooled . . . except the perpetrators, who perhaps found some relief from their anxiety by wrapping Mary's bosom as flat as a boy's and rechanneling those streams of grace from her bountiful female breasts to run the length of her sleeves and exit behind her upturned hands or else from her palms.

And what of her face? It is the face that is most like Christ's, as Dante observed.[12] What would that luminous inner beauty and divine grace look like? The reason every Catholic culture painted the physical features of the Blessed Virgin to resemble its ideal female escaped me when I was an adolescent. I found it absurd that northern European artists, for instance, depicted her with blondish hair, light-color eyes, and Nordic features. Since she was obviously a Mediterranean woman, why all the deceptive cultural chauvinism, I wondered with the self-righteous intolerance of youth. Eventually, though, I grew into an appreciation of her as a grand convergence of ethnic and racial streams. Mary is depicted *as* all women because Mary is *of* all women. This has been clear to millions of non-Western Catholics, who immediately understood the Great Mother of Christianity, Queen of Heaven and Earth, as looking like them. Hence, to the European portraits of the Blessed Virgin were added "The Madonna of the Moon-Gate" in China, "Our Lady of Japan," "Madre del Pueblo" (Mother of the People) in Latin America, and several versions in Africa, as well.[13] Moreover, the multiple depictions of Mary, sometimes several in one church, preserve the spiritual mystery by diffusing the symbolization. This diversity achieves through beauty what the "modernizers" strive to achieve through harsh denial.

In the current Marian renewal, a creative surge in the visual arts has once again brought forth new depictions of Mary. Unfortunately, those portrayals that have received the most attention from the media have been sensationalistic. A particularly aggressive image was a sculpture by Robert Gober, displayed at the Museum of Contemporary Art in Los Angeles in 1997, in which a life-size cast concrete statue of Mary was pierced through the torso by a five-foot-long bronze culvert pipe. Two years later, national media attention was focused on a controversial painting titled *Holy Virgin Mary* by a young British artist of Nigerian descent, Chris Ofili, which was exhibited in late September 1999 at the Brooklyn Museum of Art as part of the British group show titled *Sensation*. The painting featured, in common with his other works in the exhibition, shellacked clumps of elephant dung affixed to the canvas, an inspiration afforded by a "roots trip" the artist made to Zimbabwe, where he had observed that the all-important fertility of the fields depends on elephant dung as fertilizer. No dung, no life. Ofili's black madonna has distorted, cartoon-like features, yet is surrounded with the warm golden tones of a Byzantine icon. By far the most objectionable element in the work is the dozens of cut-outs of orifices and genitalia from pornographic magazines pasted all around the Virgin. Although Ofili refused to explain the painting once the furor arose (except to note that he had been an altar boy in Manchester and was still a loosely practicing Catholic), he said in an earlier interview that he had noticed in viewing paintings of the Virgin Mary "how sexually charged" some of them are.[14]

What might have been the Church's response, other than the public condemnation expressed by clergy and lay groups? Perhaps something like the following: "*Of course* Mr. Ofili perceives the erotic dimension in painters' portrayals of the Blessed Virgin Mary! *All* dimensions of beauty, allurement, and profound communion are present because she is the great matrix, the compassionate advocate with her arms outstretched, inviting all to come to her. But that Mr. Ofili can only make a straight line from this full cosmological allurement to *pornography* is literally pathetic — that is, full of pathos — and is a sign of our barren times. We pray that Mr. Ofili, a creative and religious person, will come into the fullness of the Virgin Mary's spiritual presence."

Some three years after Ofili's painting was first exhibited in London, an English sculptor named Guy Reid, who describes himself as a "deeply devout" Anglican, unveiled in St. Matthew's Church in London a commissioned statue of Jesus and Mary in which both are completely nude. In the media attention that predictably followed, he explained that the nudity is meant to denote their roles as the New Adam and the New Eve. In a review in the British Catholic newspaper *The Tablet,* however, Sarah Jane Boss coolly pointed out that images of the Incarnation must show both the humanity and the divinity of Christ, which Reid's depiction fails to do.[15]

Far from the orchestrated sensationalism of the London and New York art worlds, several galleries in the American southwest and west now hold exhibitions of new Marian art, often inspired by the image of Our Lady of Guadalupe. The Galeria Tonantzin in the picturesque mission town of San Juan Bautista, California, hosts an annual symposium, the Virgin Image Conference, to accompany their Marian exhibition. This event coincides with the exuberant theatrical presentation by El Teatro Campesino of *La Virgen del Tepeyac* on Guadalupe's day in alternate years (those ending with an even number). In December 1998 I was invited to participate in the fifth such conference and was asked to give a reading of my prose poem, "A Catechism on Mary at the New Millennium," in the Guadalupe chapel within the historical mission compound. The conference included several slide presentations by artists and art historians, half of whom were Mexican American, who have been drawn to the image of the Virgin in their work over the past twenty years.

The art presented at the conference was both poignant and delightful, covering a wide range of moods and interpretations, many of them buoyant and sometimes humorous, such as a large-scale rendition of a "green card" from the U.S. Immigration and Naturalization Service with Guadalupe's picture and name since she has, after all, traveled to *el Norte,* being carried there in the heart of nearly every Mexican whose photo stares out from the prized card. Reproductions of a monoprint shown at that conference, *Madre de las Americas,* plus several other contemporary depictions of *"big* Mary" accompany this chapter. They are but a sampling of the vibrant Marian art of our time that presents "the humanly realizable shape of the Irrepresentable," as Clarissa Pinkola Estés has put it. A Jungian analyst who was consecrated to Our Lady of Guadalupe as a young girl, Pinkola Estés understands the Holy Mother as an archetype, meaning not merely a symbol or character but a "living image of great force." She asserts that Mary, in all her forms, is the sort of living image that is "a thunder-and-lightening crashing indwelling from a force that changes and is changed through its congress with human souls."[16]

In the presentations and discussions at the conference in San Juan Bautista, two of the themes that emerged surprised me. Having heard Mexicans and Mexican Americans express pride that the Virgin of Guadalupe's spiritual presence has spread so far, I was unprepared for the resentment expressed by some of the artists about the "cultural imperialism" that results when non-Mexicans "appropriate," artistically or spiritually, Guadalupana, the Soul of Mexico. On one hand, Our Lady of Guadalupe may be seen as one of several cultural expressions of Mary that have traveled from a particular nation to the hearts of millions of Catholics around the world. On the other hand, the embrace of Our Lady of Guadalupe by citizens of a country that has long discriminated against Mexicans is obviously a sensitive area.

The other charged yet, for myself, unexpected theme that emerged was the decidedly nonspiritual attitude toward Our Lady of Guadalupe that was expressed by some Marian artists whose background is the

Chicano civil rights movement: They spoke of the image of Guadalupe as a political icon that they "appropriated" and "deconstructed" in a "very calculated and scientific" manner simply because it is the most commonplace image of and for Mexican Americans. As always, I felt a depressing pang of loss to hear that the long arm of modern "scientific" semiotic theory had once again reduced a numinous, multivalent *symbol* to a mere *sign* that "tough-minded" modern thinking uses instrumentally for a given end. Perhaps I experienced the barrenness of this perspective as being literally painful in a visceral sense because it negates so thoroughly the cosmological presence of Mary's bountiful *body* of grace. Quite soon, however, I realized that my private mourning was a case of *O, ye of little faith!* because the slides these secular women showed were so full of Guadalupe's own mystical resonance that she trumps any modern theories, even their own, about the nature of a religious icon.

A subtheme in the activist "appropriations" was a range of humorous and often charming depictions of Guadalupe (identifiable by her cloak of starry heaven, rays of the sun radiating from behind her, and crescent moon beneath her feet) as a decidedly can-do type of woman who is active in society or as a cartoon Wonder Girl dashing about with her short cape of starry heaven billowing in the breeze behind her as she runs and leaps. The images were clever and frequently delightful — though never beautiful, as was the art shown by the more spiritually inclined Mexican American artists and art historians. It seemed that the political artists sought to *add* power to the Virgin's image because modern socialization — or too many childhood sermons about Mary as the model of perfect female docility — prevented them from perceiving her *inherent* power. Similar aggressively modern stances were also played out in controversial depictions of Our Lady of Guadalupe at the Museum of International Folk Art, in Santa Fe, New Mexico, in Spring 2001, and at the Smithsonian Institution's Center for Latino Initiatives, in New York City, in December 2001. For example, the exhibition in Santa Fe included a photo collage, *Our Lady* by Alma Lopez, that features a defiant-looking Guadalupe standing with her hands on her hips and clothed in a verdant bikini made of roses and leaves. (I would not assume, however, that the artist has no spiritual connection with Our Lady of Guadalupe in the "liberated" version she has created.)

At the 1998 Virgin Image Conference, the modern, utilitarian attitude toward the Virgin's image was deftly challenged by a professor from Mexico City, Marguerita Zires, who began by noting several of the disparate groups and individuals who have communed with Guadalupe during the past 500 years and then asked: "Do the new pop appropriations cause the image to lose spiritual and political power? Does presenting the Virgin of Guadalupe as suiting a particular group destroy her as a long-standing point of integration?"

As I drove home from the conference and the exhibition in San Juan Bautista, my mind was filled with the stimulating art, the extraordinary theatrical production by El Teatro Campesino in the historical mission, and the surprising presence of so many non-Catholics at several of the events. In fact, the convenor of the conference and director of the Galeria Tonantzin, Jennifer Colby, holds a masters degree from a Protestant school of theology. No doubt ecumenical ease around Mary is achieved more often through art than doctrine. How else to explain Episcopalian groups traveling from the United States to Chartres Cathedral to hear inspiring lectures from Episcopalian spiritual teachers on the strictly biblical sense of Mary the Nazarene woman? Nothing wrong with that, of course, except that the setting seems highly incongruous: the greatest medieval monument to the *cosmological* version of Mary as Queen of Heaven. Perhaps everyone takes from great art that with which they are attuned. (In any event, the name of the popular annual excursion to Chartres Cathedral organized by the Labyrinth Project at the Episcopal Church's Grace Cathedral in San Francisco was changed in 2003 from "Let Us Walk with Mary" to "Walking a Sacred Path.")

In the national, or otherwise renowned, Marian shrines, the body of the Virgin is nearly always dark in color — usually black, brown, or gray — whether she is standing or enthroned. Mary is of dark complexion at Chartres (*Notre Dame de Sous-Terre* in the underground crypt), Rocamadour, Orleans, and Le Puy in France; Santa Maria Maggiore (Rome) and Loreto in Italy; Einsiedeln in Switzerland; Guadalupe, Saragossa, and Monserrat in Spain; Czestochowa in Poland;

Bistrica in Croatia; and Guadalupe in Mexico. These are merely the best known dark madonnas. It is estimated that, prior to destruction by Huguenots in the sixteenth century and by the French Revolution in the eighteenth century, there were some 190 small medieval black madonna statues in churches and shrines in France, mostly in the southern half of the country. (Several of those "murdered" medieval statues have been replaced with replicas in the churches.)

In Italy today, there are twenty-five significant sanctuaries of black madonnas. They are often clustered near archaeological sites in which images of a female deity have been unearthed from the neolithic era or even the upper paleolithic. For instance, the pregnant earth-mother divinity dated 26,000–18,000 B.C., called Venere Artemide by Italians, was found at Savignano (between Modena and Bologna); a black madonna has long been venerated at Bologna and several other nearby cities.[17] In Rome the church of the black Madonna of Santa Maria in Ara Coeli was built on the remains of a temple to the goddess Cybele (who was often symbolized as a black stone), while the church of the whitened madonna of Santa Maria in Cosmedin was built on the remains of a temple to the Roman goddess Ceres (the Greek goddess Demeter). Some of the black madonna iconic paintings in Italy — but not all, as is often incorrectly assumed — had Byzantine origins because numerous Marian icons were sent to Italy and elsewhere during the eighth and ninth centuries to escape destruction during the iconoclastic controversy in Constantinople.

At the national Marian shrine of Italy, the black Madonna of Loreto, the visitor registry includes, ironically, the names of many of the men later considered by history to be pioneers of the modern, post-mystical era: Descartes, Galileo, Montesquieu, Montaigne, Cervantes, and Mozart. In fact, Descartes, who intensified the Western perception of a radical discontinuity between both the mind and the body as well as the mind and the rest of the world, expressed his gratitude to the Virgin Mary, in the guest book, for illuminating his philosophical direction! The shrine itself encases a small stone house in which Mary was said to have received the Annunciation. Legend holds that it flew through the air from the Holy Land to the Balkans and then to its final resting place at Loreto. A less imaginative explanation is that the stones, which are indeed from the area surrounding Nazareth, were brought back by Crusaders, who then had the house reconstructed.

The origin of the black madonnas is complex and probably has multiple sources. The position of the Church is that these medieval statues — which are mostly carved of oak, apple, olive, pear, or cedar and painted with polychrome — turned black over time merely because of candle smoke or exposure to the elements. Regarding the latter explanation, many were indeed buried outdoors or within church walls for several hundred years to protect them during the invasions of the Moors in Spain and the Turks in the Balkans. For instance, the dark madonna called Marija Bistrica in the national shrine near Zagreb, Croatia, was sealed in a wall of a church to elude the invading army of the Ottoman Empire, which got as far north into Europe as the gates of Vienna in the sixteenth century, then retreated from Austria, Hungary, Slovenia, and Croatia to areas in and south of Bosnia, which it occupied for several hundred years.

The darkening effects of being buried, especially outdoors, sounds plausible in a few such cases, but if candle smoke is to account for all the other dark madonnas, as the Church asserts, why would not the entire statue have become black? Instead, the polychromed areas representing their clothing have remained colorful. Sometimes cleanings have revealed that the statue is indeed not black, as it had appeared, but is still quite dark. For instance, the black madonna of Tindari in Sicily, dating from the thirteenth century, was cleaned in 1997 and found to have olive-brown skin, kohl-rimmed eyes, a blue-green cloak, an Arabian-style crown, and hair flecked with copper-red in the Middle Eastern style. This example fits the other explanation that the Church accepts: Some dark statues of the Virgin were brought back from the Holy Land by the Crusaders.

What the Catholic Church does not like to discuss — since it refuses to celebrate the cultural convergence that is Mary — is the widespread Goddess religion in Europe and Africa in the era immediately preceding the appearance of the black Virgins. Black statues of Isis were common in Gaul (France under the Roman Empire) for hundreds of years, as were dark figurines of Cybele (the Magna Mater in Rome) and Diana (whose famous statue at Ephesus was black). Moreover, European Christendom in the Middle Ages became fascinated with the biblical Song of Songs, which includes the bride's declaration "Yes, I am black — and radiant!" It seems clear that the black madonna statues are themselves sites of convergence, as is the larger presence of Mary herself.

Perhaps those scholars are correct who locate the origins of the Song of Songs in an earlier tradition that celebrated the body and nature as holy, as did so many of the Goddess religions in the Near East for so long. In Canaan and elsewhere that orientation was opposed, often quite brutally, by the new Abrahamic religions (Judaism, Christianity, and Islam), which emphasized the word — that is, the textual commandment — in sharp contrast to the older ways. Still, the earliest authors of the Christian canon must have grasped that a religion based solely on Scripture, even filled with great stories, would not be as compelling as one that contained, and was contained in, some sort of embodiment. Of course, the Incarnation as the cornerstone of Christianity separated it from the realms of the purely abstract. Yet . . . something more was needed, was indeed demanded, by the Mystery, something that would resonate with deep-seated associations.

So it came to pass that the Last Supper was recalled in the gospels as a staging site for the appropriation of two extremely ancient sacred rituals, an absorption that probably seemed to the shapers of the Christian story merely natural, rather than calculated. First, Christ's elevating a piece of bread and declaring "This is my body" echoes the ritual elevation of the wheat in Demeter's Eleusinian Mysteries (the great initiation ritual at Eleusis that was undergone by nearly all citizens of Athens for centuries and later by many prominent Romans). The concept of Christ's being in the communion bread also drew upon the ancient belief in Greece and several Near Eastern cultures that the Goddess of the Fruits of the Earth, including grains, was in the seed grain and in the ritual bread. According to the Christian narrative, Jesus next subsumes into his new symbol system the extremely ancient blood mysteries and rituals of the female. He elevates the wine and declares, "This is my blood." With that act, a new version of the blood mysteries is born.

It was a grand solution at the conceptual level. Still, Mary, with her numinous maternal body, lives at a deeper level than canonic pronouncements. From the beginning, her mystical body outshone the tiresome erection of words into religious institutions.

The Catholic Church does try so hard, though. Every time a mass is celebrated, the faithful approach the altar and hear the priest say, as he holds up a communion wafer before each person arriving at the head of the line: "The Body of Christ." *The Body of Christ. The Body of Christ.* One hears it pronounced a dozen times while waiting in line and then walking away to return to the pew. The words echo in the mind, yet no incantation can keep the majority of Catholics' spiritual attention focused *solely* on the body on the cross, a tragic emblem of what men do to men. One ponders the mysteries of the Incarnation, the Crucifixion, and the Resurrection, but it is the bountiful maternal body of the Blessed Mother that holds and nourishes. Clearly Mary and Jesus are a spiritual pair, a symbolic unity with extremely ancient resonance. The dynamic of focusing sometimes on Mary and sometimes on Jesus does not feel like a competition in the minds of the faithful, only in the minds of anxious theologians and Church bureaucrats.

The liturgy that males have evolved for the Church through the ages keeps its distance from the mystical powers of Mary's bountiful body. Imagine the liturgical prayers we would have if they were composed by women, not women tamed by the ideologies of modernity and "progressive" patriarchy but women still spiritually grounded in the elemental power of the female. Here is an example of what we have been missing, a prayer written by an Episcopal priest that was read as the Prefatory (Preface) in a celebration of the mass in June 2001 at a spiritual retreat for Dominican nuns, held in Houston:

Before Jesus
was his Mother.

Before supper
in the upper room,
breakfast in the barn.

Before the Passover Feast,
a feeding trough.
And here, the altar
of Earth, fair linens
of hay and seed.

Before his cry,

her cry.
Before his sweat
of blood,
her bleeding
and tears.
Before his offering,
hers.

Before the breaking
of bread and death,
the breaking of her
body in birth.

Before the offering
of the cup,
the offering
of her breast.
Before his blood,
her blood.
And by her body and blood
alone, his body and blood
and whole human being.

The wise ones knelt
to hear the woman's word
in wonder.
Holding up her sacred child,
her God in the form of a babe,
she said: "Receive and let
your hearts be healed
and your lives be filled
with love, for
This is my body,
This is my blood."[18]

— Rev. Alla Renée Bozarth

Mystical Rose

Gate of Heaven

Our Lady of Roses

Mirror of Infinite Beauty

Epilogue

Being Mary

During the final month of the previous millennium, a series of circumstances propelled me to experience the Virgin Mary in a manner more immediate and embodied than I could have imagined. No visitation or celestial choir was involved but a transcendent perception that lodged in my bones and remains to this day.

On December 7, 1999, I conducted the last class of a graduate course on Mary and modernity at the California Institute of Integral Studies in San Francisco. The course covered the historical and contemporary issues explored in this book. Half of the thirteen students were Catholic, by birth if not practice, and two of those were nuns, a Franciscan and a Dominican. The sole male student (named after Martin Luther) had enrolled in the course out of spiritual curiosity after having found himself drawn to Our Lady of Guadalupe during a mountain-climbing trip to Mexico. As he put it, the feeling on walking into her churches was "so down deep." Like the rest of us, he was subtly transformed through our engagement with Mary over the fifteen-week semester.

Although the focus of the course was scholarly inquiry into the cultural history of the Virgin Mary and her fate in the modern era, the personal dimension of Marian spirituality gradually established itself between the lines of the reading assignments — and I made no secret of my own spiritual communion with Mary. The result was an educational experience greater than "book-learning." On that last day, then, the class thanked me for making Mary a real presence in their spiritual lives. One woman, speaking for a few of the Catholic students, assured me that experiencing the meaning of Our Blessed Mother had "given us back our religion" and also had built a bridge with their grandmothers, whose Marian spirituality they had never understood.

Perhaps the most dramatic engagement with Mary occurred in the heart and mind of the Dominican nun. She was in her early forties and was thoroughly focused on the possibility of women's ordination. She had pursued theological studies elsewhere and had come to our program in philosophy, cosmology, and cultural history to continue her intellectual pursuits. She and I discussed recent scholarship indicating that the core three or four of Christ's female disciples in his radical ministry were most likely also apostles, though they were edited out of the canonical version of the four gospels composed decades later. On a less scholarly note, I showed her an altered version of Leonardo's painting of the Last Supper with all the women and children painted in, which had appeared in *Ms.* magazine.[1] Good for a laugh . . . and more. "The Reverend," as I called her, was bright, funny, and assertively "progressive" about Catholicism. Having grown up after Vatican II, she had little feeling for Mary and commented early on, with mild disdain, that the entire rosary often had to be recited before funerals since families still request it.

When she presented the thesis of her midterm paper, written after we had covered the pre-Christian lineage that is so apparent in both the biblical Nativity story and the symbolism surrounding Mary, she employed the format of a sermon. Seated before us and facing the class, she stared straight ahead at the back wall and announced very firmly, halfway through the sermon, "It is not the job of the Catholic Church to protect the survival of the Goddess." I smiled and admired her courage. Besides, it was a common position for a representative of the Church to take: the "supersessionist" view, which emphasizes Christianity's radical break from its immediate predecessors rather than acknowledging much, if any, continuity. I was saddened to realize, though, that most female Catholic priests under age fifty, if there are to be any at all, would most likely be "progressively" post-Marian. On the other hand, our "Reverend" had made a commitment to scholarship and graduate education. As a scholar, she would be unable to dismiss the abundant evidence of continuity between Mary's biblical story and various earlier sacred stories of the Goddess. In the weeks that followed, I watched the conflict dance in her mind but did not interfere.

By the time "the Reverend" presented the thesis of her final paper on the last day of class, something had shifted. She wrote on the Immaculate Conception and the new cosmology that has emerged from science during recent decades (she was simultaneously taking a course on the new cosmology from the scientist Brian Swimme). In discussing the theological richness of the meaning of Mary, she noted, almost as a matter of course, that Mary's ancient cosmological associations inherited from the Goddess era were obviously a part of her spiritual totality. The class was as surprised as I and broke out in applause in the middle of the presentation. Moreover, the change within this Dominican nun was physical as well as intellectual: Her face had brightened; the way she held her shoulders had opened up; and her heart was infusing her presence as had not been the case earlier. She told me later that she had taken to winking or waving at the plaster statue of Mary located at the end of a long corridor in the convent where she stayed during her graduate studies with us. Previously she had seen it only as an irrelevant vestige of the old-time Church. Now she appreciated Mary's presence as the cosmological matrix of the Incarnation and a conduit of healing grace.

With so many similar stories in the class, the potluck meal I had suggested to accompany the presentation of the final papers turned into a beautiful ritual. The students brought not only food and drink but flowers, candles, and Marian statues from various cultures. A professional dancer in the group performed, as did an actress, who delivered a dramatic monologue about the Virgin Mary and Mary Magdalene. Many biblical scholars agree, by the way, that the "Mary Magdalene" figure in the gospels is a composite of three persons: Mary of Magdala (a well-to-do apostolic witness who was the favored confidant of Jesus and was also a patron of the "Jesus movement" and later a minister), Mary of Bethany, and an unnamed woman who had committed adultery.

Another student gave each of us a whimsical Christmas card with an ink drawing of a contemporary woman in a biblical cloak and dress with a halo over her head. She was smiling and holding in her hand a large glass of red wine. The inscription beside her read, "Eat, drink, and be Mary!" *Be Mary?* What a concept, I thought to myself.

Four days after holding that card in my hand at the close of a memorable course, fate steered me in a direction that was at first delightful and in the end profound. On Saturday morning I was doing errands in our town, Half Moon Bay, when I realized that the following day was the feast day of Our Lady of Guadalupe, December 12. On my way out of town, I stopped my car in front of Our Lady of the Pillar Catholic Church to see if there was a special announcement on the board listing the schedule of masses. As I peered at the board across the lawn, two men came over to the car and asked if I was looking for something. They and two others were erecting the annual living crèche scene in front of the church, so I figured correctly that they were members of the Knights of Columbus, who sponsor that project.

I asked them the time of the special mass in honor of Our Lady of Guadalupe, a bilingual grand event with beautiful singing and a reenactment of the story of the visitation. The man closest to my car window said he didn't know, but the other man, a Mexican American, had the answer immediately. I thanked him and was about to drive away when the first man said to me, "Would you like to be Mary?"

Without deliberating even a fraction of a second, I heard myself say, "Would I ever!"

He handed me the schedule of days and times during which parishioners volunteer to stand in costume in the life-size crèche scene throughout the week before Christmas. A donkey, sheep, and a couple of goats from local farms play their parts as well. When I saw the dates, I told him I couldn't do it because I had a plane ticket to my mother's for the following Friday, from December 17 to 30. Buoyantly, he assured me that that wouldn't be a problem as there was one more date for his "performers" after the New Year: the Feast of the Epiphany on January 2. Not only that, he added, but I wouldn't even have to stand outdoors because all that was required that day was to walk down the center aisle of the church with Joseph, the three wise men, and the shepherds at the 11:15 mass to present the "gifts" (the bread and wine) to be consecrated in the sacrament of holy communion. He told me his name was

Mel Schwing, a retired airline mechanic, and that I should think it over and call him the next day if I could definitely make a commitment.

When I called Mr. Schwing to confirm the arrangement, I told him that I'm tall and would need a tall Joseph. "Not a problem. I've got a couple of those," he replied. All I had to do was show up in the kitchen of the old hall at a quarter to eleven to get into my costume with the other volunteers. I wondered aloud if their Mary used a doll or a live baby. "Do you have a baby?" he asked. I told him that I do, but she's twenty-eight. He laughed and said they use his granddaughter's doll.

It was all that simple — but between the moment on Guadalupe's day when I agreed to be Mary and the enactment itself twenty days later, my "baby" tumbled into the hellish ordeal of two life-threatening health crises, one after the other, and I went with her.

On December 17, my daughter, Lissa, who lives in Los Angeles, went to the emergency room of UCLA Medical Center with severe pain in the lower left side of her groin. After a CT scan, she was admitted and operated on a few days later for an acute case of diverticulitis, which had caused a large abscess to form in her descending colon. The abscess was successfully removed before it could burst, but an entire foot of her colon also had to be removed, followed by a re-sectioning. Though the surgery went well, the abscess was so convoluted that it had to be cut open during the process of removal. In such situations, the large incision in the abdomen must then be left open during the weeks of healing; that is, it cannot be closed with stitches, in case any minute particle of infective material might have been left in the body after the abscess was opened.

Sitting and sleeping in the chair by Lissa's hospital bed, I gradually glanced over at more and more of the gaping incision each time a nurse changed the dressing. When I finally looked at the entire canyon cut into the middle of my child, I was so shocked that I felt dizzy. A twenty-eight year old! How could this have happened?

During the preceding year when she had repeatedly reported a sharp pain in that area, her doctor had reasoned, he told us, that "she was too young to have had colon trouble." Obviously, this medical "truism" no longer holds, as several of the diseases that previously manifested themselves only in mid-life now show up in twenty-somethings. Lissa found herself in a vanguard no one would want to join. Still, her tragedy, as we discovered much later when she requested a copy of her medical record, was entirely avoidable. It had occurred because apparently neither her doctor nor any of the emergency room doctors, during her previous episodes of extreme pain, had read her test results in the computer, which had clearly identified diverticulosis eleven months earlier, in January, and had even identified "acute diverticulitis with a 2.5-cm abscess" in mid-November. Neither test report seems to have been read by her doctor. Diverticulosis, if treated early on, usually requires nothing more than a restricted diet and, if the colon periodically becomes inflamed, an antibiotic. Lissa's condition, however, went undiagnosed throughout the entire year, until December 17, by which time it was not only intensely painful but dangerously acute, with the abscess then convoluted and grown to 5 cm.

Because Lissa had decided after the surgery not to look at her huge incision, I said nothing except to agree aloud with the nurses that it was "very pink and healthy." She would close her eyes or stare at the ceiling whenever the nurses changed the dressing and would chat with them as they worked. One day during the second week, though, Lissa was looking upward as usual and accidentally saw the very large, gaping incision reflected in a Christmas ornament, a shiny red metallic ball that I had hung along with a little Christmas stocking on the top bar of her i.v. stand (the six-foot-high holder for tubes and containers of intravenous solutions). There was nothing to do but believe the surgeon's assurance that her young body would effortlessly knit the "canyon" together, beginning with the deepest levels, and would restore her abdomen to a strong, resilient condition, leaving "only" a twelve-inch line of scar tissue about an inch wide. That, in fact, is what happened over the next few months, but it was nearly impossible to imagine at the time. I prayed my rosary a lot, and I lay Lissa's rosary over her incision on top of her blankets every night as she fell asleep.

Two days after her colon surgery a complication was discovered, one of the worst among the various things that can go wrong. A huge blood clot had formed, a deep vein thrombosis running from her left ankle all the way up to the area just below her heart, specifically, into the inferior *vena cava*. Her primary-care physician, her surgeon, and the hospital's reigning experts in hematology and vascular conditions were all amazed by the size of the clot. We were told that such a blood clot was extremely dangerous, as a piece might break off and travel to her heart or lungs, destroying tissue that normally enables the absorption of oxygen and causing death.

In the ten days that followed, a range of tests and measurements of her leg were taken, each eliciting a stream of contradictory interpretations. As Lissa put it, "I'm damned and saved a hundred times an hour in this place." There was general agreement, however, that such a huge clot would leave permanent damage: The afflicted leg would probably always be somewhat enlarged and painful at times; it would always be weaker internally because the collateral veins that form to recanalize the blood around a blocked area are less robust than the original vein; and attempting to carry a pregnancy in the future should not be attempted because it would most likely create "significant risk" to the weakened vein structure. As for the immediate future, they predicted that the clot would be reabsorbed within about six months, but that did not occur until much later.

Every day in the hospital the pain and redness in her leg increased until she could barely hobble, with assistance, from her bed to the bathroom a few feet away. During Lissa's waking hours, which were few since she was on a good deal of pain medication, I read aloud from a *Harry Potter* book, the perfect escapist literature. Still, we were continually interrupted by reality in the form of nurses, doctors, interns, residents, and the sharp pain in her swollen leg.

The entire ordeal was intensely stressful. My daughter, of course, was the one who suffered, but witnessing her (preventable) agony, learning to ask the crucial medical questions and remembering to do so at all times, sleeping on a chair (and finally a liberated cot), and eating depressing cafeteria food for almost two weeks took its toll on me as well.

While the experts continued to confer, Lissa's condition worsened. Her leg turned an even deeper red whenever she stood on it and the pain continued to increase. She jokingly suggested to her doctors that, being a UCLA alumna, she should at least be given the preferential treatment of being discharged by New Year's Eve — but that seemed highly unlikely. The specialists debated various treatments and finally decided on an invasive procedure called a venagram, which involves the insertion of a small apparatus through the groin to the damaged vein so that a dye can be injected into the clot and a tiny claw can tear off and remove part of the clot. What saved her from that risky course of action and finally sprang us from the hospital was the spiritual assistance of an additional Mary, specifically a Marianne.

Along with her rosary, Lissa kept next to her hospital bed a copy of *Illuminata*, a book of prayers to God written by the spiritual teacher Marianne Williamson, whose tapes and books Lissa had collected for years. On one of our grimmer days, it finally dawned on me to phone Marianne, whom I had met a couple of years earlier, and explain the situation on Lissa's behalf. I left the whole story on Marianne's voice mail, and though she did not know Lissa, she phoned her the following evening. I was sitting next to the bed during their conversation. After they talked for a while, Lissa closed her eyes and became silent for a long time, while still holding the phone to her ear. I realized that Marianne was praying (aloud) with her. I then happened to notice something remarkable during their praying: Lissa's whole body changed. Through the sheet and light blanket, the contours of her body could be seen to soften, almost to melt, as if all the tension had gone out. I nearly did a double-take because the effect was so physical and yet so improbable. After the call, Lissa fell asleep in a deeply peaceful state.

In the morning she surprised the nurse and herself by saying that she didn't think she would need the extra pain medication before the physical therapist's daily visit. In fact, when the therapist came and helped her stand up and lean on a walker, Lissa announced with amazement that there was no pain. Neither was there any redness. Moreover, she could walk all the way out into the hallway without any pain. We were thrilled simply because it meant a lessening of her suffering. Little did we know that it signaled even more to her medical team: Due to the two signs of significant improvement (the lessening of both pain and redness), they cancelled the invasive procedure and let us go home the following afternoon — with the understanding that she must stay on a high dosage of blood thinner, plus the extremely restricted diet that goes with it, for at least six months.

Lissa couldn't go home to her second-floor apartment because it wasn't safe for her to climb all those stairs yet, so we were kindly taken in by her aunt (who, icing on the cake, is a nurse) and her uncle. To say we were exhausted doesn't begin to describe our condition. It was as if we were two survivors of an ordeal we could never describe to anyone else, a relentless experience that yielded only a fraction of itself to words. We immediately fell asleep in their den, Lissa on the daybed and myself on a futon on the floor next to her. A friend of hers had brought some New Year's Eve decorations, but the most we could manage was to wake up now and then to watch bits of the PBS round-the-world broadcast of millennial celebrations in various cultures. Just before midnight, Lissa awoke enough to extend her hand to mine and say, "Happy New Year, Mom. We made it."

We slept through most of New Year's Day 2000, except for the family dinner and the arrivals of the visiting nurse to change Lissa's dressing in the wound. Lissa's pain and redness were returning in her leg, but she insisted that I not miss my opportunity to be Mary in my parish church. (After I left, her leg worsened so intensely that, four days later, we were back in the hospital for a few more days, as we would be again in March.[2]) On the plane back to San Francisco on the morning of January 2, though, I considered the hospital experience to be behind me — except that it wouldn't leave me. All the patients I had seen and sometimes spoken with as I walked the hospital corridors those many days — plus Lissa's sweet nineteen-year-old hospital roommate, who had a large malignant tumor and had had a third of her liver re-moved — floated around in my mind. Many of the patients I had met were far worse off than my child, and it felt as if they were not exactly "other" than my child. We were all linked, related now in some way. I felt that bond quite strongly as the jet propelled me away from them, though my reflections surfaced only as a swirl of half-finished thoughts in my utterly drained condition.

The plane was late in landing. My husband was waiting at the curb and drove me directly to the church. Once there, I hurried into the kitchen of the old hall only eight minutes before the 11:15 mass. I perceived immediately that the room was full of people adjusting their costumes, but the person I happened to face directly as I entered was a woman in a long cream-colored, "homespun" dress, with a white rope for a belt, and a floor-length, azure blue cloak draped over her head and shoulders.

We looked into each other's face, and I asked rather weakly, "Mary?"

To my great relief, she explained that she was merely the back-up Mary that day, as I had phoned Mr. Schwing to explain that I would be cutting it close if the shuttle flight was not on time. We went into the small restroom and transferred the costume.

I emerged as Mary. I emerged from my individual self into something larger, and I perceived instantly that everyone could feel that, not only my fellow actors at close range but, very soon, even the people in the pews as Joseph, the shepherds, the three wise men, and I grouped in the back of the church. Several women in the pews turned around to see "Mary" and perhaps to experience "Mary" looking at them. When our eyes met, I smiled, a smile that felt somehow more than my own, as if it softly radiated grace. The women smiled softly back.

As Joseph and I, followed by the others, proceeded slowly down the center aisle — once at the beginning of the mass and once later on to present the communion gifts of bread and wine — we approached the huge mural of Mary that covers the wall behind the altar. I could also see, just beyond the front pew on the right side, which was our destination, the large plaster statue of Mary, in an azure cloak and a gold crown. Next to her was a framed reproduction of the *tilma* showing Our Lady of Guadalupe. Next to that was a small bronze statue of Mary on a column of jasper, Our Lady of the Pillar.

As it happened — because the heavy cloak would slip off unless I kept my head tilted slightly forward — I was in the classic Marian posture. Like the four depictions before me, my head was bowed slightly under the weight of the suffering of the world. The suffering of the world. I had just seen a concentration of it up close for twelve days. It was in every cell of my being. The suffering of the world, weighing on my head and shoulders. Suddenly an image of Lissa — her abdomen slit wide open and her swollen leg a dark red — arose in my mind, followed by the worried face of her young roommate, the ashen-faced man down the hall from them who was undergoing chemotherapy, the African American woman who had been waiting weeks in the hospital for a liver transplant, the elderly diabetic man whose toes had been amputated, the frightened teenager on the surgical gurney who was about to receive a kidney transplant from his brother, the tiny Japanese American grandmother struggling painfully to take her first walk after a major operation, the young Mexican American family whose aunt was in critical condition after an automobile accident, and all the grim-faced relatives at the bedside inside every open door, suspended in family tableaux of stunned acquiescence. These were instantly joined by intimations of the countless suffering people I hadn't seen — the war orphans, the refugees, the victims of disasters made, or made worse, by human folly, and all the women battered and raped and the relentlessness of it always and everywhere. The suffering of the world.

I felt tears well up as I thought with exasperation of those "progressive" feminist sisters who dismissively interpret Mary's bowed head as a sign of submission, all the assertively modern Catholics who feel certain the faith can get on fine without her, and all the post-Marians who believe that a feminized, if ethereal, Holy Spirit could pick up the slack. *Can you not see? Her head is bent under the suffering of the world because she knows suffering. She knows it bodily. It shaped her earthly life. She is the cosmic dynamic who feels human suffering in her very being and absorbs it as her own. The Lamb of God may take away the sins of the world, but Mary feels our suffering.*

Our Lady of Sorrows

Our Lady of Prompt Succor

Our Lady of Consolation

Acknowledgments

F oremost, gratitude to my family — especially my mother, Donna, and my maternal grandmother, Anna — for raising my sister and me in the warm embrace of the Blessed Mother.

Oceans of appreciation, once again, to my husband, Daniel Moses; my daughter, Lissa Merkel; and my sister, Nikki Spretnak.

I thank the following friends and colleagues for reading all or parts of the manuscript and sending me their responses: Sharon Abercrombie, Thomas Berry, Brian Brown, Leo Cachat, Tyrone Cashman, Pamela Eakins, Linda Gibler, Mara Lynn Keller, Andrew Kimbrell, Lissa Merkel, Daniel Moses, Seonaid Robertson, Brian Swimme, Sarah McFarland Taylor, Mary Evelyn Tucker, and Pamela Wylie.

I am grateful for research assistance from Susan Hall Andrews, Lauren Artress, Lucia Chiavola Birnbaum, Joan Cichon, Patti Davis, Robert Ellsberg, Pozzi Escot, Catlyn Fendler, Ann Forrister, China Galland, Don Johnson, Thomas Lucas, Bonnie Niewiarowska, Ana Maria Pineda, Ricki Pollycove, Shannon Reich, Kearney Reitmann, Marguerite Rigoglioso, Barbara J. Scot, Francis Tiso, David Ulansey, Jeannette Watts, and Martin Wittenberg.

I have received friendly and valuable research assistance — in person, on the phone, and by mail — from the excellent Marian Library at the University of Dayton. In addition, I wish to thank the Information Queens in the library at the graduate institute where I teach, the California Institute of Integral Studies: Lise Dyckman, Eahr Joan, and Robyn Barker. At the University of San Francisco's Gleeson Library, three skilled information sleuths provided invaluable assistance: Vicki

Milan Rosen, Carol Spector, and Penny Scott. At the sculpture department of the Victoria and Albert Museum, in London, Stephanie Long graciously pooled her information with mine concerning the mystery of the missing crown on the Marian sculpture by Bartolomeo Buon that is featured as the frontispiece in this book.

Special thanks to Judith Braber Kenney and Lauren Tresnon Klein for encouragement and support.

For assistance in gathering striking examples of contemporary Marian art, from which the selections for the photo insert in chapter seven were made, I thank Jennifer Colby, director of Galeria Tonantzin, in San Juan Bautista, CA; Terence Dempsey, S.J., director of the Museum of Contemporary Religious Art (MOCRA), in St. Louis, MO; and Tricia Grame, a freelance curator in the San Francisco Bay Area. Gratitude to the artists who created the selected art and to their galleries for providing it.

My thanks as well as to my graduate students in the philosophy and religion program at the California Institute of Integral Studies, in San Francisco. I am also grateful for the positive and energizing responses from Sisters of Earth, a national network of ecosocially engaged Catholic nuns, to whom I presented some of the ideas in this book as the keynote address at their biennial conference in August 2002 in Massachusetts.

Gratitude also to my literary agent, Frederick Hill, for his guidance and support, and to his associate, Irene Moore. For her enthusiasm for this book from the moment she delved into the manuscript, I express heartfelt appreciation to my editor at Palgrave Macmillan, Amanda Johnson. Thanks also to her editorial assistant, Matthew Ashford, and to my eagle-eyed copyeditor, Jen Simington. Finally, special thanks to Carol P. Christ, who mentioned to Amanda Johnson that I was writing a book about Mary.

Notes

Introduction: Being Marian

1. See, for example, Andrew Greeley, *The Catholic Imagination* (Berkeley and Los Angeles: University of California Press, 2000), p. 101.
2. Mary E. Hines, *What Ever Happened to Mary?* (Notre Dame, IN: Ave Maria Press, 2001), pp. 7-9.
3. Hines, *What Ever Happened to Mary?*, p. 86.
4. Hines, *What Ever Happened to Mary?*, pp. 84 and 87.
5. Hines, *What Ever Happened to Mary?*, p. 76.
6. Rea Howarth, cited in "Feminist Rosary Prayers Written," *Network for Women's Spirituality*, March/April/May 2003, p. 4.
7. Jan Jarboe Russell, "Seeking a Promotion for the Virgin Mary," *New York Times*, 23 December 2000.
8. Leo Cachat, S.J., a critique of an early draft of the manuscript of *Missing Mary*, June 5, 2002.

Chapter One: The Virgin and the Dynamo: A Rematch

1. Henry Adams, cited in the introduction by Asa Briggs to *Mont-Saint-Michel and Chartres* (New York: Gallery Books / W. H. Smith Publishers, 1980), p. 8.
2. Henry Adams, "The Dynamo and the Virgin," in *The Education of Henry Adams*, Oxford World's Classics (New York: Oxford University Press, 1999), p. 324.
3. Henry Adams, *The Education of Henry Adams*, Oxford's World's Classics (New York: Oxford University Press, 1999), p. 325.
4. Henry Adams, *The Education of Henry Adams*, p. 317.
5. Henry Adams, *The Letters of Henry Adams*, edited by J. C. Levenson, Ernest Samuels, Charles Vandersee, and Viola Hopkins Winner (Cambridge, MA: Harvard University Press, 1982-1988), 5: 169; cited in *The Education of Henry Adams*, p. 474.
6. Henry Adams, *The Education of Henry Adams*, p. 318.

7. Henry Adams, *The Education of Henry Adams*, pp. 318-320.

8. Henry Adams, *Mont-Saint-Michel and Chartres* (New York: Gallery Books / W. H. Smith Publishers, 1980), p. 117.

9. Henry Adams, *Mont-Saint-Michel and Chartres*, p. 92.

10. Frances Kissling, "Mary Co-opted as Co-Redeemer," *On the Issues: The Progressive Woman's Quarterly* 7, no. 2 (spring 1998): 17.

11. Mary Lou Kownacki, O.S.B., "One Day at a Time," *Pax Christi USA* 12, no. 1 (spring 1987): 3. I am an admirer of Sr. Kownacki's courageous work for peace and justice over the years. I am happy to report that in this article, written when she was national coordinator of Pax Christi USA, she urged her readers to eschew what she described as the usual disdainful response of "progressives" to a Marian Year and, instead, to embrace the idea of a Pax Christi prayer to the Queen of Peace. *Pax Christi USA* is available from the Pax Christi office, 532 Eighth Street, Erie, PA 16502.

12. This political cartoon is reprinted in Philippe Thiebaut, *Gaudi: Visionary Architect* (New York: Abrams, 2001), p. 74.

13. The "progressive" view of what occurred at Vatican II is presented in extensive detail in the three-volume study *History of Vatican II*, ed. by Guiseppe Alberigo, English version ed. by Joseph A. Komonchak (Maryknoll, NY: Orbis / Peeters, 1995, 1997, 2000). Numerous summaries, commentaries, and memoirs by Catholic "progressives" are also available on the Internet. Accounts of Marian traditionalists' experiences at Vatican II are in various sources. Some of the positions they expressed are available under "Book Text" at the Vox Populi website: www.voxpopuli.org.

14. Alberto Melloni, "The Marian Question," *History of Vatican II*, vol. 3, p. 95-96; and William G. Most, "Upgrading the Downgrade," *Vatican II: Marian Council* (Athlane, Ireland: St. Paul Publications, 1972), available at the website www.petersnet.net/most.

15. See, for instance, William G. Most, "Upgrading the Downgrade," *Vatican II — Marian Council*, available at the website www.petersnet.net/most. Also see Sr. Thomas Mary McBride, O.P., "Marian Theology up to Vatican II," available at the website www.christendomawake.org/pages/mcbride.

16. Alberto Melloni, "The Marian Question," *History of Vatican II*, vol. 3, pp. 96-97.

17. See, for example, the comment by the theologian and commission secretary Charles Moeller praising Cardinal König's speech in the Marian debate as being "more nuanced," cited in Albert Melloni, "The Marian Question," *History of Vatican II*, vol. 3, p. 97.

18. Jan Grootaers, "The Schema on the Blessed Virgin Mary," *History of Vatican II*, vol. 2, p. 481.

19. Denis E. Hurley, chapter 6, "Laity, Deacons, and our Lady," in his series titled "Eyewitness to Vatican II," *The Southern Cross*, 2001, available at the website www.thesoutherncross.co.za/VaticanII.

20. Dogmatic Constitution on the Church (*Lumen Gentium*), in *The Documents of Vatican II*, ed. by Walter M. Abbot, S.J. (New York: Guild Press, 1966), p. 84.

21. Pope John XXIII, opening speech at Vatican II, October 11, 1962, available at the website www.vatican2plus40.info/topic-vatican2/v2-history/pope-john-speech.
22. See "History of the Marian Library — Part II: Vatican II and Its Aftermath," *The Marian Newsletter*, no. 27 (new series) (winter 1993-94): 4: "As the new quarters for the library were being dedicated in 1965, some wondered whether a Marian library was still necessary, 'whether it would impede ecumenical dialogue.' . . . Its previous activities were reconsidered in the light of Vatican II's directives." The article then cites the resultant cancellations that were imposed.
23. Thomas Lanigan-Schmidt, telephone conversation with Charlene Spretnak, May 1, 2003.
24. Robert Lentz, telephone conversation with Charlene Spretnak, May 5, 2003.
25. Henry Adams, *The Letters of Henry Adams,* 5: 500; cited by Ira B. Nadel in the introduction to *The Education of Henry Adams,* p. xv.

Chapter Two: The Quiet Rebellion

1. The Annunciation: Luke 1:26-38. The Visitation: Luke 1:39-45. The Magnificat: Luke 1:46-55. Infancy narratives: Matthew 1:18-25; Luke 2:1-20; Matthew 2:9-11; Matthew 2:13-15; Luke 2:33-35; Luke 2:41-52. Ministry: Mark 3:20-21, 31-35 (also Matthew 12:46-50; Luke 8:19-22); John 2:1-6, 11-12. The Passion: John 19:25-27. Pentecost: Acts 1:13-14. Revelation: Revelation 12:1-8, 13-17.
2. Mary Lee Nolan and Sidney Nolan, *Christian Pilgrimage in Modern Western Europe* (Chapel Hill, NC: The University of North Carolina Press, 1989, p. 120.
3. Cited in "Gauging Marian Devotion," *The Marian Library Newsletter,* no. 39 (new series) (winter 1999-2000): 4.
4. Thomas A. Thompson, S.M., "Pilgrimage and Shrines: A Recognition Long Delayed," *Marian Studies* 51 (2000): 117. Regarding attendance at the National Shrine of Our Lady of Lourdes, in Maryland, see "Handmaid or Feminist?," *Time* (December 30, 1991): 62.
5. *Life,* December 1996.
6. *Newsweek,* August 25, 1997.
7. Richard N. Ostling, "The Pope's Hail Mary," *Time* (June 16, 1997): 16.
8. For information about the *Vox Populi* movement, see their website: www.voxpopuli.org.
9. Andrew Greeley, e-mailed message to Charlene Spretnak, August 24, 2001.
10. See, for example, the coverage of Fr. Greeley's talk, "Recovering the Catholic Heritage," at the University of San Francisco, in Jack Smith, "Recovering Catholic Heritage: Fr. Greeley Decries the Loss of Unique Sacramental Way of Life," *Catholic San Francisco,* 2 March 2001. .
11. All citations from the published version of Fr. Greeley's article are taken from pp. 10-13 in "A Cloak of Many Colors," *Commonweal* (November 9, 2001). All citations from his original, unpublished version of the article are

from his manuscript of the article, originally titled "Recovering the Catholic Heritage," e-mailed to Charlene Spretnak on August 24, 2001.

12. Reported in "The Marianum's Position on the Dogmatic Definition," *The Marian Library Newsletter,* no. 38 (new series) (summer 1999), 4.

13. Fr. Jorge Román served at Our Lady of the Pillar Catholic Church, Half Moon Bay, CA, from 2000–2003.

14. Reported by David Scott, "Debating New Dogma for a New Millennium," *Our Sunday Visitor* (August 10, 1997); also reported by Kenneth L. Woodward, "Hail, Mary," *Newsweek* (August 25, 1997); also reported in many Catholic publications.

15. See Garry Wills, *Papal Sin: Structures of Deceit* (New York: Doubleday, 2000). I must note here that Wills attended the Jesuit seminary attached to my alma mater and often speaks appreciatively of his Jesuit education. Whether one likes it or not, though, the founder of the Jesuit order, St. Ignatius of Loyola, was inspired by spiritual communion with Mary at several key points in his life. While convalescing from a serious wound he had received in the Battle of Pamplona, he experienced a visitation from the Blessed Mother, resulting in a spiritual conversion. He vowed to live a life of holiness and chastity and to do great things for God and for Mary. He kept a prayer vigil at the Marian shrine at Aranzazu, in the Basque country. He pined for some Jewish ancestry so that he could have been related to Mary and Jesus. On leaving home, he presented his sword to Our Lady of Monserrat and spent an all-night vigil in prayer at the foot of that black madonna statue. He then spent a year in prayer near Montserrat composing his famous *Spiritual Exercises.* When St. Ignatius founded the Society of Jesus, he and six companions spoke their vow on the Feast of the Assumption in a Marian chapel in Montmartre. At the Marian shrine La Sorta, he received the answer to his prayer to Mary: "Place me with your Son." He selected for the Jesuits' headquarters a refurbished church in Rome named for the Our Lady of the Street. He advised that, when an important decision had to be made, one should begin with a conversation with Mary, Our Lady of the Society of Jesus. In particular, the Jesuit order developed an early association with the Marian shrine at Loreto in Italy, where they had an important ministry. Back in Rome, the painting titled *Mary, Solace of the Roman People,* which hangs in the Santa Maria Maggiore church and was popularly believed to have been painted by the apostle Luke, was visited often by Jesuits and their network of associates, who distributed copies of this Marian image to all the Jesuit missions worldwide, uniting them at a deep level of spiritual aesthetics. Hence, one may conclude that St. Ignatius's Marian inspiration was central in the birth and development of this impressive order: no Mary, no Jesuits.

16. Walter Burghardt, S.J., "Ignatius of Loyola and the Mother of Jesus," a homily published in *The Marian Library Newsletter,* no. 23 (new series) (winter 1991–92): 1–2 and 6–7.

17. Ambrose of Milan, *In Lucam* 2, 56, cited in Bertrand Buby, *Mary of Galilee,* vol. 3, *The Marian Heritage of the Early Church* (Staten Island, NY: Alba House, Society of St. Paul, 1997), p. 122.

18. "The Madeleva Manifesto: A Message of Hope and Courage," *America* (June 17-24, 2000): 15.

19. Elizabeth A. Johnson, "Mary of Nazareth: Friend of God and Prophet," *America* (June 17-24, 2000): 7-11 and 13.

20. Maurice Hamington, *Hail Mary?: The Struggle for Ultimate Womanhood in Catholicism* (New York: Routledge, 1995), introduction, pp. 1-7.

21. Maurice Hamington, *Hail Mary?*; citations in this paragraph are from chapter 6, "The Recasting of Marian Imgery," pp. 157, 162, and 164-170.

22. Dorothee Solle, *The Strength of the Weak: Toward a Christian Feminist Identity* (Oxford, England: Basil Blackwell, 1984), p. 47; cited in Maurice Hamington, *Hail Mary?*, p. 164.

23. Ivone Gebara and Maria Clara Bingemer, *Mary, Mother of God, Mother of the Poor* (Maryknoll, NY: Orbis, 1987), pp. 1-19; summarized and cited in Maurice Hamington, *Hail Mary?*, pp. 169-170.

24. Maurice Hamington, *Hail Mary?*, p. 177.

25. Marina Warner, *Alone of All Her Sex: The Myth and Cult of the Virgin Mary* (New York: Alfred A. Knopf, 1976), pp. 338-339. Warner has continued to write insightfully and with a deeply informed sensibility about the fate of the Mary in our times. See, for instance, Marina Warner, "Blood and Tears," *The New Yorker* (April 8, 1996).

Chapter Three: Premodern Mary Meets Postmodern Cosmology

1. St. Thomas Aquinas, "Whether the Multitude and Distinction of Things Come from God?," *Summa Theologica*, trans. by Fathers of the English Dominican Province, part I, question 47, article 1. (New York: Benziger Bros., 1947-1948), pp. 245-246.

2. See Thomas Berry, *The Dream of the Earth* (San Francisco: Sierra Club Books, 1988); *The Universe Story*, coauthored with Brian Swimme (San Francisco: HarperSanFrancisco, 1992); and *The Great Work* (New York: Bell Tower Books / Random House, 1999).

3. See Brian Swimme: *The Universe Is a Green Dragon* (Santa Fe, NM: Bear & Co., 1985); *The Universe Story*, coauthored with Thomas Berry (San Francisco: HarperSanFrancisco, 1992); and *The Hidden Heart of the Cosmos* (Maryknoll, NY: Orbis Books, 1996); plus two video series: *Canticle to the Cosmos* (Mill Valley, CA: Center for the Story of the Universe, 1990) and *Earth's Imagination* (Mill Valley, CA: Center for the Story of the Universe, 1998). Information about the video series and the Center for the Story of the Universe is available at the website www.brianswimme.org.

4. Sr. Miriam Therese MacGillis, M.A., is a Dominican sister of Caldwell, NJ, who is cofounder and director of Genesis Farm, an ecological learning center (41A Silver Lake Road, Blairstown, NJ 07825). She lectures widely on the "new cosmology" and is featured in several audio and video tapes.

5. Paul McHugh, "Church Needs to Grow Up When It Comes to Sexual Doctrine," *San Francisco Chronicle,* 5 May 2002.
6. Jane Sears, "New Age Catholicism," letter to the editor, *Catholic San Francisco,* 16 August 2002. The publication she was criticizing, *Catholic Women's Network* (available at cwn@catholicwomensnet.org), did indeed change its name eventually but largely to clarify for potential subscribers that its focus is more on the growth of the spirit than on theology or doctrine. This quarterly "progressive" newspaper, based in Sunnyvale, CA, is now titled *Network for Women's Spirituality,* published by Catholic Women's Network.
7. "Liturgical Reforms of Vatican II Need Reform, says Cardinal Ratzinger," Catholic News Service, January 10, 2002.
8. Thomas Berry, letter written to Charlene Spretnak on October 16, 2001.
9. See the discussion of this theological orientation in Kenan B. Osborne, *Christian Sacraments in a Postmodern World: A Theology for the Third Millennium* (Mahwah, NJ: Paulist Press, 1999), especially p. 47.
10. Edward Kilmartin, "Sacramental Nature of the Cosmos," in his essay "Theology of the Sacraments: Toward a New Understanding of the Chief Rites of the Church and Jesus Christ," in Regis A. Duffy, ed., *Alternative Futures for Worship,* vol. 1, general introduction (Collegeville, MN: Liturgical Press, 1987), p. 158; cited in Osborne, *Christian Sacraments in a Postmodern World,* p. 51.
11. Edward Kilmartin, *Alternative Futures for Worship,* vol. 1, general introduction, p. 159; cited in Osborne, *Christian Sacraments in a Postmodern World,* p. 51.
12. *Catechism of the Catholic Church* (New York: Doubleday, 1995), section 1374, p. 383-384.
13. Martin Luther, in Timothy F. Lull, ed., *Martin Luther's Basic Theological Writings* (Minneapolis: Fortress Press, 1989), The Smalkald Articles, part 3, section 6, p. 528. Also see John Dietzen, "Catholic and Lutheran Belief in the Real Presence," *Catholic San Francisco,* 10 January 2003.
14. John A. Hardon, S.J., "Transubstantiation," *The Catholic Faith* 2, no. 1, p. 38.
15. Mary Lee Nolan and Sidney Nolan, *Christian Pilgrimage in Modern Western Europe* (Chapel Hill, NC: University of North Carolina Press, 1989), p. 117 and 120.
16. Nolan and Nolan, *Christian Pilgrimage in Modern Western Europe,* p. 120.

Chapter Four: Where Mary Still Reigns

1. Patricia Hampl, *Virgin Time* (New York: Ballantine Books, 1993), p. 138.
2. Andrew Greeley, "A Cloak of Many Colors," *Commonweal* (November 9, 2001): 10.
3. Andrew Greeley, "The Mother Love of God," *The Catholic Imagination* (Berkeley and Los Angeles: University of California Press, 2000), p. 101.

4. Mary Gordon, "Coming to Terms with Mary," *Commonweal* (January 15, 1982): 12 and 14.
5. I had been told that the Paulist Fathers who run the Newman Center next to Ohio State University had responded to the requests of foreign students for a Marian chapel. When I visited that Newman Center on July 31, 2003, I encountered a sign over a door not to a chapel but a "Marian Room." Inside I found a most begrudging response to the students' request, although one that is certainly "in line with Vatican II." *Where's Mary?* is the question a first-time visitor might well entertain. On the wall across from the door is a tapestry featuring Jesus and the fishing boats. On the long wall to the right is a row of *bas relief* plaques depicting Jesus in the Stations of the Cross. Hanging above the Stations is a grotesque sculpture of the Holy Family, all grinning as if in a modern snapshot. Finally, if one looks sharply to the left, a narrow alcove set into the wall becomes visible. In it is a vase of flowers above which hangs a sculpture of Mary (looking somewhat pathetic and forlorn) holding the infant Jesus. The rows of chairs do not face this unimpressive Mary but face into the sanctuary. (The Marian "room" is actually a long, raised alcove that is three steps up from the main floor of the sanctuary.) Over the altar, by the way, hangs a large metal cross *that is empty,* in the Protestant style. How very ecumenical.
6. Auxiliary Bishop John Tong Hon, quoted by Patrick Joyce in "'Graced and Historic Day': Bishop Ignatius Wang Is Ordained as First U.S. Bishop of Asian Heritage," *Catholic San Francisco,* 7 February 2003.
7. The website for the Mary's Gardens movement is available at www.mgardens.org.
8. Vincenzina Krymow, *Mary's Flowers: Gardens, Legends, and Meditations* (Cincinnati, OH: St. Anthony Messenger Press, 1999).
9. St. Bernard of Clairvaux, *Homilies in Praise of the Blessed Virgin Mary by Bernard of Clairvaux* (Kalamazoo, MI: Cistercian Publications, 1993), p. 30.
10. Dante Alighieri, *The Divine Comedy: Paradiso,* translated by Allen Mandelbaum (Berkeley and Los Angeles: University of California Press, 1984), canto 33, p. 290.
11. Cindy Wooden, "Vatican Urges Respect for Popular Piety," *Catholic San Francisco,* 12 April 2002.
12. Dianne Hales, "Why Prayer Could Be Good Medicine," *Parade Magazine,* 23 March 2003, pp. 4-5.
13. See, for example, Lone Jensen, *Gifts of Grace: A Gathering of Personal Encounters with the Virgin Mary* (San Francisco: HarperSanFrancisco, 1995). Jensen relates the personal accounts of recovery from muscular sclerosis, extensive brain damage following an automobile accident, cancer, chronic pain, and drug addiction (without the agony of withdrawal symptoms). In each of these lives, the appeal to Mary's spiritual presence for help yielded remarkable results.
14. Stephan Tobler, a Reformed Evangelical theologian, University of Tübingen, Germany; cited in *The Marian Library Newsletter,* no. 46 (new series) (summer 2003), 3.

15. Pope John Paul II, cited by Cindy Wooden in "Pope Calls for Devotion to Rosary, Prayer of Consolation," *Catholic San Francisco,* 25 October 2002. Also see Frank Bruni, "Pope Will Add Five 'Mysteries' to the Rosary," reprinted from the *New York Times, San Francisco Chronicle,* 15 October 2002.

16. Domenico Marcucci, *Through the Rosary with Fra Angelico* (Staten Island, NY: Alba House, Society of St. Paul, 1989).

17. Fr. Timothy Radcliffe, O.P., "The Rosary: Prayer for Community and for the Journey," excerpted in *The Marian Library Newsletter,* no. 46 (new series) (summer 2003), 4.

18. See Sandra Zimdars-Swartz, *Encountering Mary: From LaSalette to Medjugorje* (Princeton: Princeton University Press, 1991) for a sensitive and thorough study of the processes that followed the major Marian visitations since 1846.

19. See Janice T. Connell, *Meetings with Mary: Visions of the Blessed Mother* (New York: Ballantine Books, 1995) for a succinct account of Marian visitations from 1840 to the present.

20. Kenneth L. Woodward, "The Other Jesus," *Newsweek* (March 27, 2000); available through the web service proquest.umi.com, p. 4.

21. See, for example, Michael Schultheis, Edward DeBerri, and Peter Henriot, *Our Best Kept Secret: The Rich Heritage of Catholic Social Teaching* (Washington, D.C.: Center of Concern, 1987). Also see Mary E. Hobgood, *Catholic Social Teaching and Economic Theory: Paradigms in Conflict* (Philadelphia: Temple University Press, 1991).

22. Sharon Abercrombie, "The Earth Rosary," *Columban Mission,* July-August 1999, pp. 21-23.

23. See Anne Baring and Jules Cashford, *The Myth of the Goddess: Evolution of an Image* (London and New York: Viking Arkana, 1991), especially chapter fourteen on Mary.

Chapter Five: Why the Church Deposed the Queen of Heaven

1. Richard Boudreaux and Larry B. Stammer, "Vatican Reasserts Catholic Primacy," *Los Angeles Times,* 6 September 2000.

2. "Catholics Join in Call to End Efforts to Convert Jews," *Catholic San Francisco,* 20 September 2002.

3. Avery Dulles, quoted by Don Lattin in "Surprise Cardinal at 82," *San Francisco Chronicle,* 26 January 2001.

4. Pope John Paul II, Letter to the German Cardinals, cited in "Blunt Warning to German Church," *Daily Catholic* 12, no. 73 (March 14, 2001); available at the website www.DailyCatholic.org.

5. Pope John Paul II, Letter to the German Cardinals, cited in "Blunt Warning to German Church," *Daily Catholic* 12, no. 73 (March 14, 2001), available at the website www.DailyCatholic.org.

6. See the Forum on Religion and Ecology, founded and co-directed by Mary Evelyn Tucker and John A. Grim; information available at www.harvard. edu/cswr/ecology. Also see the special issue on "The Emerging Alliance of World Religions and Ecology," edited by Professors Tucker and Grim, *Daedalus, Journal of the American Academy of Arts and Sciences* (fall 2001).

7. See Vladimir Zelinsky, "Mary in the Mystery of the Church: The Orthodox Search for Unity," in Mark Miravalle, ed., *Mary: Coredemptrix, Mediatrix, Advocate: Theological Foundations II — Papal, Pneumatological, and Ecumenical* (Santa Barbara, CA: Queenship Publishing, 1996).

8. Martin Luther, "The Magnificat," in Jaroslav Pelikan, ed., *Luther's Works* (St. Louis, MO: Concordia, 1956), vol. 21, p. 317.

9. Luther, "The Magnificat," in *Luther's Works,* vol. 21, p. 322.

10. Luther, "The Magnificat," in *Luther's Works,* vol. 21, p. 329.

11. Luther, "The Magnificat," in *Luther's Works,* vol. 21, p. 323.

12. Luther, "The Magnificat," in *Luther's Works,* vol. 21, p. 323.

13. Luther, "The Magnificat," in *Luther's Works,* vol. 21, pp. 327-328.

14. Martin Luther, "Sermon on the Afternoon of Christmas Day 1530," in John W. Doberstein, ed., *Luther's Works* (Philadelphia: Muhlenberg Press, 1959), vol. 51, p. 213.

15. Luther, "Sermon on the Afternoon of Christmas Day 1530," in *Luther's Works,* vol. 51, p. 213.

16. John Calvin, cited in Charles A. M. Hall, *With the Spirit's Sword: The Drama of Spiritual Warfare in the Theology of John Calvin* (Richmond, VA: John Knox Press, 1968), pp. 140 and 142.

17. John Calvin, cited in Hall, *With the Spirit's Sword,* p. 145.

18. See Helen Hackett, *Virgin Mother, Virgin Queen: Elizabeth I and the Cult of the Virgin Mary* (New York: St. Martin's Press, 1995).

19. Ann Douglas, quoted by Julia Vitullo-Martin in "Hearth, Home, Holiday," *Wall Street Journal,* 12 May 2000.

20. "The Blessed Virgin Mary, Mother of God in the Mystery of Christ and the Church," chapter 8 of *The Dogmatic Constitution on the Church (Lumen Gentium)* (Boston: Pauline Books & Media, 1964), pp. 54-61.

21. Pope Pius VI, cited in George H. Tavard, *The Thousand Faces of the Virgin Mary* (Collegeville, MN: The Liturgical Press, 1966), p. 205. That address was delivered only three weeks prior to the crucial vote on the Marian chapter, on October 29, 1963. Tavard, by the way, gives the following numbers for vote tally: 1,114 in favor of putting the Marian statement into the Dogmatic Constitution on the Church, and 1,074 in favor of issuing a free-standing statement on Mary instead. Various historical studies state slightly different numbers, but the margin of victory is always very small.

22. Pope Pius VI, cited in Tavard, *The Thousand Faces of the Virgin Mary,* p. 205.

23. Pope Pius VI, Closing Council Speech, in *The Teachings of the Second Vatican Council,* introduction by Gregory Baum (Westminster, MD: Newman Press, 1966), pp. 602-606; also available at the website www.christusrex.org.

24. Many modern biblical scholars feel that there is something unmanly about all the attention Luke gives to Mary and the Nativity in his gospel; hence,

some scholars refer to him derisively as "Lukey-poo." Others believe that all or parts of his gospel may have been written by a woman.

25. Luther, "The Magnificat," *Luther's Works*, vol. 21, p. 308.

26. See the second in the three-volume series titled *Celebrations for the Millennium* (New York: Catholic Book Publishing, 1998).

27. Richard Owen, "Pope Praises 'God the Mother' to Pilgrims," *London Times*, 10 September 1999.

28. "Scapular Is Sign of Dedication, Devotion to Mary, Pope Says," *Catholic San Francisco*, 20 April 2001.

29. Cindy Wooden, "Pope Entrusts Young People to Mary, Asks Her to Help Them Be Peacemakers," Catholic News Service, *Catholic San Francisco*, 18 April 2003.

30. Fr. Balasuriya relates the entire ordeal, along with the full text of the article, in *Mary and Human Liberation: The Story and the Text* (Harrisburg, PA: Trinity Press, 1997).

31. Andrew Greeley, "Our Lady's Day in Harvest Time," *Myths of Religion* (New York: Warner Books, 1989), pp. 347-348.

32. Available at the Vox Populi website, www.voxpopuli.org.

Chapter Six: Mary's Biblical and Syncretic Roots

1. See Marija Gimbutas, *The Living Goddess* (Berkeley and Los Angeles: University of California Press, 1999).

2. Marija Gimbutas, *The Language of the Goddess* (San Francisco: HarperSanFrancisco, 1989).

3. See, for example, Savina J. Teubal, *Sarah the Priestess, First Matriarch of Genesis* (1984; Athens, OH: Swallow Press, 1993).

4. See Lucia Chiavola Birnbaum, *Black Madonnas: Feminism, Religion, and Politics in Italy* (Boston: Northeastern University Press, 1993).

5. Virgil Elizondo, *Guadalupe: Mother of the New Creation* (Maryknoll, NY: Orbis Books, 1998), pp. 66-67 and 107-112.

6. Elizondo, *Guadalupe: Mother of the New Creation*, p. xi.

7. Margaret Randall, "Guadalupe, Subversive Virgin," in Ana Castillo, ed., *Goddess of the Americas: Writings on the Virgin of Guadalupe* (New York: Riverhead Books, 1996), p. 118.

8. Clarissa Pinkola Estés, "I Am Your Mother," *U.S. Catholic* 67, no. 12 (December 2002): 16-19.

9. Carl G. Jung, Answer to Job (1958; Princeton, NJ: Bollingen Series / Princeton University Press, 1969), pp. 102-103.

10. Seamus Heaney, *Preoccupations: Selected Prose 1968–1978* (New York: Noonday Press / Farrar, Straus and Giroux, 1981), p. 143; cited by Eamon Duffy in "Madonnas that Maim?: Christian Maturity and the Cult of the Virgin," available at the website www.bfpubs.demon.co.uk/duffy, p. 7.

11. Eamon Duffy, "Madonnas that Maim?: Christian Maturity and the Cult of the Virgin," available at the website www.bfpubs.demon.co.uk/duffy, p. 9.
12. Jung, *Answer to Job*, p. 103.
13. John de Satgé, cited in Geoffrey Ashe, *The Virgin* (London: Routledge & Kegan Paul, 1976), p. 7.

Chapter Seven: Her Mystical Body of Grace

1. Graham Greene, "The Assumption of Mary," *Life* (October 30, 1950): 51.
2. St. Ambrose, *In Lucam* 2, 56; cited by Bertrand Buby, *Mary of Galilee*, vol. 3, *The Marian Heritage of the Early Church* (Staten Island, NY: Alba House, Society of St. Paul, 1997), p. 122.
3. Martin Luther, "The Magnificat," in Jaroslav Pelikan, ed., *Luther's Works* (St. Louis, MO: Concordia, 1956), vol. 21, p. 308.
4. J. L. Nelson, "Microchimerism in Human Health and Disease," *American Journal of Human Biology* 15, no. 3 (May-June 2003): 330-41. Also see Sarah Blaffer Hrdy, *Mother Nurture: Maternal Instincts and How They Shape the Human Species* (New York: Ballantine Books, 1999), p. 94.
5. Blaffer Hrdy, *Mother Nurture: Maternal Instincts and How They Shape the Human Species*, p. 94.
6. Anne Winston-Allen, *Stories of the Rose: The Making of the Rosary in the Middle Ages* (University Park, PA: Pennsylvania State University Press, 1997), p. 100.
7. Cited by Henry Adams, *Mont-Saint-Michel and Chartres* (New York: W. H. Smith / Gallery Books, 1985), p. 69.
8. Adams, *Mont-Saint-Michel and Chartres*, p. 73.
9. See Johann G. Roten, "Mary and the Way of Beauty," *Marian Studies* 49 (1998): 109-127.
10. Gerard Manley Hopkins, "May Magnificat," in Norman H. Mackenzie, ed., *The Poetical Works of Gerard Manley Hopkins* (Oxford, England: Clarendon Press / New York: Oxford University Press, 1990), pp. 153-154.
11. See Judy Grahn, *Blood, Bread, and Roses* (Boston: Beacon Press, 1993) for a study of the ways in which these early rituals shaped the emergence of human cultures.
12. Dante Alighieri, *The Divine Comedy: Paradiso*, translated by Allen Mandelbaum (Berkeley and Los Angeles: University of California Press, 1984), canto 32, p. 286.
13. See Cynthia Pearl Maus, *The World's Great Madonnas* (New York: Harper & Brothers, 1947).
14. Chris Ofili, cited by Michael Kimmelman, "Separating Cynicism and Shock," *New York Times*, 24 September 1999.
15. Sarah Jane Boss, "The Naked Madonna," *The Tablet*, 17 February 2001.
16. Clarissa Pinkola Estés, "The Holy Mother: Mary, Maria, Mir-yam," *The Bloomsbury Review* (November/December 2000): 16.

17. See Lucia Chiavola Birnbaum, *Black Madonnas: Feminism, Religion, and Politics in Italy* (Boston: Northeastern University Press, 1993).
18. This prayer appears by courtesy of the author, Rev. Alla Renée Bozarth. It can also be found in Elizabeth Roberts and Elias Amidon, eds., *Life Prayers* (San Francisco: HarperSanFrancisco, 1996), p. 169. For more prayers and poetry by Alla Renée Bozarth, see her books *Book of Bliss* (iUniverse, 2000) and *Accidental Wisdom* (iUniverse, 2003).

Epilogue: Being Mary

1. Pamela Schaeffer, "Janice Sevre-Duszynska: On the Edge of Prophecy," *Ms. Magazine* (April/May 1999).
2. Several years after this ordeal, Lissa is living a normal life, although she still experiences some pain in her leg, keeps it elevated when possible, and must be careful not to strain it through too much exertion.

Related Resources

Books and Journals

Abbott, Walter M., ed. *The Documents of Vatican II.* New York: Guild Press, 1966.

Adams, Henry. *The Education of Henry Adams.* Oxford World's Classics. 1906. Reprint, New York: Oxford University Press, 1999.

———. *Mont-Saint-Michel and Chartres.* 1904. Reprint, New York: Gallery Books/W. H. Smith Publishers, 1980.

Alberigo, Guiseppe, ed. *History of Vatican II. Volume I: Announcing and Preparing Vatican Council II — Toward a New Era in Catholicism. Volume II: The Formation of the Council's Identity: First Period and Intersession, October 1962–September 1963. Volume III: The Mature Council: Second Period and Intersession, September 1963–September 1964.* English edition edited by Joseph A. Komonchak. Maryknoll, NY and Leuven, Belgium: Orbis/Peeters, 1995, 1997, and 2000.

Ali, Abdullah Yusuf. *The Story of Mary and Jesus in the Quran: Reprinted from* The Meaning of the Holy Quran. Beltsville, MD: Amana Publications, 1995.

Alghieri, Dante. *Paradiso,* third book of *The Divine Comedy,* translated by Allen Mandelbaum. Berkeley and Los Angeles: University of California Press, 1984.

Anson, Francis. *Guadalupe: What Her Eyes Say.* Manila: Sinag-tala Publishers, 1994.

Ashe, Geoffrey. *The Virgin: Mary's Cult and the Re-emergence of the Goddess.* London: Routledge & Kegan Paul, 1976; London: Arkana/Routledge, 1998.

Ashton, Joan. *Mother of All Nations: The Visitations of the Blessed Virgin Mary and Her Message for Today.* San Francisco: Harper & Row, 1989.

———. *The People's Madonna: An Account of the Visions of Mary at Medjugorje.* London: HarperCollins/Fount, 1991.

Baker, J. Robert and Barbara Budde, eds. *A Sourcebook about Mary.* Chicago: Liturgy Training Publications, 2002.

Balasuriya, Tissa. *Mary and Human Liberation: The Story and the Text.* Harrisburg, PA: Trinity Press International, 1997.

Ball, Ann. *A Litany of Mary.* Huntington, IN: Our Sunday Visitor, 1988.

Barbaric, Slavko. *The Way of the Cross: With Jesus and Mary from Golgotha to the Resurrection.* Medugorje, Bosnia-Hercegovina: Medugorje Information Center, 1999.

Baring, Anne and Jules Cashford. *The Myth of the Goddess: Evolution of an Image.* London and New York: Viking Arkana, 1991.

Begg, Ean. *The Cult of the Black Virgin.* London: Penguin/Arkana, 1985.

Belan, Kyra. *Madonnas: From Medieval to Modern.* New York: Parkstone Press, 2000.

Bernard of Clairvaux. *Homilies in Praise of the Blessed Virgin Mary.* Kalamazoo, MI: Cistercian Publications, 1993.

Berry, Thomas. *The Dream of the Earth.* San Francisco: Sierra Club Books, 1988.

———. *Befriending the Earth: A Theology of Reconciliation between Humans and the Earth* (with Thomas Clarke). Mystic, CT: Twenty-Third Publications, 1991.

———. *The Great Work.* New York: Bell Tower Books/Random House, 1999.

Berry, Thomas and Brian Swimme. *The Universe Story: A Celebration of the Unfolding of the Cosmos.* San Francisco: HarperSanFrancisco, 1992.

Beyer, Richard J. *Blessed Art Thou: A Treasury of Marian Prayers and Devotions with Summaries of Current Apparitions.* Notre Dame, IN: Ave Maria Press, 1996.

Birnbaum, Lucia Chiavola. *Black Madonnas: Feminism, Religion, and Politics in Italy.* Boston: Northeastern University Press, 1993.

———. *Dark Mother: African Origins and Godmothers.* San Jose and New York: Authors Choice/iUniverse, 2002.

Boff, Leonardo. *The Maternal Face of God: The Feminine and Its Religious Expressions.* San Francisco: Harper & Row, 1988.

Borchard, Therese Johnson. *Our Blessed Mother: Mary in Catholic Tradition.* New York: Crossroad, 1999.

Boss, Sarah Jane. *Empress and Handmaid: On Nature and Gender in the Cult of the Virgin Mary.* London and New York: Cassell, 2000.

Boyer, Marie-France. *The Cult of the Virgin: Offerings, Ornaments, and Festivals.* London and New York: Thames & Hudson, 2000.

Boyer, Mark G. *Mary's Day — Saturday: Meditations for Marian Celebrations.* Collegeville, MN: Liturgical Press, 1993.

Braiding, D. A. *Mexican Phoenix: Our Lady of Guadalupe — Image and Tradition Across Five Centuries.* Cambridge, England: Cambridge University Press, 2001.

Brennan, Walter. *The Sacred Memory of Mary.* New York: Paulist Press, 1988.

Brown, Michael H. *Seven Days with Mary.* Milford, OH: Faith Publishing Co., 1998.

Buono, Anthony M. *The Greatest Marian Prayers: Their History, Meaning and Usage.* New York: Alba House (Society of St. Paul), 1999.

———. *Favorite Prayers to Our Lady.* New York: Catholic Book Publishing Co., 1991.

Calkins, Arthur Burton. *Totus Tuus: John Paul II's Program of Marian Consecration and Entrustment.* Libertyville, IL: Academy of the Immaculate, 1992.

Carroll, Eamon R. *Understanding the Mother of Jesus.* Wilmington, DE: Michael Glazier, 1979.

Castillo, Ana, ed. *Goddess of the Americas / LaDiosa de las Americas: Writings on the Virgin of Guadalupe.* New York: Riverhead Books, 1996.

Chiffolo, Anthony F. *100 Names of Mary: Stories and Prayers.* Cincinnati: St. Anthony Messenger Press, 2002.

Collection of Masses of the Blessed Virgin Mary. Edited by International Commission on English in the Liturgy, and National Conference of Catholic Bishops. Collegeville, MN: Liturgical Press, 1992.

Connell, Janice T. *Meetings with Mary: Visions of the Blessed Mother.* New York: Ballantine Books, 1995.

————. *Praying with Mary: Sacred Prayers to the Blessed Mother for All Occasions.* San Francisco: HarperSanFrancisco, 1997.

————. *Queen of Angels: Mary's Answers to Universal Questions.* New York: Tarcher/Putnam, 1999.

————. *The Triumph of the Immaculate Heart.* Santa Barbara, CA: Queenship Publishing, 1997.

————. *The Visions of the Children: The Apparitions of the Blessed Mother.* New York: St. Martin's Press, 1998.

Cruz, Joan Carroll. *Miraculous Images of Our Lady: 100 Famous Catholic Portraits and Statues.* Rockford, IL: Tan Books, 1993.

Cunneen, Sally. *In Search of Mary: The Woman and the Symbol.* New York: Ballantine Books, 1996.

————. "Breaking Mary's Silence," *Theology Today* (October 1999).

Cunningham, Agnes. *The Significance of Mary.* Allen, TX: Thomas More Press, 1988.

Czarnopys, Theresa Santa and Thomas M. Santa. *Marian Shrines of the United States: A Pilgrim's Travel Guide.* Liguori, MO: Liguori, 1998.

D., Michael. *The Healing Rosary: Rosary Meditations for Those in Recovery from Alcoholism and Addiction.* New York: Resurrection Press/Catholic Book Publishing Co., 1998.

Delaney, John J., ed. *A Woman Clothed with the Sun: Eight Great Appearances of Our Lady.* New York: Image Books / Doubleday, 1961.

Dictionary of Mary: "Behold Your Mother." New York: Catholic Book Publishing Co., 1999.

Directory on Popular Piety and Liturgy: Principles and Guidelines. Boston: Pauline Books and Media, 2002.

Dobraczynski, Jan. *Meetings with the Madonna.* Warsaw: Polonia Publishers, 1988.

Dogmatic Constitution on the Church (Lumen Gentium). Unofficial translation based on the Latin text appearing in *L'Osservatore Romano* on 25 November 1964. Boston: Pauline Books & Media, 1964.

Donofrio, Beverly. *Looking for Mary: Or, the Blessed Mother and Me.* New York: Viking Press, 2000.

Dubruiel, Michael. *(Mention Your Request Here): The Church's Most Powerful Novenas.* Huntington, IN: Our Sunday Visitor Publishing Division, 2000.

Duggan, Paul E. *The Assumption Dogma: Some Reactions and Ecumenical Implications in the Thought of English-Speaking Theologians.* Cleveland, OH: The Emerson Press, 1989.

Durham, Michael S. *Miracles of Mary: Apparitions, Legends, and Miraculous Works of the Blessed Virgin Mary.* San Francisco: HarperSanFrancisco, 1995.

Ebertshauser, Caroline, Herbert Haag, Joe H. Kirchberger, and Dorothee Solle. *Mary: Art, Culture, and Religion through the Ages.* New York: Crossroad, 1997.

Elizondo, Virgil. *Guadalupe: Mother of the New Creation*. Maryknoll, NY: Orbis Books, 1997.

Faccenda, Luigi. *One More Gift: Total Consecration to the Immaculata According to the Spirituality of Saint Maximilian Kolbe*. West Covina, CA: Immaculata 1990.

Feeney, Robert. *The Rosary through Biblical Meditations and Masterpieces of Italian Art*. New Hope, KY: Urbi et Orbi Communications, 1995.

Fiorenza, Elisabeth Schussler. *Jesus: Miriam's Child, Sophia's Prophet*. New York: Continuum, 1994.

Gadon, Elinor W. *The Once and Future Goddess: A Symbol for Our Time*. San Francisco: Harper & Row, 1989.

Galland, China. *Longing for Darkness: Tara and the Black Madonna*. New York: Viking Press, 1990.

———. *The Bond between Women: A Journey to Fierce Compassion*. New York: Riverhead Books, 1998.

Gatta, John. *American Madonna: Images of the Divine Woman in Literary Culture*. New York: Oxford University Press, 1997.

Gaventa, Beverly Roberts and Cynthia L. Rigby, eds. *Blessed One: Protestant Perspectives on Mary*. Louisville, KY: Westminster John Knox Press, 2002.

Gebara, Ivone and Maria Clara Bingemer. *Mary: Mother of God, Mother of the Poor*. Maryknoll, NY: Orbis Books, 1989.

Gerakas, Andrew J. *The Rosary and Devotion to Mary*. Boston: Pauline Books & Media, 1992.

Gershten, Donna M. *Kissing the Virgin's Mouth* (a novel). New York: HarperCollins, 2001.

Gimbutas, Marija. *The Living Goddess*. Berkeley and Los Angeles: University of California Press, 1999.

Graef, Hilda. *Mary: A History of Doctrine and Devotion*. 1963. Reprint, Milwaukee: Sheed & Ward, 1999.

Greeley, Andrew M. *The Mary Myth: On the Feminity of God*. New York: Seabury Press, 1977.

———. *The Catholic Imagination*. Berkeley and Los Angeles: University of California Press, 2000.

———. "A Cloak of Many Colors," *Commonweal* 128, no. 19 (November 9, 2001): 10-13.

Gribble, Richard. *The History and Devotion of the Rosary*. Huntington, IN: Our Sunday Visitor, 1992.

Guardini, Romano. *The Rosary of Our Lady*. Manchester, NH: Sophia Institute Press, 1999.

Gustafson, Fred. *The Black Madonna*. Boston: Sigo Press, 1990.

Hackett, Helen. *Virgin Mother, Maiden Queen: Elizabeth I and the Cult of the Virgin Mary*. New York: St. Martin's Press, 1995.

Hahn, Scott. *Hail, Holy Queen: The Mother of God in the Word of God*. New York: Doubleday, 2001.

Hamington, Maurice. *Hail Mary? The Struggle for Ultimate Womanhood in Catholicism*. New York and London: Routledge, 1995.

Hampl, Patricia. *Virgin Time*. New York: Ballantine Books, 1992.

Hanut, Eryk. *The Road to Guadalupe: A Modern Pilgrimage to the Goddess of the Americas*. New York: Tarcher/Putnam, 2001.

Harris, Ruth. *Lourdes: Body and Spirit in the Secular Age*. New York: Viking, 2000.

Harvey, Andrew and Anne Baring. *The Divine Feminine: Exploring the Feminine Face of God Around the World*. Berkeley, CA: ConariPress, 1996.

Harvey, Andrew and Eryk Hanut. *Mary's Vineyard: Daily Meditations, Readings, and Revelations*. Wheaton, IL: Quest Books, 1996.

Hines, Mary E. *What Ever Happened to Mary?* Notre Dame, IN: Ave Maria Press, 2001.

Holy Apostles Convent Staff, *The Life of the Virgin Mary, the Theotokos*. Buena Vista, CO: Holy Apostles Convent Publications, 1997.

Jameson, Anna Brownell. *Legends of the Madonna as Represented in the Fine Arts*. 1890. Reprint, Detroit, MI: Omnigraphics, 1990.

Jensen, Lone. *Gifts of Grace: A Gathering of Personal Encounters with the Virgin Mary*. San Francisco: HarperSanFrancisco, 1995.

John Paul II. *John Paul II's Book on Mary*, compiled by Margaret Bunson. Huntington, IN: Our Sunday Visitor, 1996.

———. *Mother of the Redeemer*. A papal encyclical letter. Boston: Pauline Books & Media, 1987.

———. *Rosarium Virginis Mariae (The Rosary of the Virgin Mary)*. The title in the translated American edition is *Apostolic Letter of Pope John Paul II on the Most Holy Rosary* (including the five new Mysteries of Light). Boston: Pauline Books & Media, 2003.

———. *Theotokos: Woman, Mother, Disciple — A Catechesis on Mary, Mother of God*. Boston: Pauline Books & Media, 2000.

———. *A Year with Mary: Daily Meditations*. New York: Catholic Book Publishing Co., 1986.

Johnson, Elizabeth A. *She Who Is: The Mystery of God in Feminist Theological Discourse*. New York: Crossroad, 1992.

———. *Truly Our Sister: A Theology of Mary in the Communion of Saints*. New York: Continuum, 2003.

Johnson, Francis. *The Wonder of Guadalupe: The Origin and Cult of the Miraculous Image of the Blessed Virgin in Mexico*. Rockford, IL: Tan Books, 1981.

Johnson, Kevin Orlin. *Rosary: Mysteries, Meditations, and the Telling of the Beads*. Dallas, TX: Pangaeus Books, 1997.

Jung, C. G. *Answer to Job*. 1958. Reprint, Princeton, NJ: Princeton University Press, 1973.

Katz, Melissa R., ed. *Divine Mirrors: The Virgin Mary in the Visual Arts*. New York: Oxford University Press, 2001.

Kavelage, Mary Francis, ed. *Marian Shrines of Italy*. San Francisco: Ignatius Press, 2000.

Kelly, Liz. *The Seeker's Guide to the Rosary*. Chicago: Loyola Press, 2001.

Kidd, Sue Monk. *The Secret Life of Bees* (a novel). New York: Viking, 2002.

Laurentin, René. *A Short Treatise on the Virgin Mary*. 1967. Reprint, Washington, NJ: AMI Press, 1991.

Laurentin, René and René Lejeune. *Messages and Teachings of Mary at Medjugorje: Chronological Corpus of the Messages*. Milford, OH: Riehle Foundation, 1988.

LeBlanc, Mary Francis. *Cause of Our Joy*. Boston: Pauline Books & Media, 1991.

Legion of Mary. *The Official Handbook of the Legion of Mary*. Dublin, Ireland: De Monfort House, 1953.

de Liguori, Alfonso Maria. *The Glories of Mary*. 1750. Reprint, Liguori, MO: Liguori Publications, 2000.

Lynch, William. *A Woman Wrapped in Silence*. 1941. Reprint, Mahwah, NJ: Paulist Press, 1968.

Male, Emile. *Religious Art in France: The Thirteenth Century*. Princeton, NJ: Princeton University Press, 1984.

Maloney, George A. *Mary: The Womb of God*. Denville, NJ: Dimension Books,1976.

Marcucci, Domenico. *Through the Rosary with Fra Angelico*. New York: Alba House (Society of St. Paul), 1989.

The Marian Library Newsletter. The Marian Library, University of Dayton, Dayton, OH 45469. Information is available at "Publications" at www.udayton.edu/mary/.

Marian Studies: Annual Publication of the Mariological Society of America. The Marian Library, University of Dayton, Dayton, OH 45469.

Martin, John. *Roses, Fountains, and Gold: The Virgin Mary in History, Art and Apparition*. San Francisco: Ignatius Press, 1998.

Mary, Francis, ed. *A Handbook on Guadalupe*. San Francisco: Ignatius Press, 1997.

Mary's Miraculous Medal: The Novena Prayers, Origin, and Story. Vienna, OH: S.I.H.M., 1999 (P.O. Box 524, Vienna, OH 44473).

Mateo, Father. *Refuting the Attack on Mary: A Defense of Marian Doctrines*. El Cajon, CA: Catholic Answers, 1999.

Mato, Tataya. *The Black Madonna Within: Drawings, Dreams, Reflections*. Peru, IL: Open Court, 1994.

Maus, Cynthia Pearl. *The World's Great Madonnas*. New York: Harper & Brothers, 1947.

Maximovitch, John. *The Orthodox Veneration of Mary the Birthgiver of God*. Platina, CA: St. Herman Press, 1997.

McBride, Alfred. *Images of Mary*. Cincinnati: St. Anthony Messenger Press, 1999.

McKenna, Megan. *Mary, Mother of All Nations: Reflections*. Icons by William Hart Nichols. Maryknoll, NY: Orbis Books, 2000.

McManus, Jim. *All Generations Will Call Me Blessed: Mary at the Millennium*. New York: Crossroad, 1999.

Miles, Margaret. *Image as Insight: Visual Understanding in Western Christianity and Secular Culture*. Boston: Beacon Press, 1985.

Miravalle, Mark. *Mary: Coredemptrix, Mediatrix, Advocate* (the short version of the theological argument put forth by the Vox Populi movement). Santa Barbara, CA: Queenship Pubishing, 1993.

———. *Introduction to Mary: The Heart of Marian Doctrine and Devotion*. Santa Barbara, CA: Queenship Publishing, 1993.

Miravalle, Mark, ed. *Mary, Coredemptrix, Mediatrix, Advocate: Theological Foundations II — Papal, Pneumatological, Ecumenical.* Santa Barbara, CA: Queenship Publishing, 1996.

de Monfort, Louis-Marie Grignion. *The Secret of the Rosary.* Bay Shore, NY: Monfort Publications, 1992.

———. *True Devotion to the Blessed Virgin.* Bay Shore, NY: Monfort Publications, 1996; also published as *True Devotion to Mary.* Rockford, IL: Tan Books & Publishers, 1992.

Mullen, Peter. *Shrines of Our Lady: A Guide to Over Fifty of the World's Most Famous Marian Shrines.* New York: St. Martin's Press, 1998.

Newman, John Henry. *The Mystical Rose: Thoughts on the Blessed Virgin from the Writings of John Henry Cardinal Newman,* edited by Joseph Regina. New York: Scepter Publications, 1996.

Nolan, Mary Lee and Sidney Nolan. *Christian Pilgrimage in Modern Western Europe.* Chapel Hill, NC: University of North Carolina Press, 1989.

Norris, Kathleen. *Meditations on Mary.* New York: Viking Studio, 1999.

Obbard, Elizabeth Ruth. *A Year with Mary: Prayers and Readings for Marian Feasts and Festivals.* Mystic, CT: Twenty-Third Publications, 1998.

Orsini, Jacqueline. *Mary: Images of the Holy Mother.* San Francisco: Chronicle Books, 2000.

Osborne, Kenan B. *Christian Sacraments in a Postmodern World: A Theology for the Third Millennium.* Mahwah, NJ: Paulist Press, 1999.

Paulos, Dan, ed. *He's Put the Whole World in Her Hands* (quotations from Mother Teresa with silhouette paper-cuttings by Dan Paulos). San Francisco: Ignatius Press, 1993.

Pelikan, Jaroslav. *Mary through the Centuries: Her Place in the History of Culture.* New Haven, CT: Yale University Press, 1996.

Pennington, Basil. *Praying by Hand: Rediscovering the Rosary as a Way of Prayer.* San Francisco: HarperCollins, 1991.

Rodriguez, Jeanette. *Our Lady of Guadalupe: Faith and Empowerment among Mexican-American Women.* Austin: University of Texas Press, 1994.

Rosage, David E. *Mary, Star of the New Millennium: Guiding Us to Renewal.* Ann Arbor, MI: Charis/Servant Publications, 1997.

Rosikon, Janusz. *The Madonnas of Europe: Pilgrimages to the Great Marian Shrines of Europe.* Warsaw, Poland: Rosikon Press, 1998.

Roten, Johann G. "Mary and the Way of Beauty," *Marian Studies,* annual publication of the Mariological Society of America, The Marian Library, University of Dayton, Dayton, OH 45469, vol. 49 (1998).

Ruggles, Robin. *Christian Apparition Shrines: Places of Pilgrimage and Prayer.* Boston: Pauline Books and Media, 1999.

Schipflinger, Thomas. *Sophia-Maria: A Holistic Vision of Creation.* York Beach, ME: Weiser, 1998.

Schoemperlen, Diane. *Our Lady of the Lost and Found: A Novel of Mary, Faith, and Friendship.* New York: Viking, 2001.

Schultheis, Michael, Edward DeBerri, and Peter Henriot. *Our Best Kept Secret: The Rich Heritage of Catholic Social Teaching.* Washington, DC: Center of Concern, 1987.

Sheen, Fulton J. *The World's First Love.* 1952. Reprint, San Francisco: Ignatius Press, 1996.

Sousa, Lisa, Stafford Poole, and James Lockhart, eds. *The Story of Guadalupe: Luis Laso de la Vega's Huei tlamahuicoltica of 1649.* Palo Alto, CA: Stanford University Press, 1997.

Starbird, Margaret. *The Woman with the Alabaster Jar: Mary Magdalen and the Holy Grail.* Santa Fe, NM: Bear & Co., 1993.

Stone, Merlin. *When God Was a Woman.* New York: Dial Press, 1976.

Swimme, Brian. *The Hidden Heart of the Cosmos.* Maryknoll, NY: Orbis Books, 1996.

———. *The Universe Is a Green Dragon.* Santa Fe, NM: Bear & Company, 1985.

Swimme, Brian and Thomas Berry. *The Universe Story.* San Francisco: HarperSanFrancisco, 1992.

Tavard, George H. *The Thousand Faces of the Virgin Mary.* Collegeville, MN: The Liturgical Press, 1996.

Teilhard de Chardin, Pierre. *The Divine Milieu.* New York: Harper & Row, 1960.

Terrien, Samuel. *The Magnificat: Musicians as Biblical Interpreters.* New York: Paulist Press, 1995.

Teubal, Savina J. *Sarah the Priestess: The First Matriarch of Genesis.* 1984. Reprint, Athens, OH: Swallow Press, 1993.

Theology Today, special section on Mary (seven articles including "Breaking Mary's Silence" by Sally Cunneen and "Mary in Catholic Doctrine and Practice" by Lawrence S. Cunningham), 56, no. 3 (October 1999).

Turner, Kay. *Beautiful Necessity: The Art and Meaning of Women's Altars.* New York: Thames & Hudson, 1999.

Tweed, Thomas A. *Our Lady of the Exile: Diasporic Religion at a Cuban Catholic Shrine in Miami.* New York: Oxford University Press, 1997.

Vail, Anne. *The Story of the Rosary.* San Francisco: HarperSanFrancisco, 1995.

———. *Joy of the Rosary: A Way into Meditative Prayer,* with prayers by Caryll Houselander and woodcut engravings by David Jones. Liguori, MO: Liguori Publications, 1997.

Vann, Gerald Seven Swords. *At the Foot of the Cross: The Seven Lessons of Mary for the Sorrowing Heart.* Manchester, NH: Sophia Institute Press, 1998.

Van Straaten, Werenfried, ed. *We Fly to Thy Patronage: Praying the Rosary.* San Francisco: Ignatius Press, 2000. (This book includes texts from the Byzantine Liturgy; it is an invitation for Orthodox and Roman Catholics to pray the rosary together.)

Varghese, Roy Abraham. *God-Sent: A History of the Accredited Apparitions of Mary.* New York: Crossroad Publishing/Herder & Herder, 2000.

Viano, Joseph A. *Mary with Us: Readings and Prayers.* New York: Alba House (Society of St. Paul), 1989.

Von Balthasar, Hans Urs. *Mary for Today.* San Francisco: Ignatius Press, 1988.

———. *Threefold Garland.* San Francisco: Ignatius Press, 1982.

Ward, Maisie. *The Splendor of the Rosary.* New York: Sheed & Ward, 1945.

Warner, Marina. *Alone of All Her Sex: The Myth and Cult of the Virgin Mary.* New York: Knopf, 1976.

Weber, Christin Lore. *Circle of Mysteries: The Women's Rosary Book.* St. Paul, MN: Yes International Publishers, 1997.

Williams, Rowan. *Ponder These Things: Praying with Icons of the Virgin.* Norwich, England: Canterbury Press, 2002.

Winston-Allen, Anne. *Stories of the Rose: The Making of the Rosary in the Middle Ages.* College Park, PA: Pennsylvania State University Press, 1997.

Wolter, Allan B. and Blane O'Neill. *John Duns Scotus: Mary's Architect.* Quincy, IL: Franciscan Press, 1993.

Woodman, Marion. *The Pregnant Virgin.* Toronto: Inner City Books, 1985.

Wright, Kevin J. *Catholic Shrines of Central and Eastern Europe: A Pilgrim's Guide.* Liguori, MO: Liguori, 1999.

Zelinsky, Vladimir. "Mary in the Mystery of the Church: The Orthodox Search for Unity," in *Mary: Coredemptrix, Mediatrix, Advocate: Theological Foundations II,* Santa Barbara, CA: Queenship Publishing, 1996.

Zimdars-Swartz, Sandra L. *Encountering Mary: From La Salette to Medjugorje.* Princeton, NJ: Princeton University Press, 1991.

Books for Children

Codina, Josep. *I Meet Mary!* Boston: Pauline Books & Media, 2002.

De Avalle-Arce, Diane, Nancy Conkle, and Alma Munoz Maya. *Madonnas of Mexico/Madonas de Mexico* (bilingual). Santa Barbara, CA: Bellerophon Books, 2000.

De Paola, Tomie. *The Lady of Guadeloupe.* New York: Holiday House, 1988.

————. *Mary: The Mother of Jesus.* New York: Holiday House, 1995.

De Santis, Zerlina. *Journeys with Mary: Apparitions of Our Lady.* Boston: Pauline Books & Media, 2001.

Halpin, D. Thomas. *My Rosary Coloring and Activity Book,* illustrated by Virginia Helen Richards. Boston: Pauline Books & Media, 2003.

Heffernan, Anne Eileen and Patricia Edward Jablonski. *Blesseds Jacinta and Francisco Marto: Shepherds of Fatima.* Boston: Pauline Books & Media, 2000.

Heffernan, Anne Eileen and Mary Elizabeth Tebo. *Saint Bernadette Soubirous: Light in the Grotto.* Boston: Pauline Books & Media, 1999.

Jablonski, Patricia Edward. *Saint Maximillan Kolbe: Mary's Knight.* Boston: Pauline Books & Media, 2001.

Martinez, Homer T., Jr. *Rosary: A Child's Prayer* (Spanish edition: *El Rosario*). Mahwah, NJ: Paulist Press, 1997 (Spanish edition: 1995).

Nobisso, Josephine. *Saint Juan Diego — and Our Lady of Guadalupe.* Boston: Pauline Books & Media, 2002.

Orfeo, Christine Virginia. *My First Book about Mary.* Boston: Pauline Books & Media, 1996.

Pastore, Vicki, illustrator. *The "Hail Mary" / The Lord's Prayer*. Mahwah, NJ: Paulist Press, 2003.

Musical Recordings

There are several fine recordings of two of the Marian classics, *Vespers of the Blessed Virgin* by Monteverdi and *Magnificat in D Major* by Bach. In addition, the following are contemporary recordings of Marian music that have gained a large audience in recent years:

Ave Maria. The Benedictine Monks of Santo Domingo de Silos. Milan Entertainment/BMG, 1995. Gregorian chants to the Virgin Mary.

La Bele Marie: Songs to the Virgin from 13th-Century France. The Anonymous 4. Harmonia Mundi France, 2002. Selections drawn from both the Latin liturgy and *chansons* that were adopted from the French *trouvère* tradition of secular love songs.

Cozzolani, Chiara Margarita. *Vespro della Beata Vergine* and *Magnificat*. Musica Omnia, 2001. Two works by a seventeenth-century Milanese nun. Cozzolani's compositions have been acclaimed by critics for their melodic freshness and formal ingenuity. Her Vespers service, in particular, is harmonically adventurous, featuring many suggestive chromatic shifts.

An English Ladymass: 13th- and 14th-Century Chant and Polyphony in Honor of the Virgin Mary. The Anonymous 4. Harmonia Mundi USA, 1992. This recording is a composite of English liturgical polyphony and other devotional works that were sung during masses in honor of Mary, which in large cathedrals and churches were held in a Lady chapel. These votive masses were celebrated either daily or on Saturday, Mary's special day.

Gounod, Charles, Franz Schubert, and Giuseppe Verdi. *The Ave Maria Album.* Leontyne Price, Placido Domingo, Enrico Caruso, Rosa Ponselle, Marian Anderson, John McCormack ("The Irish Lark"), Jeanette MacDonald, and Mario Lanza. RCA/BMG Classics, 1998. An anthology of performances of the three great musical expressions of this prayer.

Handmaiden of the Lord: Songs of Mary. The Daughters of St. Paul (Boston). Daughters of St. Paul, 1988. A homey recording of classic hymns sung in English.

Leonard, Isabella, Bianca Maria Meda, Chiara Margarita Cozzolani, et al. *Rosa Mistica.* Cappella Artemisia. Tactus Records, 2000. Marian music composed by seventeenth-century nuns of the Lombard region of Italy, performed by a women's chorus.

Da Palestrina, Giovanni, Josquin Desprez, Vasily Titov, et al. *Magnificat.* Chanitcleer. Teldec, 2000. A selection of early compositions dedicated to the Virgin Mary, performed by a men's choir.

Pergolesi, Giovanni. *Marian Vespers.* Sophie Daneman, Noemi Kiss, the Choir of New College Oxford, and the Academy of Ancient Music. Atlantic, 2003. A reconstruction of the Baroque composer's Marian Vespers, consisting of pieces from various stages of the composer's brief but impressive career; he died at 26.

———. *Stabat Mater/Salve Regina.* Emma Kirkby, James Bowman, and the Academy of Ancient Music. Polygram Records, 1990. A remarkable Baroque expression of two famous Marian prayers, characterized by somber and passionate glory.

Rachmaninoff, Sergei. *Vespers.* Robert Shaw Festival Singers. Telarc, 1990. Hymns for an all-night vigil, many of which are written to or about Mary, composed in 1915 in Moscow.

Rossini, Gioacchino. *Stabat Mater.* Luba Orgonasova, Cecilia Bartoli, Raul Gimenez, Roberto Scandiuzzi, and the Vienna Philharmonic Orchestra. Deutsche Grammophon, 1996. A passionate nineteenth-century operatic treatment of a lyric poem about Mary's vigil at the foot of the Cross that is attributed to Jacopone da Todi, a thirteenth-century Franciscan monk, for the Feast of the Seven Sorrows of the Blessed Virgin Mary.

Tavener, John. *The Protecting Veil.* Yo-Yo Ma with the Baltimore Symphony Orchestra. Sony Classical, 1998. Tavener composed this "lyrical icon in sound" in 1987 using Byzantine modes to create a meditative piece in which he "tried to capture some of the almost cosmic power of the Mother of God," according to the liner notes.

The Virgin's Lament. Noirin Ni Riain and the Monks of Glenstal Abbey. Sounds True, 1996. Irish songs to the Virgin Mary beautifully performed by the Irish soprano.

Annual Conferences and Juried Art Exhibitions

Virgin Image Conference and Art Exhibition. Dr. Jennifer Colby, director. Galeria Tonantzin, San Juan Bautista, CA. Second weekend of December. Telephone: 831-623-ARTE. Website available at www.galeriatonantzin.com

Index

Art Credits

Frontispiece:

Madonna Platytera / Madonna Miscericordia by Bartolomeo Buon, from the portal of the Abbazia della Misericordia, Venice, 1448-50. Courtesy of V&A Images, the Victoria and Albert Museum, London.
Note: The fate of this sculpture reflects the deposing of Mary as Queen of Heaven. Originally Buon sculpted a tall crown on the Blessed Virgin, but it was later chiseled away. The crown was still present when Giovanni Grevembroch made a drawing of the sculpture in the mid-eighteenth century. The crown and the colorful medieval polychrome were apparently removed by the end of that century, the Age of Enlightenment.

Twentieth- and twenty-first-century Marian art featured in chapter seven:

Untitled (Madonna) by Joe Brainard (1942-1994). Collection of Kenward Elmslie. Courtesy of the Estate of Joe Brainard and of Gallery Tibor de Nagy, New York.

Untitled (Mary/Mary) by Petah Coyne. Courtesy of Petah Coyne and Galerie Lelong, New York. Artist Contact: Galerie Lelong (www.galerielelong.com)

Lady-Unique-Inclination-of-the-Night by Susan Plum. Courtesy of Susan Plum. Artist Contact: William Traver Gallery, Seattle (www.travergallery.com)

La Frontera (The Border) by Graciela Iturbide. Courtesy of Graciela Iturbide and the Aperture Foundation, New York. Artist Contact: Galeria Emma Molina, Mexico (www.galeriaemmamolina.com)

Homage to Our Lady of Guadalupe by Raechel Marie Running. Courtesy of Raechel Marie Running and Charlene Spretnak. Collection of Charlene Spretnak. Artist Contact: RMR Studio, Flagstaff, AZ (www.rmrunningfoto.com)

The Virgin by Joseph Stella (1877-1946). Courtesy of the Brooklyn Museum of Art, Brooklyn, NY.

Madonna of the Vines by Christopher Castle. Courtesy of Christopher Castle and the Estate of Judith Stronach. Collection of the late Judith Stronach. Artist Contact: animamundi@jps.net

Madre de los Desaparecidos / Mother of the Disappeared by Robert Lentz. Courtesy of Robert Lentz and Trinity Stores (www.trinitystores.com)

An Irish Mary: Our Lady for Girls in All Seasons by Kayla Komito. Courtesy of Kayla Komito. Artist Contact: www.komito.com

Our Lady of Mount Carmel / Nuestra Señora del Carmen by Mario Parial. Courtesy of Mario Parial and Mrs. Yolando Q. M. Sulit. Collection of Mrs. Yolando Q. M. Sulit. Artist Contact: mvap@compass.com.ph

Mother of Sorrows by Ioana Datcu. Courtesy of Ioana Datcu. Artist Contact: c/o Marian Library Gallery (www.udayton.edu/mary/gallery)

Pietà by Mary Zarbano. Courtesy of Mary Zarbano and the Sarah Bain Gallery, Brea, CA. Artist Contact: Sarah Bain Gallery (www.sarahbaingallery.com)

Star of the Sea: Star of Evening, Star of Morning, Radiant Queen by Rose Wognum Frances. Courtesy of Rose Wognum Frances. Artist Contact: www.rosewognumfrances.com

Mary of the Cosmos by Bernadette Bostwick. Courtesy of Bernadette Bostwick and Charlene Spretnak. Collection of Charlene Spretnak. Artist Contact: Green Mountain Monastery (srgail@together.net)

In Her Tender Arms by Kate McKenzie. Courtesy of Kate McKenzie and Ron Pellegrini. Collection of Ron Pellegrini. Artist Contact: katemckenzie@earthlink.net

Madre de las Americas / Mother of the Americas by Rosa M. Huerta-Williamson. Courtesy of Rosa M. Huerta-Williamson. Photograph by Haddad's Fine Arts, Anaheim, CA. Artist Contact: Galeria Tonantzin (www.galeriatonantzin.com)

Mother of Grace by Pamela Eakins. Courtesy of Pamela Eakins. Artist Contact: Pacific Center, P.O. Box 3191, Half Moon Bay, CA 94019